T&P BOOKS

I0145088

PORTUGUESE
VOCABULARY

ENGLISH
PORTUGUESE

The most useful words
To expand your lexicon and sharpen
your language skills

7000 words

Brazilian Portuguese vocabulary for English speakers - 7000 words

By Andrey Taranov

T&P Books vocabularies are intended for helping you learn, memorize and review foreign words. The dictionary is divided into themes, covering all major spheres of everyday activities, business, science, culture, etc.

The process of learning words using T&P Books' theme-based dictionaries gives you the following advantages:

- Correctly grouped source information predetermines success at subsequent stages of word memorization
- Availability of words derived from the same root allowing memorization of word units (rather than separate words)
- Small units of words facilitate the process of establishing associative links needed for consolidation of vocabulary
- Level of language knowledge can be estimated by the number of learned words

T&P Books Publishing
www.tpbooks.com

ISBN: 978-1-78767-449-3

This book is also available in E-book formats.
Please visit www.tpbooks.com or the major online bookstores.

BRAZILIAN PORTUGUESE VOCABULARY
for English speakers

T&P Books vocabularies are intended to help you learn, memorize, and review foreign words. The vocabulary contains over 7000 commonly used words arranged thematically.

- Vocabulary contains the most commonly used words
- Recommended as an addition to any language course
- Meets the needs of beginners and advanced learners of foreign languages
- Convenient for daily use, revision sessions, and self-testing activities
- Allows you to assess your vocabulary

Special features of the vocabulary

- Words are organized according to their meaning, not alphabetically
- Words are presented in three columns to facilitate the reviewing and self-testing processes
- Words in groups are divided into small blocks to facilitate the learning process
- The vocabulary offers a convenient and simple transcription of each foreign word

The vocabulary has 198 topics including:

Basic Concepts, Numbers, Colors, Months, Seasons, Units of Measurement, Clothing & Accessories, Food & Nutrition, Restaurant, Family Members, Relatives, Character, Feelings, Emotions, Diseases, City, Town, Sightseeing, Shopping, Money, House, Home, Office, Working in the Office, Import & Export, Marketing, Job Search, Sports, Education, Computer, Internet, Tools, Nature, Countries, Nationalities and more ...

TABLE OF CONTENTS

NATURE   170
The Earth. Part 1   170

The Earth. Part 2   178

Fauna   180

Flora   190

PRONUNCIATION GUIDE

T&P phonetic alphabet	Portuguese example	English example

Vowels

[a]	baixo ['baɪʃu]	shorter than in ask
[e]	erro ['eʀu]	elm, medal
[ɛ]	leve ['lɛvə]	man, bad
[i]	lancil [lã'sil]	shorter than in feet
[o], [ɔ]	boca, orar ['bokə], [ɔ'rar]	drop, baught
[u]	urgente [ur̩'ʒẽtə]	book
[ã]	toranja [tu'rãʒe]	nasal [a]
[ẽ]	gente ['ʒẽtɛ]	fang
[ĩ]	seringa [sə̃'ɾgɐ]	nasal [i]
[õ]	ponto ['põtu]	strong
[ũ]	umbigo [ũ'bɨgu]	nasal [u]

Consonants

[b]	banco ['bãku]	baby, book
[d]	duche ['duʃə]	day, doctor
[dʒ]	abade [a'bɛdʒi]	joke, general
[f]	facto ['faktu]	face, food
[g]	gorila [gu'rilɐ]	game, gold
[j]	feira ['fejrɐ]	yes, New York
[k]	claro ['klaru]	clock, kiss
[l]	Londres ['lõdrəʃ]	lace, people
[ʎ]	molho ['moʎu]	daily, million
[m]	montanha [mõ'tɐɲɐ]	magic, milk
[n]	novela [nu'vɛlɐ]	name, normal
[ɲ]	senhora [sə'ɲorɐ]	canyon, new
[ŋ]	marketing ['markətiŋ]	ring
[p]	prata ['pratɐ]	pencil, private
[s]	safira [sɐ'firɐ]	city, boss
[ʃ]	texto ['tɛʃtu]	machine, shark
[t]	teto ['tɛtu]	tourist, trip
[tʃ]	doente [do'ẽtʃi]	church, French

T&P phonetic alphabet	Portuguese example	English example
[v]	alvo ['alvu]	very, river
[z]	vizinha [vi'ziɲɐ]	zebra, please
[ʒ]	juntos ['ʒũtuʃ]	forge, pleasure
[w]	sequoia [se'kwɔjɐ]	vase, winter

ABBREVIATIONS
used in the vocabulary

English abbreviations

ab.	-	about
adj	-	adjective
adv	-	adverb
anim.	-	animate
as adj	-	attributive noun usec as adjective
e.g.	-	for example
etc.	-	et cetera
fam.	-	familiar
fem.	-	feminine
form.	-	formal
inanim.	-	inanimate
masc.	-	masculine
math	-	mathematics
mil.	-	military
n	-	noun
pl	-	plural
pron.	-	pronoun
sb	-	somebody
sing.	-	singular
sth	-	something
v aux	-	auxiliary verb
vi	-	intransitive verb
vi, vt	-	intransitive, transitive verb
vt	-	transitive verb

Portuguese abbreviations

f	-	feminine noun
f pl	-	feminine plural
m	-	masculine noun
m pl	-	masculine plural
m, f	-	masculine, feminine
pl	-	plural
v aux	-	auxiliary verb

vi	-	intransitive verb
vi, vt	-	intransitive, transitive verb
vr	-	reflexive verb
vt	-	transitive verb

BASIC CONCEPTS

Basic concepts. Part 1

1. Pronouns

I, me	eu	['ew]
you	você	[vɔ'se]
he	ele	['ɛli]
she	ela	['ɛla]
we	nós	[nɔs]
you (to a group)	vocês	[vɔ'ses]
they (masc.)	eles	['ɛlis]
they (fem.)	elas	['ɛlas]

2. Greetings. Salutations. Farewells

Hello! (fam.)	Oi!	[ɔj]
Hello! (form.)	Olá!	[o'la]
Good morning!	Bom dia!	[bõ 'dʒia]
Good afternoon!	Boa tarde!	['boa 'tardʒi]
Good evening!	Boa noite!	['boa 'nojtʃi]
to say hello	cumprimentar (vt)	[kũprimẽ'tar]
Hi! (hello)	Oi!	[ɔj]
greeting (n)	saudação (f)	[sawda'sãw]
to greet (vt)	saudar (vt)	[saw'dar]
How are you? (form.)	Como você está?	['kɔmu vo'se is'ta]
How are you? (fam.)	Como vai?	['kɔmu 'vaj]
What's new?	E aí, novidades?	[a a'i novi'dadʒis]
Bye-Bye! Goodbye!	Tchau!	['tʃaw]
See you soon!	Até breve!	[a'tɛ 'brɛvi]
Farewell!	Adeus!	[a'dews]
to say goodbye	despedir-se (vr)	[dʒispe'dʒirsi]
So long!	Até mais!	[a'tɛ majs]
Thank you!	Obrigado! -a!	[obri'gadu, -a]
Thank you very much!	Muito obrigado! -a!	['mwĩtu obri'gadu, -a]
You're welcome	De nada	[de 'nada]
Don't mention it!	Não tem de quê	['nãw tẽj de ke]

It was nothing	Não foi nada!	['nãw foj 'nada]
Excuse me! (fam.)	Desculpa!	[dʒis'kuwpa]
Excuse me! (form.)	Desculpe!	[dʒis'kuwpe]
to excuse (forgive)	desculpar (vt)	[dʒiskuw'par]

to apologize (vi)	desculpar-se (vr)	[dʒiskuw'parsi]
My apologies	Me desculpe	[mi dʒis'kuwpe]
I'm sorry!	Desculpe!	[dʒis'kuwpe]
to forgive (vt)	perdoar (vt)	[per'dwar]
It's okay! (that's all right)	Não faz mal	['nãw fajʒ maw]
please (adv)	por favor	[por fa'vor]

Don't forget!	Não se esqueça!	['nãw si is'kesa]
Certainly!	Com certeza!	[kõ ser'teza]
Of course not!	Claro que não!	['klaru ki 'nãw]
Okay! (I agree)	Está bem! De acordo!	[is'ta bẽj], [de a'kordu]
That's enough!	Chega!	['ʃega]

3. Cardinal numbers. Part 1

0 zero	zero	['zɛru]
1 one	um	[ũ]
2 two	dois	['dojs]
3 three	três	[tres]
4 four	quatro	['kwatru]

5 five	cinco	['sĩku]
6 six	seis	[sejs]
7 seven	sete	['sɛtʃi]
8 eight	oito	['ojtu]
9 nine	nove	['nɔvi]

10 ten	dez	[dɛz]
11 eleven	onze	['õzi]
12 twelve	doze	['dozi]
13 thirteen	treze	['trezi]
14 fourteen	catorze	[ka'torzi]

15 fifteen	quinze	['kĩzi]
16 sixteen	dezesseis	[deze'sejs]
17 seventeen	dezessete	[dezi'setʃi]
18 eighteen	dezoito	[dʒi'zojtu]
19 nineteen	dezenove	[deze'nɔvi]

20 twenty	vinte	['vĩtʃi]
21 twenty-one	vinte e um	['vĩtʃi i ũ]
22 twenty-two	vinte e dois	['vĩtʃi i 'dojs]
23 twenty-three	vinte e três	['vĩtʃi i 'tres]
30 thirty	trinta	['trĩta]
31 thirty-one	trinta e um	['trĩta i ũ]

| 32 thirty-two | trinta e dois | ['trĩta i 'dojs] |
| 33 thirty-three | trinta e três | ['trĩta i 'tres] |

40 forty	quarenta	[kwa'rẽta]
41 forty-one	quarenta e um	[kwa'rẽta i 'ũ]
42 forty-two	quarenta e dois	[kwa'rẽta i 'dojs]
43 forty-three	quarenta e três	[kwa'rẽta i 'tres]

50 fifty	cinquenta	[sĩ'kwẽta]
51 fifty-one	cinquenta e um	[sĩ'kwẽta i ũ]
52 fifty-two	cinquenta e dois	[sĩ'kwẽta i 'dojs]
53 fifty-three	cinquenta e três	[sĩ'kwẽta i 'tres]

60 sixty	sessenta	[se'sẽta]
61 sixty-one	sessenta e um	[se'sẽta i ũ]
62 sixty-two	sessenta e dois	[se'sẽta i 'dojs]
63 sixty-three	sessenta e três	[se'sẽta i 'tres]

70 seventy	setenta	[se'tẽta]
71 seventy-one	setenta e um	[se'tẽta i ũ]
72 seventy-two	setenta e dois	[se'tẽta i 'dojs]
73 seventy-three	setenta e três	[se'tẽta i 'tres]

80 eighty	oitenta	[oj'tẽta]
81 eighty-one	oitenta e um	[oj'tẽta i 'ũ]
82 eighty-two	oitenta e dois	[oj'tẽta i 'dojs]
83 eighty-three	oitenta e três	[oj'tẽta i 'tres]

90 ninety	noventa	[no'vẽta]
91 ninety-one	noventa e um	[no'vẽta i 'ũ]
92 ninety-two	noventa e dois	[no'vẽta i 'dojs]
93 ninety-three	noventa e três	[no'vẽta i 'tres]

4. Cardinal numbers. Part 2

100 one hundred	cem	[sẽ]
200 two hundred	duzentos	[du'zẽtus]
300 three hundred	trezentos	[tre'zẽtus]
400 four hundred	quatrocentos	[kwatro'sẽtus]
500 five hundred	quinhentos	[ki'ɲẽtus]

600 six hundred	seiscentos	[sej'sẽtus]
700 seven hundred	setecentos	[sete'sẽtus]
800 eight hundred	oitocentos	[ojtu'sẽtus]
900 nine hundred	novecentos	[nove'sẽtus]

1000 one thousand	mil	[miw]
2000 two thousand	dois mil	['dojs miw]
3000 three thousand	três mil	['tres miw]
10000 ten thousand	dez mil	['dɛz miw]

one hundred thousand	cem mil	[sẽ miw]
million	um milhão	[ũ mi'ʎãw]
billion	um bilhão	[ũ bi'ʎãw]

5. Numbers. Fractions

fraction	fração (f)	[fra'sãw]
one half	um meio	[ũ 'meju]
one third	um terço	[ũ 'tersu]
one quarter	um quarto	[ũ 'kwartu]

one eighth	um oitavo	[ũ oj'tavu]
one tenth	um décimo	[ũ 'dɛsimu]
two thirds	dois terços	['dojs 'tersus]
three quarters	três quartos	[tres 'kwartus]

6. Numbers. Basic operations

subtraction	subtração (f)	[subtra'sãw]
to subtract (vi, vt)	subtrair (vi, vt)	[subtra'ir]
division	divisão (f)	[dʒivi'zãw]
to divide (vt)	dividir (vt)	[dʒivi'dʒir]

addition	adição (f)	[adʒi'sãw]
to add up (vt)	somar (vt)	[so'mar]
to add (vi, vt)	adicionar (vt)	[adʒisjo'nar]
multiplication	multiplicação (f)	[muwtʃiplika'sãw]
to multiply (vt)	multiplicar (vt)	[muwtʃipli'kar]

7. Numbers. Miscellaneous

digit, figure	algarismo, dígito (m)	[awga'rizmu], ['dʒiʒitu]
number	número (m)	['numeru]
numeral	numeral (m)	[nume'raw]
minus sign	sinal (m) de menos	[si'naw de 'menus]
plus sign	mais (m)	[majs]
formula	fórmula (f)	['fɔrmula]

calculation	cálculo (m)	['kawkulu]
to count (vi, vt)	contar (vt)	[kõ'tar]
to count up	calcular (vt)	[kawku'lar]
to compare (vt)	comparar (vt)	[kõpa'rar]

How much?	Quanto?	['kwãtu]
How many?	Quantos? -as?	['kwãtus, -as]
sum, total	soma (f)	['sɔma]

result	resultado (m)	[hezuw'tadu]
remainder	resto (m)	['hɛstu]
a few (e.g., ~ years ago)	alguns, algumas ...	[aw'gũs], [aw'gumas]
few (I have ~ friends)	poucos, poucas	['pokus], ['pokas]
a little (~ water)	um pouco ...	[ũ 'poku]
the rest	resto (m)	['hɛstu]
one and a half	um e meio	[ũ i 'meju]
dozen	dúzia (f)	['duzja]
in half (adv)	ao meio	[aw 'meju]
equally (evenly)	em partes iguais	[ẽ 'partʃis i'gwais]
half	metade (f)	[me'tadʒi]
time (three ~s)	vez (·)	[vez]

to advise (vt)	aconselhar (vt)	[akõse'ʎɛr]
to agree (say yes)	concordar (vi)	[kõkor'dar]
to answer (vi, vt)	responder (vt)	[hespõ'der]
to apologize (vi)	desculpar-se (vr)	[dʒiskuw'parsi]
to arrive (vi)	chegar (vi)	[ʃe'gar]
to ask (~ oneself)	perguntar (vt)	[pergũ'tar]
to ask (~ sb to do sth)	pedir (vt)	[pe'dʒir]
to be (~ a teacher)	ser (·)	[ser]
to be (~ on a diet)	estar (vi)	[is'tar]
to be afraid	ter medo	[ter 'medɹ]
to be hungry	ter fome	[ter 'fomi]
to be interested in ...	interessar-se (vr)	[ĩtere'sarsi]
to be needed	ser necessário	[ser nese'sarju]
to be surprised	surpreender-se (vr)	[surprjẽ'dersi]
to be thirsty	ter sede	[ter 'sedʒi]
to begin (vt)	começar (vt)	[kome'sɛr]
to belong to ...	pertencer (vt)	[pertẽ'ser]
to boast (vi)	gabar-se (vr)	[ga'barsi]
to break (split into pieces)	quebrar (vt)	[ke'brar]
to call (~ for help)	chamar (vt)	[ʃa'mar]
can (v aux)	poder (vi)	[po'der]
to catch (vt)	pegar (vt)	[pe'gar]
to change (vt)	mudar (vt)	[mu'dar]
to choose (select)	escolher (vt)	[isko'ʎer]
to come down (the stairs)	descer (vi)	[de'ser]
to compare (vt)	comparar (vt)	[kõpa'rar]
to complain (vi, vt)	queixar-se (vr)	[kej'ʃarsi]
to confuse (mix up)	confundir (vt)	[kõfũ'dʒir]

to continue (vt)	**continuar** (vt)	[kõtʃi'nwar]
to control (vt)	**controlar** (vt)	[kõtro'lar]
to cook (dinner)	**preparar** (vt)	[prepa'rar]
to cost (vt)	**custar** (vt)	[kus'tar]
to count (add up)	**contar** (vt)	[kõ'tar]
to count on ...	**contar com ...**	[kõ'tar kõ]
to create (vt)	**criar** (vt)	[krjar]
to cry (weep)	**chorar** (vi)	[ʃo'rar]

9. The most important verbs. Part 2

to deceive (vi, vt)	**enganar** (vt)	[ẽga'nar]
to decorate (tree, street)	**decorar** (vt)	[deko'rar]
to defend (a country, etc.)	**defender** (vt)	[defẽ'der]
to demand (request firmly)	**exigir** (vt)	[ezi'ʒir]
to dig (vt)	**cavar** (vt)	[ka'var]
to discuss (vt)	**discutir** (vt)	[dʒisku'tʃir]
to do (vt)	**fazer** (vt)	[fa'zer]
to doubt (have doubts)	**duvidar** (vt)	[duvi'dar]
to drop (let fall)	**deixar cair** (vt)	[dej'ʃar ka'ir]
to enter (room, house, etc.)	**entrar** (vi)	[ẽ'trar]
to excuse (forgive)	**desculpar** (vt)	[dʒiskuw'par]
to exist (vi)	**existir** (vi)	[ezis'tʃir]
to expect (foresee)	**prever** (vt)	[pre'ver]
to explain (vt)	**explicar** (vt)	[ispli'kar]
to fall (vi)	**cair** (vi)	[ka'ir]
to find (vt)	**encontrar** (vt)	[ẽkõ'trar]
to finish (vt)	**acabar, terminar** (vt)	[aka'bar], [termi'nar]
to fly (vi)	**voar** (vi)	[vo'ar]
to follow ... (come after)	**seguir ...**	[se'gir]
to forget (vi, vt)	**esquecer** (vt)	[iske'ser]
to forgive (vt)	**perdoar** (vt)	[per'dwar]
to give (vt)	**dar** (vt)	[dar]
to give a hint	**dar uma dica**	[dar 'uma 'dʒika]
to go (on foot)	**ir** (vi)	[ir]
to go for a swim	**ir nadar**	[ir na'dar]
to go out (for dinner, etc.)	**sair** (vi)	[sa'ir]
to guess (the answer)	**adivinhar** (vt)	[adʒivi'ɲar]
to have (vt)	**ter** (vt)	[ter]
to have breakfast	**tomar café da manhã**	[to'mar ka'fɛ da ma'ɲã]
to have dinner	**jantar** (vi)	[ʒã'tar]
to have lunch	**almoçar** (vi)	[awmo'sar]

to hear (vt)	ouvir (vt)	[o'vir]
to help (vt)	ajudar (vt)	[aʒu'dar]
to hide (vt)	esconder (vt)	[iskõ'der]
to hope (vi, vt)	esperar (vi, vt)	[ispe'rar]
to hunt (vi, vt)	caçar (vi)	[ka'sar]
to hurry (vi)	apressar-se (vr)	[apre'sarsi]

10. The most important verbs. Part 3

to inform (vt)	informar (vt)	[ĩfor'mar]
to insist (vi, vt)	insistir (vi)	[ĩsis'tʃir]
to insult (vt)	insultar (vt)	[ĩsuw'tar]
to invite (vt)	convidar (vt)	[kõvi'dar]
to joke (vi)	brincar (vi)	[brĩ'kar]

to keep (vt)	guardar (vt)	[gwar'dar]
to keep silent, to hush	ficar em silêncio	[fi'kar ẽ si'lẽsju]
to kill (vt)	matar (vt)	[ma'tar]
to know (sb)	conhecer (vt)	[koɲe'sər]
to know (sth)	saber (vt)	[sa'ber]
to laugh (vi)	rir (vi)	[hir]

to liberate (city, etc.)	libertar, liberar (vt)	[liber'tar], [libe'rar]
to like (I like ...)	gostar (vt)	[gos'tar]
to look for ... (search)	buscar (vt)	[bus'kar]
to love (sb)	amar (vt)	[a'mar]
to make a mistake	errar (vi)	[e'har]

to manage, to run	dirigir (vt)	[dʒiri'ʒi-]
to mean (signify)	significar (vt)	[signifi'kar]
to mention (talk about)	mencionar (vt)	[mẽsjo'nar]
to miss (school, etc.)	faltar a ...	[faw'tar a]
to notice (see)	perceber (vt)	[perse'ber]

to object (vi, vt)	objetar (vt)	[obʒe'tar]
to observe (see)	observar (vt)	[obser'var]
to open (vt)	abrir (vt)	[a'brir]
to order (meal, etc.)	pedir (vt)	[pe'dʒi-]
to order (mil.)	ordenar (vt)	[orde'nar]
to own (possess)	possuir (vt)	[po'swir]

to participate (vi)	participar (vi)	[partʃisi'par]
to pay (vi, vt)	pagar (vi, vt)	[pa'ga-]
to permit (vt)	permitir (vt)	[permi'tʃir]
to plan (vt)	planejar (vt)	[plane'ʒar]
to play (children)	brincar, jogar (vi, vt)	[brĩ'ka-], [ʒo'gar]

to pray (vi, vt)	rezar, orar (vi)	[he'zar], [o'rar]
to prefer (vt)	preferir (vt)	[prefe'rir]
to promise (vt)	prometer (vt)	[promə'ter]

to pronounce (vt)	**pronunciar** (vt)	[pronũ'sjar]
to propose (vt)	**propor** (vt)	[pro'por]
to punish (vt)	**punir** (vt)	[pu'nir]

11. The most important verbs. Part 4

to read (vi, vt)	**ler** (vt)	[ler]
to recommend (vt)	**recomendar** (vt)	[hekomẽ'dar]
to refuse (vi, vt)	**negar-se** (vt)	[ne'garsi]
to regret (be sorry)	**arrepender-se** (vr)	[ahepẽ'dersi]
to rent (sth from sb)	**alugar** (vt)	[alu'gar]

to repeat (say again)	**repetir** (vt)	[hepe'tʃir]
to reserve, to book	**reservar** (vt)	[hezer'var]
to run (vi)	**correr** (vi)	[ko'her]
to save (rescue)	**salvar** (vt)	[saw'var]
to say (~ thank you)	**dizer** (vt)	[dʒi'zer]

to scold (vt)	**ralhar, repreender** (vt)	[ha'ʎar], [heprjẽ'der]
to see (vt)	**ver** (vt)	[ver]
to sell (vt)	**vender** (vt)	[vẽ'der]
to send (vt)	**enviar** (vt)	[ẽ'vjar]
to shoot (vi)	**disparar, atirar** (vi)	[dʒispa'rar], [atʃi'rar]

to shout (vi)	**gritar** (vi)	[gri'tar]
to show (vt)	**mostrar** (vt)	[mos'trar]
to sign (document)	**assinar** (vt)	[asi'nar]
to sit down (vi)	**sentar-se** (vr)	[sẽ'tarsi]

to smile (vi)	**sorrir** (vi)	[so'hir]
to speak (vi, vt)	**falar** (vi)	[fa'lar]
to steal (money, etc.)	**roubar** (vt)	[ho'bar]
to stop (for pause, etc.)	**parar** (vi)	[pa'rar]
to stop (please ~ calling me)	**cessar** (vt)	[se'sar]

to study (vt)	**estudar** (vt)	[istu'dar]
to swim (vi)	**nadar** (vi)	[na'dar]
to take (vt)	**pegar** (vt)	[pe'gar]
to think (vi, vt)	**pensar** (vi, vt)	[pẽ'sar]
to threaten (vt)	**ameaçar** (vt)	[amea'sar]

to touch (with hands)	**tocar** (vt)	[to'kar]
to translate (vt)	**traduzir** (vt)	[tradu'zir]
to trust (vt)	**confiar** (vt)	[kõ'fjar]
to try (attempt)	**tentar** (vt)	[tẽ'tar]
to turn (e.g., ~ left)	**virar** (vi)	[vi'rar]

| to underestimate (vt) | **subestimar** (vt) | [subestʃi'mar] |
| to understand (vt) | **entender** (vt) | [ẽtẽ'der] |

| to unite (vt) | unir (vt) | [u'nir] |
| to wait (vt) | esperar (vt) | [ispe'rar] |

to want (wish, desire)	querer (vt)	[ke'rer]
to warn (vt)	advertir (vt)	[adʒiver tʃir]
to work (vi)	trabalhar (vi)	[traba'ʎar]
to write (vt)	escrever (vt)	[iskre'ver]
to write down	anotar (vt)	[ano'tar]

12. Colors

color	cor (f)	[kɔr]
shade (tint)	tom (m)	[tõ]
hue	tonalidade (m)	[tonali'dadʒi]
rainbow	arco-íris (m)	['arku 'iris]

white (adj)	branco	['brãku]
black (adj)	preto	['pretu]
gray (adj)	cinza	['sĩza]

green (adj)	verde	['verdʒi]
yellow (adj)	amarelo	[ama'rɛu]
red (adj)	vermelho	[ver'meʎu]

blue (adj)	azul	[a'zuw]
light blue (adj)	azul claro	[a'zuw 'klaru]
pink (adj)	rosa	['hoza]
orange (adj)	laranja	[la'rãʒa]
violet (adj)	violeta	[vjo'leta]
brown (adj)	marrom	[ma'hõ]

| golden (adj) | dourado | [do'radu] |
| silvery (adj) | prateado | [pra'tʃjadu] |

beige (adj)	bege	['bɛʒi]
cream (adj)	creme	['krɛmi]
turquoise (adj)	turquesa	[tur'keza]
cherry red (adj)	vermelho cereja	[ver'meʎu se'reʒa]
lilac (adj)	lilás	[li'las]
crimson (adj)	carmim	[kah'mĩ]

light (adj)	claro	['klaru]
dark (adj)	escuro	[is'kuru]
bright, vivid (adj)	vivo	['vivu]

colored (pencils)	de cor	[de kɔr]
color (e.g., ~ film)	a cores	[a 'kores]
black-and-white (adj)	preto e branco	['pretu i 'brãku]
plain (one-colored)	de uma só cor	[de 'uma sɔ kɔr]
multicolored (adj)	multicolor	[muwtʃiko'lor]

13. Questions

Who?	Quem?	[kẽj]
What?	O que?	[u ki]
Where? (at, in)	Onde?	['õdʒi]
Where (to)?	Para onde?	['para 'õdʒi]
From where?	De onde?	[de 'õdʒi]
When?	Quando?	['kwãdu]
Why? (What for?)	Para quê?	['para ke]
Why? (~ are you crying?)	Por quê?	[por 'ke]

What for?	Para quê?	['para ke]
How? (in what way)	Como?	['kɔmu]
What? (What kind of ...?)	Qual?	[kwaw]
Which?	Qual?	[kwaw]

To whom?	A quem?	[a kẽj]
About whom?	De quem?	[de kẽj]
About what?	Do quê?	[du ke]
With whom?	Com quem?	[kõ kẽj]

How many?	Quantos? -as?	['kwãtus, -as]
How much?	Quanto?	['kwãtu]
Whose?	De quem?	[de kẽj]

14. Function words. Adverbs. Part 1

Where? (at, in)	Onde?	['õdʒi]
here (adv)	aqui	[a'ki]
there (adv)	lá, ali	[la], [a'li]

| somewhere (to be) | em algum lugar | [ẽ aw'gũ lu'gar] |
| nowhere (not in any place) | em lugar nenhum | [ẽ lu'gar ne'ɲũ] |

| by (near, beside) | perto de ... | ['pɛrtu de] |
| by the window | perto da janela | ['pɛrtu da ʒa'nɛla] |

Where (to)?	Para onde?	['para 'õdʒi]
here (e.g., come ~!)	aqui	[a'ki]
there (e.g., to go ~)	para lá	['para la]
from here (adv)	daqui	[da'ki]
from there (adv)	de lá, dali	[de la], [da'li]

| close (adv) | perto | ['pɛrtu] |
| far (adv) | longe | ['lõʒi] |

near (e.g., ~ Paris)	perto de ...	['pɛrtu de]
nearby (adv)	à mão, perto	[a mãw], ['pɛrtu]
not far (adv)	não fica longe	['nãw 'fika 'lõʒi]

left (adj)	esquerdo	[is'kerdu]
on the left	à esquerda	[a is'kerda]
to the left	para a esquerda	['para a is'kerda]

right (adj)	direito	[dʒi'rejtu]
on the right	à direita	[a dʒi'rejta]
to the right	para a direita	['para a dʒi'rejta]

in front (adv)	em frente	[ẽ 'frẽtʃi]
front (as adj)	da frente	[da 'frẽtʃi]
ahead (the kids ran ~)	adiante	[a'dʒãtʃi]

behind (adv)	atrás de …	[a'trajs de]
from behind	de tras	[de trajs]
back (towards the rear)	para trás	['para trajs]

| middle | meio (m), metade (f) | ['meju], [me'tadʒi] |
| in the middle | no meio | [nu 'meju] |

at the side	do lado	[du 'ladu]
everywhere (adv)	em todo lugar	[ẽ 'todu lu'gar]
around (in all directions)	por todos os lados	[por 'todus os 'ladus]

from inside	de dentro	[de 'dẽtru]
somewhere (to go)	para algum lugar	['para av'gũ lu'gar]
straight (directly)	diretamente	[dʒireta'mẽtʃi]
back (e.g., come ~)	de volta	[de 'vowta]

| from anywhere | de algum lugar | [de aw'gũ lu'gar] |
| from somewhere | de algum lugar | [de aw'gũ lu'gar] |

firstly (adv)	em primeiro lugar	[ẽ pri'mejru lu'gar]
secondly (adv)	em segundo lugar	[ẽ se'gũdu lu'gar]
thirdly (adv)	em terceiro lugar	[ẽ ter'sejru lu'gar]

suddenly (adv)	de repente	[de he'pẽtʃi]
at first (in the beginning)	no início	[nu i'nisju]
for the first time	pela primeira vez	['pɛla pri'mejra 'vez]
long before …	muito antes de …	['mwĩtu 'ãtʃis de]
anew (over again)	de novo	[de 'novu]
for good (adv)	para sempre	['para 'sẽpri]

never (adv)	nunca	['nũka]
again (adv)	de novo	[de 'novu]
now (at present)	agora	[a'gora]
often (adv)	frequentemente	[frekwẽ:ʃi'mẽtʃi]
then (adv)	então	[ẽ'tãw]
urgently (quickly)	urgentemente	[urʒẽte'mẽtʃi]
usually (adv)	normalmente	[normaw'mẽtʃi]

| by the way, … | a propósito, … | [a pro'pozitu] |
| possibly | é possível | [ɛ po'sivew] |

probably (adv)	provavelmente	[provavɛw'mētʃi]
maybe (adv)	talvez	[taw'vez]
besides ...	além disso, ...	[a'lēj 'dʒisu]
that's why ...	por isso ...	[por 'isu]
in spite of ...	apesar de ...	[ape'zar de]
thanks to ...	graças a ...	['grasas a]

what (pron.)	que	[ki]
that (conj.)	que	[ki]
something	algo	[awgu]
anything (something)	alguma coisa	[aw'guma 'kojza]
nothing	nada	['nada]

who (pron.)	quem	[kēj]
someone	alguém	[aw'gēj]
somebody	alguém	[aw'gēj]

nobody	ninguém	[nĩ'gēj]
nowhere (a voyage to ~)	para lugar nenhum	['para lu'gar ne'ɲũ]
nobody's	de ninguém	[de nĩ'gēj]
somebody's	de alguém	[de aw'gēj]

so (I'm ~ glad)	tão	[tãw]
also (as well)	também	[tã'bēj]
too (as well)	também	[tã'bēj]

15. Function words. Adverbs. Part 2

Why?	Por quê?	[por 'ke]
for some reason	por alguma razão	[por aw'guma ha'zãw]
because ...	porque ...	[por'ke]
for some purpose	por qualquer razão	[por kwaw'ker ha'zãw]

and	e	[i]
or	ou	['o]
but	mas	[mas]
for (e.g., ~ me)	para	['para]

too (~ many people)	muito, demais	['mwĩtu], [dʒi'majs]
only (exclusively)	só, somente	[sɔ], [so'mētʃi]
exactly (adv)	exatamente	[ɛzata'mētʃi]
about (more or less)	cerca de ...	['serka de]

approximately (adv)	aproximadamente	[aprosimada'mēti]
approximate (adj)	aproximado	[aprosi'madu]
almost (adv)	quase	['kwazi]
the rest	resto (m)	['hɛstu]

| the other (second) | o outro | [u 'otru] |
| other (different) | outro | ['otru] |

each (adj)	cada	['kada]
any (no matter which)	qualquer	[kwaw'kər]
many (adj)	muitos, muitas	['mwĩtos], ['mwĩtas]
much (adv)	muito	['mwĩtu]
many people	muitas pessoas	['mwĩtas pe'soas]
all (everyone)	todos	['todus]
in return for …	em troca de …	[ẽ 'trɔka de]
in exchange (adv)	em troca	[ẽ 'trɔka]
by hand (made)	à mão	[a mãw]
hardly (negative opinion)	pouco provável	['poku pro'vavew]
probably (adv)	provavelmente	[provavɛw'mẽtʃi]
on purpose (intentionally)	de propósito	[de pro'ɔozitu]
by accident (adv)	por acidente	[por asi'dẽtʃi]
very (adv)	muito	['mwĩtu]
for example (adv)	por exemplo	[por e'zẽplu]
between	entre	['ẽtri]
among	entre, no meio de …	['ẽtri], [ɲu 'meju de]
so much (such a lot)	tanto	['tãtu]
especially (adv)	especialmente	[ispesjal'mẽte]

Basic concepts. Part 2

16. Opposites

rich (adj)	rico	['hiku]
poor (adj)	pobre	['pɔbri]
ill, sick (adj)	doente	[do'ẽtʃi]
well (not sick)	bem	[bẽj]
big (adj)	grande	['grãdʒi]
small (adj)	pequeno	[pe'kenu]
quickly (adv)	rapidamente	[hapida'mẽtʃi]
slowly (adv)	lentamente	[lẽta'mẽtʃi]
fast (adj)	rápido	['hapidu]
slow (adj)	lento	['lẽtu]
glad (adj)	alegre, feliz	[a'lɛgri], [fe'liz]
sad (adj)	triste	['tristʃi]
together (adv)	juntos	['ʒũtus]
separately (adv)	separadamente	[separada'mẽtʃi]
aloud (to read)	em voz alta	[ẽ vɔz 'awta]
silently (to oneself)	para si	['para si]
tall (adj)	alto	['awtu]
low (adj)	baixo	['baɪʃu]
deep (adj)	profundo	[pro'fũdu]
shallow (adj)	raso	['hazu]
yes	sim	[sĩ]
no	não	[nãw]
distant (in space)	distante	[dʒis'tãtʃi]
nearby (adj)	próximo	['prɔsimu]
far (adv)	longe	['lõʒi]
nearby (adv)	perto	['pɛrtu]
long (adj)	longo	['lõgu]
short (adj)	curto	['kurtu]
good (kindhearted)	bom, bondoso	[bõ], [bõ'dozu]

evil (adj)	mal	[maw]
married (adj)	casado	[ka'zadu]
single (adj)	solteiro	[sow'tejru]
to forbid (vt)	proibir (vt)	[proi'bir]
to permit (vt)	permitir (vt)	[permi'tʃir]
end	fim (m)	[fi]
beginning	início (m)	[i'nisju]
left (adj)	esquerdo	[is'kerdʋ]
right (adj)	direito	[dʒi'rejtu]
first (adj)	primeiro	[pri'mejru]
last (adj)	último	['uwtʃimu]
crime	crime (m)	['krimi]
punishment	castigo (m)	[kas'tʃigu]
to order (vt)	ordenar (vt)	[orde'nɛr]
to obey (vi, vt)	obedecer (vt)	[obede'ser]
straight (adj)	reto	['hɛtu]
curved (adj)	curvo	['kurvu]
paradise	paraíso (m)	[para'izu]
hell	inferno (m)	[ĩ'fɛrnu]
to be born	nascer (vi)	[na'ser]
to die (vi)	morrer (vi)	[mo'her]
strong (adj)	forte	['fɔrtʃi]
weak (adj)	fraco, débil	['fraku], ['debiw]
old (adj)	velho, idoso	['vɛʎu], [i'dozu]
young (adj)	jovem	['ʒɔvẽ]
old (adj)	velho	['vɛʎu]
new (adj)	novo	['novu]
hard (adj)	duro	['duru]
soft (adj)	macio	[ma'siu]
warm (tepid)	quente	['kẽtʃi]
cold (adj)	frio	['friu]
fat (adj)	gordo	['gordu]
thin (adj)	magro	['magru]
narrow (adj)	estreito	[is'trejtu]
wide (adj)	largo	['largu]
good (adj)	bom	[bõ]

bad (adj)	mau	[maw]
brave (adj)	valente, corajoso	[va'lẽtʃi], [kora'ʒozu]
cowardly (adj)	covarde	[ko'vardʒi]

17. Weekdays

Monday	segunda-feira (f)	[se'gũda-'fejra]
Tuesday	terça-feira (f)	['tersa 'fejra]
Wednesday	quarta-feira (f)	['kwarta-'fejra]
Thursday	quinta-feira (f)	['kĩta-'fejra]
Friday	sexta-feira (f)	['sesta-'fejra]
Saturday	sábado (m)	['sabadu]
Sunday	domingo (m)	[do'mĩgu]

today (adv)	hoje	['oʒi]
tomorrow (adv)	amanhã	[ama'ɲã]
the day after tomorrow	depois de amanhã	[de'pojs de ama'ɲã]
yesterday (adv)	ontem	['õtẽ]
the day before yesterday	anteontem	[ãtʃi'õtẽ]

day	dia (m)	['dʒia]
working day	dia (m) de trabalho	['dʒia de tra'baʎu]
public holiday	feriado (m)	[fe'rjadu]
day off	dia (m) de folga	['dʒia de 'fɔwga]
weekend	fim (m) de semana	[fĩ de se'mana]

all day long	o dia todo	[u 'dʒia 'todu]
the next day (adv)	no dia seguinte	[nu 'dʒia se'gĩtʃi]
two days ago	há dois dias	[a 'dojs 'dʒias]
the day before	na véspera	[na 'vɛspera]
daily (adj)	diário	['dʒjarju]
every day (adv)	todos os dias	['todus us 'dʒias]

week	semana (f)	[se'mana]
last week (adv)	na semana passada	[na se'mana pa'sada]
next week (adv)	semana que vem	[se'mana ke vẽj]
weekly (adj)	semanal	[sema'naw]
every week (adv)	toda semana	['tɔda se'mana]
twice a week	duas vezes por semana	['duas 'vezis por se'mana]
every Tuesday	toda terça-feira	['tɔda tersa 'fejra]

18. Hours. Day and night

morning	manhã (f)	[ma'ɲã]
in the morning	de manhã	[de ma'ɲã]
noon, midday	meio-dia (m)	['meju 'dʒia]
in the afternoon	à tarde	[a 'tardʒi]
evening	tardinha (f)	[tar'dʒiɲa]

in the evening	à tardinha	[a tar'dʒiɲa]
night	noite (f)	['nojtʃi]
at night	à noite	[a 'nojtʃi]
midnight	meia-noite (f)	['meja 'ncjtʃi]

second	segundo (m)	[se'gũdu]
minute	minuto (m)	[mi'nutu]
hour	hora (f)	['ɔra]
half an hour	meia hora (f)	['meja 'ɔra]
a quarter-hour	quarto (m) de hora	['kwartu de 'ɔra]
fifteen minutes	quinze minutos	['kĩzi mi'nutus]
24 hours	vinte e quatro horas	['vĩtʃi i 'kwatru 'ɔras]

sunrise	nascer (m) do sol	[na'ser du sɔw]
dawn	amanhecer (m)	[amaɲe'ser]
early morning	madrugada (f)	[madru'gada]
sunset	pôr-do-sol (m)	[por du 'sɔw]

early in the morning	de madrugada	[de madru'gada]
this morning	esta manhã	['ɛsta ma'ɲã]
tomorrow morning	amanhã de manhã	[ama'ɲã de ma'ɲã]

this afternoon	esta tarde	['ɛsta 'tardʒi]
in the afternoon	à tarde	[a 'tardʒi]
tomorrow afternoon	amanhã à tarde	[ama'ɲã a 'tardʒi]

| tonight (this evening) | esta noite, hoje à noite | ['ɛsta 'nojtʃi], ['oʒi a 'nojtʃi] |
| tomorrow night | amanhã à noite | [ama'ɲã a 'nojtʃi] |

at 3 o'clock sharp	às três horas em ponto	[as tres 'ɔras ẽ 'põtu]
about 4 o'clock	por volta das quatro	[por 'vɔwta das 'kwatru]
by 12 o'clock	às doze	[as 'dozi]

in 20 minutes	em vinte minutos	[ẽ 'vĩtʃi mi'nutus]
in an hour	em uma hora	[ẽ 'uma 'ɔra]
on time (adv)	a tempo	[a 'tẽpu]

a quarter to ...	... um quarto para	[... ũ 'kwartu 'para]
within an hour	dentro de uma hora	['dẽtru de 'uma 'ɔra]
every 15 minutes	a cada quinze minutos	[a 'kada 'kĩzi mi'nutus]
round the clock	as vinte e quatro horas	[as 'vĩtʃi i 'kwatru 'oras]

19. Months. Seasons

January	janeiro (m)	[ʒa'nejru]
February	fevereiro (m)	[feve'rejru]
March	março (m)	['marsu]
April	abril (m)	[a'briw]
May	maio (m)	['maju]
June	junho (m)	['ʒuɲu]

July	julho (m)	['ʒuʎu]
August	agosto (m)	[a'gostu]
September	setembro (m)	[se'tẽbru]
October	outubro (m)	[o'tubru]
November	novembro (m)	[no'vẽbru]
December	dezembro (m)	[de'zẽbru]

spring	primavera (f)	[prima'vɛra]
in spring	na primavera	[na prima'vɛra]
spring (as adj)	primaveril	[primave'riw]

summer	verão (m)	[ve'rãw]
in summer	no verão	[nu ve'rãw]
summer (as adj)	de verão	[de ve'rãw]

fall	outono (m)	[o'tɔnu]
in fall	no outono	[nu o'tɔnu]
fall (as adj)	outonal	[oto'naw]

winter	inverno (m)	[ĩ'vɛrnu]
in winter	no inverno	[nu ĩ'vɛrnu]
winter (as adj)	de inverno	[de ĩ'vɛrnu]

month	mês (m)	[mes]
this month	este mês	['estʃi mes]
next month	mês que vem	['mes ki vẽj]
last month	no mês passado	[no mes pa'sadu]

a month ago	um mês atrás	[ũ 'mes a'trajs]
in a month (a month later)	em um mês	[ẽ ũ mes]
in 2 months (2 months later)	em dois meses	[ẽ dojs 'mezis]
the whole month	todo o mês	['todu u mes]
all month long	um mês inteiro	[ũ mes ĩ'tejru]

monthly (~ magazine)	mensal	[mẽ'saw]
monthly (adv)	mensalmente	[mẽsaw'mẽtʃi]
every month	todo mês	['todu 'mes]
twice a month	duas vezes por mês	['duas 'vezis por mes]

year	ano (m)	['anu]
this year	este ano	['estʃi 'anu]
next year	ano que vem	['anu ki vẽj]
last year	no ano passado	[nu 'anu pa'sadu]

a year ago	há um ano	[a ũ 'anu]
in a year	em um ano	[ẽ ũ 'anu]
in two years	dentro de dois anos	['dẽtru de 'dojs 'anus]
the whole year	todo o ano	['todu u 'anu]
all year long	um ano inteiro	[ũ 'anu ĩ'tejru]
every year	cada ano	['kada 'anu]
annual (adj)	anual	[a'nwaw]

annually (adv)	anualmente	[anwaw'mɛte]
4 times a year	quatro vezes por ano	['kwatru 'vezis por 'anu]
date (e.g., today's ~)	data (f)	['data]
date (e.g., ~ of birth)	data (f)	['data]
calendar	calendário (m)	[kalẽ'darju]
half a year	meio ano	['meju 'anu]
six months	seis meses	[sejs 'mezis]
season (summer, etc.)	estação (f)	[ista'sãw]
century	século (m)	['sɛkulu]

20. Time. Miscellaneous

time	tempo (m)	['tẽpu]
moment	momento (m)	[mo'mẽtu]
instant (n)	instante (n)	[is'tãtʃi]
instant (adj)	instantâneo	[ĩstã'tanju]
lapse (of time)	lapso (m) de tempo	['lapsu de 'tẽpu]
life	vida (f)	['vida]
eternity	eternidade (f)	[eterni'dadʒi]
epoch	época (f)	['ɛpoka]
era	era (f)	['ɛra]
cycle	ciclo (m)	['siklu]
period	período (m)	[pe'riodu]
term (short-~)	prazo (m)	['prazu]
the future	futuro (m)	[fu'turu]
future (as adj)	futuro	[fu'turu]
next time	da próxima vez	[da 'prɔsima vez]
the past	passado (m)	[pa'sadu]
past (recent)	passado	[pa'sadu]
last time	na última vez	[na 'uwtʃima 'vez]
later (adv)	mais tarde	[majs 'tardʒi]
after (prep.)	depois	[de'pojs]
nowadays (adv)	atualmente	[atwaw'mẽtʃi]
now (at this moment)	agora	[a'gora]
immediately (adv)	imediatamente	[imedʒata'mẽtʃi]
soon (adv)	em breve	[ẽ 'brɛvi]
in advance (beforehand)	de antemão	[de ante'mãw]
a long time ago	há muito tempo	[a 'mwĩtu 'tẽpu]
recently (adv)	recentemente	[hesẽtʃi'mẽtʃi]
destiny	destino (m)	[des'tʃinu]
memories (childhood ~)	recordações (f pl)	[hekorda'sõjs]
archives	arquivo (m)	[ar'kivu]
during ...	durante ...	[du'rãtʃi]
long, a long time (adv)	durante muito tempo	[du'rãtʃi 'mwĩtu 'tẽpu]

not long (adv)	pouco tempo	['poku 'tẽpu]
early (in the morning)	cedo	['sedu]
late (not early)	tarde	['tardʒi]

forever (for good)	para sempre	['para 'sẽpri]
to start (begin)	começar (vt)	[kome'sar]
to postpone (vt)	adiar (vt)	[a'dʒjar]

at the same time	ao mesmo tempo	['aw 'mezmu 'tẽpu]
permanently (adv)	permanentemente	[permanẽtʃi'mẽtʃi]
constant (noise, pain)	constante	[kõs'tãtʃi]
temporary (adj)	temporário	[tẽpo'rarju]

sometimes (adv)	às vezes	[as 'vezis]
rarely (adv)	raras vezes, raramente	['harus 'vezis]' [hara'mẽtʃi]
often (adv)	frequentemente	[frekwẽtʃi'mẽtʃi]

21. Lines and shapes

square	quadrado (m)	[kwa'dradu]
square (as adj)	quadrado	[kwa'dradu]
circle	círculo (m)	['sirkulu]
round (adj)	redondo	[he'dõdu]
triangle	triângulo (m)	['trjãgulu]
triangular (adj)	triangular	[trjãgu'lar]

oval	oval (f)	[o'vaw]
oval (as adj)	oval	[o'vaw]
rectangle	retângulo (m)	[he'tãgulu]
rectangular (adj)	retangular	[hetãgu'lar]

pyramid	pirâmide (f)	[pi'ramidʒi]
rhombus	losango (m)	[lo'zãgu]
trapezoid	trapézio (m)	[tra'pɛzju]
cube	cubo (m)	['kubu]
prism	prisma (m)	['prizma]

circumference	circunferência (f)	[sirkũfe'rẽsja]
sphere	esfera (f)	[is'fɛra]
ball (solid sphere)	globo (m)	['globu]
diameter	diâmetro (m)	['dʒjametru]
radius	raio (m)	['haju]
perimeter (circle's ~)	perímetro (m)	[pe'rimetru]
center	centro (m)	['sẽtru]

horizontal (adj)	horizontal	[orizõ'taw]
vertical (adj)	vertical	[vertʃi'kaw]
parallel (n)	paralela (f)	[para'lɛla]
parallel (as adj)	paralelo	[para'lɛlu]
line	linha (f)	['liɲa]

stroke	traço (m)	['trasu]
straight line	reta (f)	['hɛta]
curve (curved line)	curva (f)	['kurva]
thin (line, etc.)	fino	['finu]
contour (outline)	contorno (m)	[kõ'tornu]

intersection	interseção (f)	[ĩterse'sãw]
right angle	ângulo (m) reto	[ãgulu 'hɛtu]
segment	segmento (m)	[sɛ'gmẽtu]
sector (circular ~)	setor (m)	[sɛ'tor]
side (of triangle)	lado (m)	['ladu]
angle	ângulo (m)	[ãgulu]

22. Units of measurement

weight	peso (m)	['pezu]
length	comprimento (m)	[kõpri'mẽtu]
width	largura (f)	[lar'gura]
height	altura (f)	[aw'tura]
depth	profundidade (f)	[profũdʒi'dadʒi]
volume	volume (m)	[vo'lumi]
area	área (f)	['arja]

gram	grama (m)	['grama]
milligram	miligrama (m)	[mili'grama]
kilogram	quilograma (m)	[kilo'grama]
ton	tonelada (f)	[tune'lɛda]
pound	libra (f)	['libra]
ounce	onça (f)	['õsa]

meter	metro (m)	['mɛtru]
millimeter	milimetro (m)	[mi'limetru]
centimeter	centímetro (m)	[sẽ'tʃimetru]
kilometer	quilômetro (m)	[ki'lometru]
mile	milha (f)	['miʎa]

inch	polegada (f)	[pole'gada]
foot	pé (m)	[pɛ]
yard	jarda (f)	['ʒardɐ]

| square meter | metro (m) quadrado | ['mɛtru kwa'dradu] |
| hectare | hectare (m) | [ek'tari] |

liter	litro (m)	['litru]
degree	grau (m)	[graw]
volt	volt (m)	['vɔwtʃ]
ampere	ampère (m)	[ã'pɛri]
horsepower	cavalo (m) de potência	[ka'valu de po'tẽsja]
quantity	quantidade (f)	[kwãtʃi'dadʒi]
a little bit of ...	um pouco de ...	[ũ 'poku de]

half	metade (f)	[me'tadʒi]
dozen	dúzia (f)	['duzja]
piece (item)	peça (f)	['pɛsa]

| size | tamanho (m), dimensão (f) | [ta'maɲu], [dʒimẽ'sãw] |
| scale (map ~) | escala (f) | [is'kala] |

minimal (adj)	mínimo	['minimu]
the smallest (adj)	menor, mais pequeno	[me'nɔr], [majs pe'kenu]
medium (adj)	médio	['mɛdʒju]
maximal (adj)	máximo	['masimu]
the largest (adj)	maior, mais grande	[ma'jɔr], [majs 'grãdʒi]

23. Containers

canning jar (glass ~)	pote (m) de vidro	['pɔtʃi de 'vidru]
can	lata (f)	['lata]
bucket	balde (m)	['bawdʒi]
barrel	barril (m)	[ba'hiw]

wash basin (e.g., plastic ~)	bacia (f)	[ba'sia]
tank (100L water ~)	tanque (m)	['tãki]
hip flask	cantil (m) de bolso	[kã'tʃiw dʒi 'bowsu]
jerrycan	galão (m) de gasolina	[ga'lãw de gazo'lina]
tank (e.g., tank car)	cisterna (f)	[sis'tɛrna]

mug	caneca (f)	[ka'nɛka]
cup (of coffee, etc.)	xícara (f)	['ʃikara]
saucer	pires (m)	['piris]
glass (tumbler)	copo (m)	['kɔpu]
wine glass	taça (f) de vinho	['tasa de 'viɲu]
stock pot (soup pot)	panela (f)	[pa'nɛla]

| bottle (~ of wine) | garrafa (f) | [ga'hafa] |
| neck (of the bottle, etc.) | gargalo (m) | [gar'galu] |

carafe (decanter)	jarra (f)	['ʒaha]
pitcher	jarro (m)	['ʒahu]
vessel (container)	recipiente (m)	[hesi'pjẽtʃi]
pot (crock, stoneware ~)	pote (m)	['pɔtʃi]
vase	vaso (m)	['vazu]

flacon, bottle (perfume ~)	frasco (m)	['frasku]
vial, small bottle	frasquinho (m)	[fras'kiɲu]
tube (of toothpaste)	tubo (m)	['tubu]

sack (bag)	saco (m)	['saku]
bag (paper ~, plastic ~)	sacola (f)	[sa'kɔla]
pack (of cigarettes, etc.)	maço (m)	['masu]
box (e.g., shoebox)	caixa (f)	['kaɪʃa]

| crate | caixote (m) | [kaj'ʃotʃi] |
| basket | cesto (m) | ['sestu] |

24. Materials

material	material (m)	[mate'rjaw]
wood (n)	madeira (f)	[ma'dejra]
wood-, wooden (adj)	de madeira	[de ma'dejra]

| glass (n) | vidro (m) | ['vidru] |
| glass (as adj) | de vidro | [de 'vidru] |

| stone (n) | pedra (f) | ['pɛdra] |
| stone (as adj) | de pedra | [de 'pɛdra] |

| plastic (n) | plástico (m) | ['plastʃiku] |
| plastic (as adj) | plástico | ['plastʃiku] |

| rubber (n) | borracha (f) | [bo'haʃa] |
| rubber (as adj) | de borracha | [de bo'haʃa] |

| cloth, fabric (n) | tecido, pano (m) | [te'sidu], ['panu] |
| fabric (as adj) | de tecido | [de te'sidu] |

| paper (n) | papel (m) | [pa'pɛw] |
| paper (as adj) | de papel | [de pa'pɛw] |

| cardboard (n) | papelão (m) | [pape'lãw] |
| cardboard (as adj) | de papelão | [de pape'lãw] |

polyethylene	polietileno (m)	[poljetʃi'lɛnu]
cellophane	celofane (m)	[selo'fani]
linoleum	linóleo (m)	[li'nɔlju]
plywood	madeira (f) compensada	[ma'dejra kõpẽ'sada]

porcelain (n)	porcelana (f)	[porse'lana]
porcelain (as adj)	de porcelana	[de porse'lana]
clay (n)	argila (f), barro (m)	[ar'ʒila], ['bahu]
clay (as adj)	de barro	[de 'bahu]
ceramic (n)	cerâmica (f)	[se'ramika]
ceramic (as adj)	de cerâmica	[de se'ramika]

25. Metals

metal (n)	metal (m)	[me'taw]
metal (as adj)	metálico	[me'taliku]
alloy (n)	liga (f)	['liga]
gold (n)	ouro (m)	['oru]

gold, golden (adj)	de ouro	[de 'oru]
silver (n)	prata (f)	['prata]
silver (as adj)	de prata	[de 'prata]
iron (n)	ferro (m)	['fɛhu]
iron-, made of iron (adj)	de ferro	[de 'fɛhu]
steel (n)	aço (m)	['asu]
steel (as adj)	de aço	[de 'asu]
copper (n)	cobre (m)	['kɔbri]
copper (as adj)	de cobre	[de 'kɔbri]
aluminum (n)	alumínio (m)	[alu'minju]
aluminum (as adj)	de alumínio	[de alu'minju]
bronze (n)	bronze (m)	['brõzi]
bronze (as adj)	de bronze	[de 'brõzi]
brass	latão (m)	[la'tãw]
nickel	níquel (m)	['nikew]
platinum	platina (f)	[pla'tʃina]
mercury	mercúrio (m)	[mer'kurju]
tin	estanho (m)	[is'taɲu]
lead	chumbo (m)	['ʃũbu]
zinc	zinco (m)	['zĩku]

HUMAN BEING

Human being. The body

26. Humans. Basic concepts

human being	ser (m) humano	[ser u'manu]
man (adult male)	homem (m)	['ɔmẽ]
woman	mulher (f)	[mu'ʎer]
child	criança (f)	['krjãsa]
girl	menina (f)	[me'nina]
boy	menino (m)	[me'ninu]
teenager	adolescente (m)	[adole'sẽtʃi]
old man	velho (m)	['vɛʎu]
old woman	velha (f)	['vɛʎa]

27. Human anatomy

organism (body)	organismo (m)	[orga'nizmu]
heart	coração (m)	[kora'sãw]
blood	sangue (m)	['sãgi]
artery	artéria (f)	[ar'tɛrja]
vein	veia (f)	['veja]
brain	cérebro (m)	['sɛrebru]
nerve	nervo (m)	['nervu]
nerves	nervos (m pl)	['nervus]
vertebra	vértebra (f)	['vɛrtebra]
spine (backbone)	coluna (f) vertebral	[ko'luna verte'braw]
stomach (organ)	estômago (m)	[is'tomagu]
intestines, bowels	intestinos (m pl)	[ĩtes'tʃinus]
intestine (e.g., large ~)	intestino (m)	[ĩtes'tʃinu]
liver	fígado (m)	['figadu]
kidney	rim (m)	[hĩ]
bone	osso (m)	['osu]
skeleton	esqueleto (m)	[iske'letu]
rib	costela (f)	[kos'tɛla]
skull	crânio (m)	['kranju]
muscle	músculo (m)	['muskulu]
biceps	bíceps (m)	['biseps]

triceps	tríceps (m)	['triseps]
tendon	tendão (m)	[tẽ'dãw]
joint	articulação (f)	[artʃikula'sãw]
lungs	pulmões (m pl)	[puw'mãws]
genitals	órgãos (m pl) genitais	['ɔrgãws ʒeni'tajs]
skin	pele (f)	['pɛli]

28. Head

head	cabeça (f)	[ka'besa]
face	rosto, cara (f)	['hostu], ['kara]
nose	nariz (m)	[na'riz]
mouth	boca (f)	['boka]

eye	olho (m)	['oʎu]
eyes	olhos (m pl)	['oʎus]
pupil	pupila (f)	[pu'pila]
eyebrow	sobrancelha (f)	[sobrã'seʎa]
eyelash	cílio (f)	['silju]
eyelid	pálpebra (f)	['pawpebra]

tongue	língua (f)	['lĩgwa]
tooth	dente (m)	['dẽtʃi]
lips	lábios (m pl)	['labjus]
cheekbones	maçãs (f pl) do rosto	[ma'sãs du 'hostu]
gum	gengiva (f)	[ʒẽ'ʒiva]
palate	palato (m)	[pa'latu]

nostrils	narinas (f pl)	[na'rinas]
chin	queixo (m)	['kejʃu]
jaw	mandíbula (f)	[mã'dʒibula]
cheek	bochecha (f)	[bo'ʃeʃa]

forehead	testa (f)	['tɛsta]
temple	têmpora (f)	['tẽpora]
ear	orelha (f)	[o'reʎa]
back of the head	costas (f pl) da cabeça	['kɔstas da ka'besa]
neck	pescoço (m)	[pes'kosu]
throat	garganta (f)	[gar'gãta]

hair	cabelo (m)	[ka'belu]
hairstyle	penteado (m)	[pẽ'tʃjadu]
haircut	corte (m) de cabelo	['kɔrtʃi de ka'belu]
wig	peruca (f)	[pe'ruka]

mustache	bigode (m)	[bi'gɔdʒi]
beard	barba (f)	['barba]
to have (a beard, etc.)	ter (vt)	[ter]
braid	trança (f)	['trãsa]
sideburns	suíças (f pl)	['swisas]

red-haired (adj)	ruivo	['hwivu]
gray (hair)	grisalho	[gri'zaʎu]
bald (adj)	careca	[ka'rɛka]
bald patch	calva (f)	['kawvu]
ponytail	rabo-de-cavalo (m)	['habu-de-ka'valu]
bangs	franja (f)	['frãʒa]

29. Human body

hand	mão (f)	[mãw]
arm	braço (m)	['brasu]
finger	dedo (m)	['dedu]
toe	dedo (m) do pé	['dedu du pɛ]
thumb	polegar (m)	[pole'gar]
little finger	dedo (m) mindinho	['dedu mĩ'dʒiɲu]
nail	unha (f)	['uɲa]
fist	punho (m)	['puɲu]
palm	palma (f)	['pawma]
wrist	pulso (m)	['puwsu]
forearm	antebraço (m)	[ãtʃi'brasu]
elbow	cotovelo (m)	[koto'velu]
shoulder	ombro (m)	['õbru]
leg	perna (f)	['pɛrna]
foot	pé (m)	[pɛ]
knee	joelho (m)	[ʒo'eʎu]
calf (part of leg)	panturrilha (f)	[pãtu'hiʎa]
hip	quadril (m)	[kwa'driw]
heel	calcanhar (m)	[kawka'ɲar]
body	corpo (m)	['korpu]
stomach	barriga (f), ventre (m)	[ba'higa], ['vẽtri]
chest	peito (m)	['pejtu]
breast	seio (m)	['seju]
flank	lado (m)	['ladu]
back	costas (f pl)	['kɔstas]
lower back	região (f) lombar	[he'ʒjãw lõ'bar]
waist	cintura (f)	[sĩ'tura]
navel (belly button)	umbigo (m)	[ũ'bigu]
buttocks	nádegas (f pl)	['nadegas]
bottom	traseiro (m)	[tra'zejru]
beauty mark	sinal (m), pinta (f)	[si'naw], ['pĩta]
birthmark (café au lait spot)	sinal (m) de nascença	[si'naw de na'sẽsa]
tattoo	tatuagem (f)	[ta'twaʒẽ]
scar	cicatriz (f)	[sika'triz]

Clothing & Accessories

30. Outerwear. Coats

clothes	**roupa** (f)	['hopa]
outerwear	**roupa** (f) **exterior**	['hopa iste'rjor]
winter clothing	**roupa** (f) **de inverno**	['hopa de ĩ'vɛrnu]
coat (overcoat)	**sobretudo** (m)	[sobri'tudu]
fur coat	**casaco** (m) **de pele**	[kaz'aku de 'pɛli]
fur jacket	**jaqueta** (f) **de pele**	[ʒa'keta de 'pɛli]
down coat	**casaco** (m) **acolchoado**	[ka'zaku akow'ʃwadu]
jacket (e.g., leather ~)	**casaco** (m), **jaqueta** (f)	[kaz'aku], [ʒa'keta]
raincoat (trenchcoat, etc.)	**impermeável** (m)	[ĩper'mjavew]
waterproof (adj)	**a prova d'água**	[a 'prɔva 'dagwa]

31. Men's & women's clothing

shirt (button shirt)	**camisa** (f)	[ka'miza]
pants	**calça** (f)	['kawsa]
jeans	**jeans** (m)	['dʒins]
suit jacket	**paletó, terno** (m)	[pale'tɔ], ['tɛrnu]
suit	**terno** (m)	['tɛrnu]
dress (frock)	**vestido** (m)	[ves'tʃidu]
skirt	**saia** (f)	['saja]
blouse	**blusa** (f)	['bluza]
knitted jacket (cardigan, etc.)	**casaco** (m) **de malha**	[ka'zaku de 'maʎa]
jacket (of woman's suit)	**casaco, blazer** (m)	[ka'zaku], ['blejzer]
T-shirt	**camiseta** (f)	[kami'zɛta]
shorts (short trousers)	**short** (m)	['ʃortʃi]
tracksuit	**training** (m)	['trejnĩŋ]
bathrobe	**roupão** (m) **de banho**	[ho'pãw de 'baɲu]
pajamas	**pijama** (m)	[pi'ʒama]
sweater	**suéter** (m)	['swɛter]
pullover	**pulôver** (m)	[pu'lover]
vest	**colete** (m)	[ko'letʃi]
tailcoat	**fraque** (m)	['fraki]
tuxedo	**smoking** (m)	[iz'mokĩs]

uniform	**uniforme** (m)	[uni'fɔrmi]
workwear	**roupa** (f) **de trabalho**	['hopa də tra'baʎu]
overalls	**macacão** (m)	[maka'kãws]
coat (e.g., doctor's smock)	**jaleco** (m), **bata** (f)	[ʒa'lɛku], ['bata]

32. Clothing. Underwear

underwear	**roupa** (f) **íntima**	['hopa 'ĩʃima]
boxers, briefs	**cueca boxer** (f)	['kwɛka bɔkser]
panties	**calcinha** (f)	[kaw'siɲa]
undershirt (A-shirt)	**camiseta** (f)	[kami'zɛta]
socks	**meias** (f pl)	['mejas]
nightdress	**camisola** (f)	[kami'zɔla]
bra	**sutiã** (m)	[su'tʃiã]
knee highs (knee-high socks)	**meias longas** (f pl)	['mejas 'lõgas]
pantyhose	**meias-calças** (f pl)	['mejas 'kalsas]
stockings (thigh highs)	**meias** (f pl)	['mejas]
bathing suit	**maiô** (m)	[ma'jo]

33. Headwear

hat	**chapéu** (m), **touca** (f)	[ʃa'pɛw], ['toka]
fedora	**chapéu** (m) **de feltro**	[ʃa'pɛw de 'fewtru]
baseball cap	**boné** (m) **de beisebol**	[bo'nɛ de bejsi'bɔw]
flatcap	**boina** (f)	['bojna]
beret	**boina** (f) **francesa**	['bojna frã'seza]
hood	**capuz** (m)	[ka'puz]
panama hat	**chapéu panamá** (m)	[ʃa'pɛw pana'ma]
knit cap (knitted hat)	**touca** (f)	['toka]
headscarf	**lenço** (m)	['lẽsu]
women's hat	**chapéu** (m) **feminino**	[ʃa'pɛw femi'ninu]
hard hat	**capacete** (m)	[kapa'setʃi]
garrison cap	**bibico** (m)	[bi'biko]
helmet	**capacete** (m)	[kapa'setʃi]
derby	**chapéu-coco** (m)	[ʃa'pɛw koku]
top hat	**cartola** (f)	[kar'tɔla]

34. Footwear

footwear	**calçado** (m)	[kaw'sadu]
shoes (men's shoes)	**botinas** (f pl), **sapatos** (m pl)	[bo'tʃinas], [sapa'tõjs]

shoes (women's shoes)	sapatos (m pl)	[sa'patus]
boots (e.g., cowboy ~)	botas (f pl)	['bɔtas]
slippers	pantufas (f pl)	[pã'tufas]

tennis shoes (e.g., Nike ~)	tênis (m pl)	['tenis]
sneakers	tênis (m pl)	['tenis]
(e.g., Converse ~)		
sandals	sandálias (f pl)	[sã'dalias]

cobbler (shoe repairer)	sapateiro (m)	[sapa'tejru]
heel	salto (m)	['sawtu]
pair (of shoes)	par (m)	[par]

shoestring	cadarço (m)	[ka'darsu]
to lace (vt)	amarrar os cadarços	[ama'har us ka'darsus]
shoehorn	calçadeira (f)	[kawsa'dejra]
shoe polish	graxa (f) para calçado	['graʃa 'para kaw'sadu]

35. Textile. Fabrics

cotton (n)	algodão (m)	[awgo'dãw]
cotton (as adj)	de algodão	[de awgo'dãw]
flax (n)	linho (m)	['liɲu]
flax (as adj)	de linho	[de 'liɲu]

silk (n)	seda (f)	['seda]
silk (as adj)	de seda	[de 'seda]
wool (n)	lã (f)	[lã]
wool (as adj)	de lã	[de lã]

velvet	veludo (m)	[ve'ludu]
suede	camurça (f)	[ka'mursa]
corduroy	veludo (m) cotelê	[ve'ludu kɔte'le]

nylon (n)	nylon (m)	['najlɔn]
nylon (as adj)	de nylon	[de 'najlɔn]
polyester (n)	poliéster (m)	[po'ljɛster]
polyester (as adj)	de poliéster	[de po'ljɛster]

leather (n)	couro (m)	['koru]
leather (as adj)	de couro	[de 'koru]
fur (n)	pele (f)	['pɛli]
fur (e.g., ~ coat)	de pele	[de 'pɛli]

36. Personal accessories

| gloves | luva (f) | ['luva] |
| mittens | mitenes (f pl) | [mi'tɛnes] |

scarf (muffler)	cachecol (m)	[kaʃe'kɔw]
glasses (eyeglasses)	óculos (m pl)	['ɔkulus]
frame (eyeglass ~)	armação (f)	[arma'sãw]
umbrella	guarda-chuva (m)	['gwarda 'ʃuva]
walking stick	bengala (f)	[bẽ'gala]
hairbrush	escova (f) para o cabelo	[is'kova 'para u ka'belu]
fan	leque (m)	['lɛki]
tie (necktie)	gravata (f)	[gra'vata]
bow tie	gravata-borboleta (f)	[gra'vata borbo'leta]
suspenders	suspensórios (m pl)	[suspẽ'sɔrjus]
handkerchief	lenço (m)	['lẽsu]
comb	pente (m)	['pẽtʃi]
barrette	fivela (f) para cabelo	[fi'vɛla para ka'belu]
hairpin	grampo (m)	['grãpu]
buckle	fivela (f)	[fi'vɛla]
belt	cinto (m)	['sĩtu]
shoulder strap	alça (f) de ombro	['awsa de 'õbru]
bag (handbag)	bolsa (f)	['bowsa]
purse	bolsa, carteira (f)	['bowsa], [kar'tejra]
backpack	mochila (f)	[mo'ʃila]

37. Clothing. Miscellaneous

fashion	moda (f)	['mɔda]
in vogue (adj)	na moda	[na 'mɔda]
fashion designer	estilista (m)	[istʃi'lista]
collar	colarinho (m)	[kola'riɲu]
pocket	bolso (m)	['bowsu]
pocket (as adj)	de bolso	[de 'bowsu]
sleeve	manga (f)	['mãga]
hanging loop	ganchinho (m)	[gã'ʃiɲu]
fly (on trousers)	bragueta (f)	[bra'gwetʃi]
zipper (fastener)	zíper (m)	['ziper]
fastener	colchete (m)	[kow'ʃetʃi]
button	botão (m)	[bo'tãw]
buttonhole	botoeira (f)	[bo'twejra]
to come off (ab. button)	soltar-se (vr)	[sow'tarsi]
to sew (vi, vt)	costurar (vi)	[kostu'rar]
to embroider (vi, vt)	bordar (vt)	[bor'dar]
embroidery	bordado (m)	[bor'dadu]
sewing needle	agulha (f)	[a'guʎa]
thread	fio, linha (f)	['fiu], ['liɲa]
seam	costura (f)	[kos'tura]

to get dirty (vi)	sujar-se (vr)	[su'ʒarsi]
stain (mark, spot)	mancha (f)	['mãʃa]
to crease, crumple (vi)	amarrotar-se (vr)	[amaho'tarse]
to tear, to rip (vt)	rasgar (vt)	[haz'gar]
clothes moth	traça (f)	['trasa]

38. Personal care. Cosmetics

toothpaste	pasta (f) de dente	['pasta de 'dẽtʃi]
toothbrush	escova (f) de dente	[is'kova de 'dẽtʃi]
to brush one's teeth	escovar os dentes	[isko'var us 'dẽtʃis]

razor	gilete (f)	[ʒi'lɛtʃi]
shaving cream	creme (m) de barbear	['krɛmi de bar'bjar]
to shave (vi)	barbear-se (vr)	[bar'bjarsi]

| soap | sabonete (m) | [sabo'netʃi] |
| shampoo | xampu (m) | [ʃã'pu] |

scissors	tesoura (f)	[te'zora]
nail file	lixa (f) de unhas	['liʃa de 'uɲas]
nail clippers	corta-unhas (m)	['kɔrta 'uɲas]
tweezers	pinça (f)	['pĩsa]

cosmetics	cosméticos (m pl)	[koz'mɛtʃikus]
face mask	máscara (f)	['maskara]
manicure	manicure (f)	[mani'kuri]
to have a manicure	fazer as unhas	[fa'zer as 'uɲas]
pedicure	pedicure (f)	[pedi'kure]

make-up bag	bolsa (f) de maquiagem	['bowsa de ma'kjaʒẽ]
face powder	pó (m)	[pɔ]
powder compact	pó (m) compacto	[pɔ kõ'paktu]
blusher	blush (m)	[blaʃ]

perfume (bottled)	perfume (m)	[per'fumi]
toilet water (lotion)	água-de-colônia (f)	['agwa de ko'lonja]
lotion	loção (f)	[lo'sãw]
cologne	colônia (f)	[ko'lonja]

eyeshadow	sombra (f) de olhos	['sõbra de 'oʎus]
eyeliner	delineador (m)	[delinja'dor]
mascara	máscara (f), rímel (m)	['maskara], ['himew]

lipstick	batom (m)	['batõ]
nail polish, enamel	esmalte (m)	[iz'mawtʃi]
hair spray	laquê (m), spray fixador (m)	[la'ke], [is'prej fiksa'dor]
deodorant	desodorante (m)	[dʒizodo'rãtʃi]
cream	creme (m)	['krɛmi]

face cream	creme (m) de rosto	['krɛmi de 'hostu]
hand cream	creme (m) de mãos	['krɛmi de 'mãws]
anti-wrinkle cream	creme (m) antirrugas	['krɛmi ãtʃi'hugas]
day cream	creme (m) de dia	['krɛmi de 'dʒia]
night cream	creme (m) de noite	['krɛmi de 'nojtʃi]
day (as adj)	de dia	[de 'dʒia]
night (as adj)	da noite	[da 'nojtʃi]
tampon	absorvente (m) interno	[absor'vẽtʃi ĩ'tɛrnu]
toilet paper (toilet roll)	papel (m) higiênico	[pa'pɛw i'ʒjeniku]
hair dryer	secador (m) de cabelo	[seka'dor de ka'belu]

39. Jewelry

jewelry, jewels	joias (f pl)	['ʒɔjas]
precious (e.g., ~ stone)	precioso	[pre'sjɔzu]
hallmark stamp	marca (f) de contraste	['marka de kõ'trastʃi]
ring	anel (m)	[a'nɛw]
wedding ring	aliança (f)	[a'ljãsa]
bracelet	pulseira (f)	[puw'sejra]
earrings	brncos (m pl)	['brĩkus]
necklace (~ of pearls)	colar (m)	[ko'lar]
crown	coroa (f)	[ko'roa]
bead necklace	colar (m) de contas	[ko'lar de 'kõtas]
diamond	diamante (m)	[dʒia'mãtʃi]
emerald	esmeralda (f)	[izme'rawda]
ruby	rubi (m)	[hu'bi]
sapphire	safira (f)	[sa'fira]
pearl	pérola (f)	['pɛrola]
amber	âmbar (m)	[ãbar]

40. Watches. Clocks

watch (wristwatch)	relógio (m) de pulso	[he'lɔʒu de 'puwsu]
dial	mostrador (m)	[mostra'dor]
hand (of clock, watch)	ponteiro (m)	[põ'tejru]
metal watch band	bracelete (f) em aço	[brase'letʃi ẽ 'asu]
watch strap	bracelete (f) em couro	[brase'letʃi ẽ 'koru]
battery	pilha (f)	['piʎa]
to be dead (battery)	acabar (vi)	[aka'bar]
to change a battery	trocar a pilha	[tro'kar a 'piʎa]
to run fast	estar adiantado	[is'tar adʒjã'tadu]
to run slow	estar atrasado	[is'tar atra'zadu]
wall clock	relógio (m) de parede	[he'lɔʒu de pa'redʒi]

hourglass	ampulheta (f)	[ãpu'ʎeta]
sundial	relógio (m) de sol	[he'lɔʒu de sɔw]
alarm clock	despertador (m)	[dʒisperta'dor]
watchmaker	relojoeiro (m)	[helo'ʒwejru]
to repair (vt)	reparar (vt)	[hepa'rar]

Food. Nutricion

41. Food

meat	carne (f)	['karni]
chicken	galinha (f)	[ga'liɲa]
Rock Cornish hen (poussin)	frango (m)	['frãgu]
duck	pato (m)	['patu]
goose	ganso (m)	['gãsu]
game	caça (f)	['kasa]
turkey	peru (m)	[pe'ru]
pork	carne (f) de porco	['karni də 'porku]
veal	carne (f) de vitela	['karni də vi'tɛla]
lamb	carne (f) de carneiro	['karni də kar'nejru]
beef	carne (f) de vaca	['karni də 'vaka]
rabbit	carne (f) de coelho	['karni də ko'eʎu]
sausage (bologna, etc.)	linguiça (f), salsichão (m)	[lĩ'gwisa], [sawsi'ʃãw]
vienna sausage (frankfurter)	salsicha (f)	[saw'siʃa]
bacon	bacon (m)	['bejkõ]
ham	presunto (m)	[pre'zũtu]
gammon	pernil (m) de porco	[per'niw de 'porku]
pâté	patê (m)	[pa'te]
liver	fígado (m)	['figadu]
hamburger (ground beef)	guisado (m)	[gi'zadu]
tongue	língua (f)	['lĩgwa]
egg	ovo (m)	['ovu]
eggs	ovos (m pl)	['ɔvus]
egg white	clara (f) de ovo	['klara də 'ovu]
egg yolk	gema (f) de ovo	['ʒɛma de 'ovu]
fish	peixe (m)	['pejʃi]
seafood	mariscos (m pl)	[ma'riskᴧs]
crustaceans	crustáceos (m pl)	[krus'tasjus]
caviar	caviar (m)	[ka'vjar]
crab	caranguejo (m)	[karã'geʒu]
shrimp	camarão (m)	[kama'rãw]
oyster	ostra (f)	['ostra]
spiny lobster	lagosta (f)	[la'gosta]
octopus	polvo (m)	['powvu]

squid	**lula** (f)	['lula]
sturgeon	**esturjão** (m)	[istur'ʒãw]
salmon	**salmão** (m)	[saw'mãw]
halibut	**halibute** (m)	[ali'butʃi]

cod	**bacalhau** (m)	[baka'ʎaw]
mackerel	**cavala, sarda** (f)	[ka'vala], ['sarda]
tuna	**atum** (m)	[a'tũ]
eel	**enguia** (f)	[ẽ'gia]

trout	**truta** (f)	['truta]
sardine	**sardinha** (f)	[sar'dʒiɲa]
pike	**lúcio** (m)	['lusju]
herring	**arenque** (m)	[a'rẽki]

| bread | **pão** (m) | [pãw] |
| cheese | **queijo** (m) | ['kejʒu] |

| sugar | **açúcar** (m) | [a'sukar] |
| salt | **sal** (m) | [saw] |

rice	**arroz** (m)	[a'hoz]
pasta (macaroni)	**massas** (f pl)	['masas]
noodles	**talharim, miojo** (m)	[taʎa'rĩ], [mi'oʒu]

| butter | **manteiga** (f) | [mã'tejga] |
| vegetable oil | **óleo** (m) **vegetal** | ['ɔlju veʒe'taw] |

| sunflower oil | **óleo** (m) **de girassol** | ['ɔlju de ʒira'sɔw] |
| margarine | **margarina** (f) | [marga'rina] |

| olives | **azeitonas** (f pl) | [azej'tɔnas] |
| olive oil | **azeite** (m) | [a'zejtʃi] |

milk	**leite** (m)	['lejtʃi]
condensed milk	**leite** (m) **condensado**	['lejtʃi kõdẽ'sadu]
yogurt	**iogurte** (m)	[jo'gurtʃi]

| sour cream | **creme azedo** (m) | ['krɛmi a'zedu] |
| cream (of milk) | **creme** (m) **de leite** | ['krɛmi de 'lejtʃi] |

| mayonnaise | **maionese** (f) | [majo'nɛzi] |
| buttercream | **creme** (m) | ['krɛmi] |

groats (barley ~, etc.)	**grãos** (m pl) **de cereais**	['grãws de se'rjajs]
flour	**farinha** (f)	[fa'riɲa]
canned food	**enlatados** (m pl)	[ẽla'tadus]

cornflakes	**flocos** (m pl) **de milho**	['flɔkus de 'miʎu]
honey	**mel** (m)	[mɛw]
jam	**geleia** (m)	[ʒe'lɛja]
chewing gum	**chiclete** (m)	[ʃi'klɛtʃi]

42. Drinks

water	água (f)	['agwa]
drinking water	água (f) potável	['agwa pu'tavɛw]
mineral water	água (f) mineral	['agwa mine'raw]

still (adj)	sem gás	[sẽ gajs]
carbonated (adj)	gaseificada	[gazejfi kadu]
sparkling (adj)	com gás	[kõ gajs]
ice	gelo (m)	['ʒelu]
with ice	com gelo	[kõ 'ʒelu]

non-alcoholic (adj)	não alcoólico	[nãw aw'kɔliku]
soft drink	refrigerante (m)	[hefriʒe'rãtʃi]
refreshing drink	refresco (m)	[he'fresku]
lemonade	limonada (f)	[limo'nada]

liquors	bebidas (f pl) alcoólicas	[be'bidas aw'kɔlikas]
wine	vinho (m)	['viɲu]
white wine	vinho (m) branco	['viɲu 'brãku]
red wine	vinho (m) tinto	['viɲu 'tĩtu]

liqueur	licor (m)	[li'kor]
champagne	champanhe (m)	[ʃã'paɲĩ]
vermouth	vermute (m)	[ver'mutʃi]

whiskey	uísque (m)	['wiski]
vodka	vodca (f)	['vɔdʒka]
gin	gim (m)	[ʒĩ]
cognac	conhaque (m)	[ko'ɲaki]
rum	rum (m)	[hũ]

coffee	café (m)	[ka'fɛ]
black coffee	café (m) preto	[ka'fɛ 'pretu]
coffee with milk	café (m) com leite	[ka'fɛ kõ 'lejtʃi]
cappuccino	cappuccino (m)	[kapu'tʃinu]
instant coffee	café (m) solúvel	[ka'fɛ so'luvew]

milk	leite (m)	['lejtʃi]
cocktail	coquetel (m)	[koke'tɛw]
milkshake	batida (f), milkshake (m)	[ba'tʃida], ['milkʃejk]

juice	suco (m)	['suku]
tomato juice	suco (m) de tomate	['suku de to'matʃi]
orange juice	suco (m) de laranja	['suku de la'rãʒa]
freshly squeezed juice	suco (m) fresco	['suku 'fresku]

beer	cerveja (f)	[ser'veʒa]
light beer	cerveja (f) clara	[ser'veʒa 'klara]
dark beer	cerveja (f) preta	[ser'veʒa 'preta]
tea	chá (m)	[ʃa]

51

| black tea | chá (m) preto | [ʃa 'pretu] |
| green tea | chá (m) verde | [ʃa 'verdʒi] |

43. Vegetables

| vegetables | vegetais (m pl) | [veʒe'tajs] |
| greens | verdura (f) | [ver'dura] |

tomato	tomate (m)	[to'matʃi]
cucumber	pepino (m)	[pe'pinu]
carrot	cenoura (f)	[se'nora]
potato	batata (f)	[ba'tata]
onion	cebola (f)	[se'bola]
garlic	alho (m)	['aʎu]

cabbage	couve (f)	['kovi]
cauliflower	couve-flor (f)	['kovi 'flɔr]
Brussels sprouts	couve-de-bruxelas (f)	['kovi de bru'ʃelas]
broccoli	brócolis (m pl)	['brɔkolis]

beet	beterraba (f)	[bete'haba]
eggplant	berinjela (f)	[beri'ʒɛla]
zucchini	abobrinha (f)	[abo'briɲa]
pumpkin	abóbora (f)	[a'bɔbora]
turnip	nabo (m)	['nabu]

parsley	salsa (f)	['sawsa]
dill	endro, aneto (m)	['ẽdru], [a'netu]
lettuce	alface (f)	[aw'fasi]
celery	aipo (m)	['ajpu]
asparagus	aspargo (m)	[as'pargu]
spinach	espinafre (m)	[ispi'nafri]

pea	ervilha (f)	[er'viʎa]
beans	feijão (m)	[fej'ʒãw]
corn (maize)	milho (m)	['miʎu]
kidney bean	feijão (m) roxo	[fej'ʒãw 'hoʃu]

bell pepper	pimentão (m)	[pimẽ'tãw]
radish	rabanete (m)	[haba'netʃi]
artichoke	alcachofra (f)	[awka'ʃofra]

44. Fruits. Nuts

fruit	fruta (f)	['fruta]
apple	maçã (f)	[ma'sã]
pear	pera (f)	['pera]
lemon	limão (m)	[li'mãw]

orange	laranja (f)	[la'raʒa]
strawberry (garden ~)	morango (m)	[mo'rãgu]
mandarin	tangerina (f)	[tãʒe'rina]
plum	ameixa (f)	[a'mejʃa]
peach	pêssego (m)	['pesegu]
apricot	damasco (m)	[da'masku]
raspberry	framboesa (f)	[frãbo'eza]
pineapple	abacaxi (m)	[abaka'ʃi]
banana	banana (f)	[ba'nana]
watermelon	melancia (f)	[melã'sia]
grape	uva (f)	['uva]
sour cherry	ginja (f)	['ʒĩʒa]
sweet cherry	cereja (f)	[se'reʒa]
melon	melão (m)	[me'lãw]
grapefruit	toranja (f)	[to'rãʒa]
avocado	abacate (m)	[aba'kaːʃi]
papaya	mamão (m)	[ma'mãw]
mango	manga (f)	['mãga]
pomegranate	romã (f)	['homa]
redcurrant	groselha (f) vermelha	[[gro'zɛʎa ver'meʎa]
blackcurrant	groselha (f) negra	[gro'zɛʎa 'negra]
gooseberry	groselha (f) espinhosa	[gro'zɛʎa ispi'ɲoza]
bilberry	mirtilo (m)	[mih'tʃilu]
blackberry	amora (f) silvestre	[a'mɔra siw'vɛstri]
raisin	passa (f)	['pasa]
fig	figo (m)	['figu]
date	tâmara (f)	['tamara]
peanut	amendoim (m)	[amẽdo'ĩ]
almond	amêndoa (f)	[a'mẽdwa]
walnut	noz (f)	[nɔz]
hazelnut	avelã (f)	[ave'lã]
coconut	coco (m)	['koku]
pistachios	pistaches (m pl)	[pis'taʃis]

45. Bread. Candy

bakers' confectionery (pastry)	pastelaria (f)	[pastela'ria]
bread	pão (m)	[pãw]
cookies	biscoito (m), bolacha (f)	[bis'kojtu], [bo'laʃa]
chocolate (n)	chocolate (m)	[ʃoko'latʃi]
chocolate (as adj)	de chocolate	[de ʃoko'latʃi]
candy (wrapped)	bala (f)	['bala]

| cake (e.g., cupcake) | doce (m),
bolo (m) pequeno | ['dosi],
['bolu pe'kenu] |
| cake (e.g., birthday ~) | bolo (m) de aniversário | ['bolu de aniver'sarju] |

| pie (e.g., apple ~) | torta (f) | ['tɔrta] |
| filling (for cake, pie) | recheio (m) | [he'ʃeju] |

jam (whole fruit jam)	geleia (m)	[ʒe'lɛja]
marmalade	marmelada (f)	[marme'lada]
wafers	wafers (m pl)	['wafers]
ice-cream	sorvete (m)	[sor'vetʃi]
pudding	pudim (m)	[pu'dʒĩ]

46. Cooked dishes

course, dish	prato (m)	['pratu]
cuisine	cozinha (f)	[ko'ziɲa]
recipe	receita (f)	[he'sejta]
portion	porção (f)	[por'sãw]

| salad | salada (f) | [sa'lada] |
| soup | sopa (f) | ['sopa] |

clear soup (broth)	caldo (m)	['kawdu]
sandwich (bread)	sanduíche (m)	[sand'wiʃi]
fried eggs	ovos (m pl) fritos	['ɔvus 'fritus]

| hamburger (beefburger) | hambúrguer (m) | [ã'burger] |
| beefsteak | bife (m) | ['bifi] |

side dish	acompanhamento (m)	[akõpaɲa'mẽtu]
spaghetti	espaguete (m)	[ispa'geti]
mashed potatoes	purê (m) de batata	[pu're de ba'tata]
pizza	pizza (f)	['pitsa]
porridge (oatmeal, etc.)	mingau (m)	[mĩ'gaw]
omelet	omelete (f)	[ome'letʃi]

boiled (e.g., ~ beef)	fervido	[fer'vidu]
smoked (adj)	defumado	[defu'madu]
fried (adj)	frito	['fritu]
dried (adj)	seco	['seku]
frozen (adj)	congelado	[kõʒe'ladu]
pickled (adj)	em conserva	[ẽ kõ'serva]

sweet (sugary)	doce	['dosi]
salty (adj)	salgado	[saw'gadu]
cold (adj)	frio	['friu]
hot (adj)	quente	['kẽtʃi]
bitter (adj)	amargo	[a'margu]
tasty (adj)	gostoso	[gos'tozu]

to cook in boiling water	cozinhar em água fervente	[kozi'ɲar ẽ 'agwa fer'vẽtʃi]
to cook (dinner)	preparar (vt)	[prepa'rar]
to fry (vt)	fritar (vt)	[fri'tar]
to heat up (food)	aquecer (vt)	[ake'ser]

to salt (vt)	salgar (vt)	[saw'gar]
to pepper (vt)	apimentar (vt)	[apimẽ'tar]
to grate (vt)	ralar (vt)	[ha'lar]
peel (n)	casca (f)	['kaska]
to peel (vt)	descascar (vt)	[dʒiskas'kar]

47. Spices

salt	sal (m)	[saw]
salty (adj)	salgado	[saw'gadu]
to salt (vt)	salgar (vt)	[saw'gar]

black pepper	pimenta-do-reino (f)	[pi'mẽta-du-hejnu]
red pepper (milled ~)	pimenta (f) vermelha	[pi'mẽta ver'meʎa]
mustard	mostarda (f)	[mos'tarda]
horseradish	raiz-forte (f)	[ha'iz fɔrtʃi]

condiment	condimento (m)	[kõdʒi'mẽtu]
spice	especiaria (f)	[ispesja'ria]
sauce	molho (m)	['moʎu]
vinegar	vinagre (m)	[vi'nagri]

anise	anis (m)	[a'nis]
basil	manjericão (m)	[mãʒeri'kãw]
cloves	cravo (m)	['kravu]
ginger	gengibre (m)	[ʒẽ'ʒibri]
coriander	coentro (m)	[ko'ẽtru]
cinnamon	canela (f)	[ka'nɛla]

sesame	gergelim (m)	[ʒerʒe'lĩ]
bay leaf	folha (f) de louro	['foʎaʃ de 'loru]
paprika	páprica (f)	['paprika]
caraway	cominho (m)	[ko'miɲu]
saffron	açafrão (m)	[asa'frãw]

48. Meals

food	comida (f)	[ko'mida]
to eat (vi, vt)	comer (vt)	[ko'mer]

breakfast	café (m) da manhã	[ka'fɛ da ma'ɲã]
to have breakfast	tomar café da manhã	[to'mar ka'fɛ da ma'ɲã]

lunch	**almoço** (m)	[aw'mosu]
to have lunch	**almoçar** (vi)	[awmo'sar]
dinner	**jantar** (m)	[ʒã'tar]
to have dinner	**jantar** (vi)	[ʒã'tar]

appetite	**apetite** (m)	[ape'tʃitʃi]
Enjoy your meal!	**Bom apetite!**	[bõ ape'tʃitʃi]

to open (~ a bottle)	**abrir** (vt)	[a'brir]
to spill (liquid)	**derramar** (vt)	[deha'mar]
to spill out (vi)	**derramar-se** (vr)	[deha'marsi]

to boil (vi)	**ferver** (vi)	[fer'ver]
to boil (vt)	**ferver** (vt)	[fer'ver]
boiled (~ water)	**fervido**	[fer'vidu]
to chill, cool down (vt)	**esfriar** (vt)	[is'frjar]
to chill (vi)	**esfriar-se** (vr)	[is'frjarse]

taste, flavor	**sabor, gosto** (m)	[sa'bor], ['gostu]
aftertaste	**fim** (m) **de boca**	[fĩ de 'boka]

to slim down (lose weight)	**emagrecer** (vi)	[imagre'ser]
diet	**dieta** (f)	['dʒjɛta]
vitamin	**vitamina** (f)	[vita'mina]
calorie	**caloria** (f)	[kalo'ria]

vegetarian (n)	**vegetariano** (m)	[veʒeta'rjanu]
vegetarian (adj)	**vegetariano**	[veʒeta'rjanu]

fats (nutrient)	**gorduras** (f pl)	[gor'duras]
proteins	**proteínas** (f pl)	[prote'inas]
carbohydrates	**carboidratos** (m pl)	[karboi'dratus]

slice (of lemon, ham)	**fatia** (f)	[fa'tʃia]
piece (of cake, pie)	**pedaço** (m)	[pe'dasu]
crumb	**migalha** (f), **farelo** (m)	[mi'gaʎa], [fa'rɛlu]
(of bread, cake, etc.)		

49. Table setting

spoon	**colher** (f)	[ko'ʎer]
knife	**faca** (f)	['faka]
fork	**garfo** (m)	['garfu]

cup (e.g., coffee ~)	**xícara** (f)	['ʃikara]
plate (dinner ~)	**prato** (m)	['pratu]

saucer	**pires** (m)	['piris]
napkin (on table)	**guardanapo** (m)	[gwarda'napu]
toothpick	**palito** (m)	[pa'litu]

50. Restaurant

restaurant	restaurante (m)	[hestaw'rãtʃi]
coffee house	cafeteria (f)	[kafete'ria]
pub, bar	bar (m), cervejaria (f)	[bar], [serveʒa'ria]
tearoom	salão (m) de chá	[sa'lãw de ʃa]
waiter	garçom (m)	[gar'sõ]
waitress	garçonete (f)	[garso'r etʃi]
bartender	barman (m)	[bar'mã]
menu	cardápio (m)	[kar'dapju]
wine list	lista (f) de vinhos	['lista de 'viɲus]
to book a table	reservar uma mesa	[hezer'var 'uma 'meza]
course, dish	prato (m)	['pratu]
to order (meal)	pedir (vt)	[pe'dʒir]
to make an order	fazer o pedido	[fa'zer u pe'dʒidu]
aperitif	aperitivo (m)	[aperi'tʃivu]
appetizer	entrada (f)	[ẽ'trada]
dessert	sobremesa (f)	[sobri'meza]
check	conta (f)	['kõta]
to pay the check	pagar a conta	[pa'gar a 'kõta]
to give change	dar o troco	[dar u 'troku]
tip	gorjeta (f)	[gor'ʒeta]

Family, relatives and friends

51. Personal information. Forms

name (first name)	nome (m)	['nɔmi]
surname (last name)	sobrenome (m)	[sobri'nɔmi]
date of birth	data (f) de nascimento	['data de nasi'mẽtu]
place of birth	local (m) de nascimento	[lo'kaw de nasi'mẽtu]
nationality	nacionalidade (f)	[nasjonali'dadʒi]
place of residence	lugar (m) de residência	[lu'gar de hezi'dẽsja]
country	país (m)	[pa'jis]
profession (occupation)	profissão (f)	[profi'sãw]
gender, sex	sexo (m)	['sɛksu]
height	estatura (f)	[ista'tura]
weight	peso (m)	['pezu]

52. Family members. Relatives

mother	mãe (f)	[mãj]
father	pai (m)	[paj]
son	filho (m)	['fiʎu]
daughter	filha (f)	['fiʎa]
younger daughter	caçula (f)	[ka'sula]
younger son	caçula (m)	[ka'sula]
eldest daughter	filha (f) mais velha	['fiʎa majs 'vɛʎa]
eldest son	filho (m) mais velho	['fiʎu majs 'vɛʎu]
brother	irmão (m)	[ir'mãw]
elder brother	irmão (m) mais velho	[ir'mãw majs 'vɛʎu]
younger brother	irmão (m) mais novo	[ir'mãw majs 'novu]
sister	irmã (f)	[ir'mã]
elder sister	irmã (f) mais velha	[ir'mã majs 'vɛʎa]
younger sister	irmã (f) mais nova	[ir'mã majs 'nɔva]
cousin (masc.)	primo (m)	['primu]
cousin (fem.)	prima (f)	['prima]
mom, mommy	mamãe (f)	[ma'mãj]
dad, daddy	papai (m)	[pa'paj]
parents	pais (pl)	['pajs]
child	criança (f)	['krjãsa]
children	crianças (f pl)	['krjãsas]

grandmother	avó (f)	[a'vo]
grandfather	avô (m)	[a'vɔ]
grandson	neto (m)	['nɛtu]
granddaughter	neta (f)	['nɛta]
grandchildren	netos (pl)	['nɛtus]
uncle	tio (m)	['tʃiu]
aunt	tia (f)	['tʃia]
nephew	sobrinho (m)	[so'briɲu]
niece	sobrinha (f)	[so'briɲa]

mother-in-law (wife's mother)	sogra (f)	['sɔgra]
father-in-law (husband's father)	sogro (m)	['sogru]
son-in-law (daughter's husband)	genro (m)	['ʒẽhu]
stepmother	madrasta (f)	[ma'drasta]
stepfather	padrasto (m)	[pa'drastu]

infant	criança (f) de colo	['krjãsa de 'kɔlu]
baby (infant)	bebê (m)	[be'be]
little boy, kid	menino (m)	[me'ninʉ]
wife	mulher (f)	[mu'ʎeɾ]
husband	marido (m)	[ma'ridu]
spouse (husband)	esposo (m)	[is'pozʉ]
spouse (wife)	esposa (f)	[is'pozɐ]

married (masc.)	casado	[ka'zadʉ]
married (fem.)	casada	[ka'zada]
single (unmarried)	solteiro	[sow'te ru]
bachelor	solteirão (m)	[sowtej rãw]
divorced (masc.)	divorciado	[dʒivor'sjadu]
widow	viúva (f)	['vjuva]
widower	viúvo (m)	['vjuvu]

relative	parente (m)	[pa'rẽtʃ]
close relative	parente (m) próximo	[pa'rẽtʃ 'prɔsimu]
distant relative	parente (m) distante	[pa'rẽtʃ dʒis'tãtʃi]
relatives	parentes (m pl)	[pa'rẽtʃs]

orphan (boy)	órfão (m)	['ɔrfãw]
orphan (girl)	órfã (f)	['ɔrfã]
guardian (of a minor)	tutor (m)	[tu'tor]
to adopt (a boy)	adotar (vt)	[ado'tar]
to adopt (a girl)	adotar (vt)	[ado'tar]

53. Friends. Coworkers

friend (masc.)	amigo (m)	[a'migu]
friend (fem.)	amiga (f)	[a'miga]

friendship	**amizade** (f)	[ami'zadʒi]
to be friends	**ser amigos**	[ser a'migus]

buddy (masc.)	**amigo** (m)	[a'migu]
buddy (fem.)	**amiga** (f)	[a'miga]
partner	**parceiro** (m)	[par'sejru]

chief (boss)	**chefe** (m)	['ʃɛfi]
superior (n)	**superior** (m)	[supe'rjor]
owner, proprietor	**proprietário** (m)	[proprje'tarju]
subordinate (n)	**subordinado** (m)	[subordʒi'nadu]
colleague	**colega** (m, f)	[ko'lɛga]

acquaintance (person)	**conhecido** (m)	[koɲe'sidu]
fellow traveler	**companheiro** (m) **de viagem**	[kõpa'ɲejru de 'vjaʒẽ]
classmate	**colega** (m) **de classe**	[ko'lɛga de 'klasi]

neighbor (masc.)	**vizinho** (m)	[vi'ziɲu]
neighbor (fem.)	**vizinha** (f)	[vi'ziɲa]
neighbors	**vizinhos** (pl)	[vi'ziɲus]

54. Man. Woman

woman	**mulher** (f)	[mu'ʎer]
girl (young woman)	**menina** (f)	[me'nina]
bride	**noiva** (f)	['nojva]

beautiful (adj)	**bonita, bela**	[bo'nita], ['bɛla]
tall (adj)	**alta**	['awta]
slender (adj)	**esbelta**	[iz'bɛwta]
short (adj)	**baixa**	['baɪʃa]

blonde (n)	**loira** (f)	['lojra]
brunette (n)	**morena** (f)	[mo'rena]

ladies' (adj)	**de senhora**	[de se'ɲora]
virgin (girl)	**virgem** (f)	['virʒẽ]
pregnant (adj)	**grávida**	['gravida]

man (adult male)	**homem** (m)	['ɔmẽ]
blond (n)	**loiro** (m)	['lojru]
brunet (n)	**moreno** (m)	[mo'renu]
tall (adj)	**alto**	['awtu]
short (adj)	**baixo**	['baɪʃu]

rude (rough)	**rude**	['hudʒi]
stocky (adj)	**atarracado**	[ataha'kadu]
robust (adj)	**robusto**	[ho'bustu]
strong (adj)	**forte**	['fɔrtʃi]

strength	força (f)	['forsa]
stout, fat (adj)	gordo	['gordu]
swarthy (adj)	moreno	[mo'renu]
slender (well-built)	esbelto	[iz'bɛwtu]
elegant (adj)	elegante	[ele'gãtʃi]

55. Age

age	idade (f)	[i'dadʒi]
youth (young age)	juventude (f)	[ʒuvẽ'tudʒi]
young (adj)	jovem	['ʒɔvẽ]

| younger (adj) | mais novo | [majs 'ncvu] |
| older (adj) | mais velho | [majs 'vɛʎu] |

young man	jovem (m)	['ʒɔvẽ]
teenager	adolescente (m)	[adole'sẽtʃi]
guy, fellow	rapaz (m)	[ha'pajz]

| old man | velho (m) | ['vɛʎu] |
| old woman | velha (f) | ['vɛʎa] |

adult (adj)	adulto	[a'duwtu]
middle-aged (adj)	de meia-idade	[de meja i'dadʒi]
elderly (adj)	idoso, de idade	[i'dozu], [de i'dade]
old (adj)	velho	['vɛʎu]

retirement	aposentadoria (f)	[apozẽtado'ria]
to retire (from job)	aposentar-se (vr)	[apozẽ'tarsi]
retiree	aposentado (m)	[apozẽ'tadu]

56. Children

child	criança (f)	['krjãsa]
children	crianças (f pl)	['krjãsas]
twins	gêmeos (m pl), gêmeas (f pl)	['ʒemjus], ['ʒemjas]

cradle	berço (m)	['bersu]
rattle	chocalho (m)	[ʃo'kaʎu]
diaper	fralda (f)	['frawdɛ]

pacifier	chupeta (f), bico (m)	[ʃu'peta], ['biku]
baby carriage	carrinho (m) de bebê	[ka'hiɲu de be'be]
kindergarten	jardim (m) de infância	[ʒar'dʒĩ de ĩ'fãsja]
babysitter	babysitter, babá (f)	[bebi'sitter], [ba'ba]

| childhood | infância (f) | [ĩ'fãsja] |
| doll | boneca (f) | [bo'nɛka] |

toy	brinquedo (m)	[brĩ'kedu]
construction set (toy)	jogo (m) de montar	['ʒogu de mõ'tar]
well-bred (adj)	bem-educado	[bẽj edu'kadu]
ill-bred (adj)	malcriado	[maw'krjadu]
spoiled (adj)	mimado	[mi'madu]
to be naughty	ser travesso	[ser tra'vɛsu]
mischievous (adj)	travesso, traquinas	[tra'vɛsu], [tra'kinas]
mischievousness	travessura (f)	[trave'sura]
mischievous child	criança (f) travessa	['krjãsa tra'vɛsa]
obedient (adj)	obediente	[obe'dʒẽtʃi]
disobedient (adj)	desobediente	[dʒizobe'dʒjẽtʃi]
docile (adj)	dócil	['dɔsiw]
clever (smart)	inteligente	[ĩteli'ʒẽtʃi]
child prodigy	prodígio (m)	[pro'dʒiʒu]

57. Married couples. Family life

to kiss (vt)	beijar (vt)	[bej'ʒar]
to kiss (vi)	beijar-se (vr)	[bej'ʒarsi]
family (n)	família (f)	[fa'milja]
family (as adj)	familiar	[fami'ljar]
couple	casal (m)	[ka'zaw]
marriage (state)	matrimônio (m)	[matri'monju]
hearth (home)	lar (m)	[lar]
dynasty	dinastia (f)	[dʒinas'tʃia]
date	encontro (m)	[ẽ'kõtru]
kiss	beijo (m)	['bejʒu]
love (for sb)	amor (m)	[a'mor]
to love (sb)	amar (vt)	[a'mar]
beloved	amado, querido	[a'madu], [ke'ridu]
tenderness	ternura (f)	[ter'nura]
tender (affectionate)	afetuoso	[afe'twozu]
faithfulness	fidelidade (f)	[fideli'dadʒi]
faithful (adj)	fiel	[fjɛw]
care (attention)	cuidado (m)	[kwi'dadu]
caring (~ father)	carinhoso	[kari'ɲozu]
newlyweds	recém-casados (pl)	[he'sẽ-ka'zadus]
honeymoon	lua (f) de mel	['lua de mɛw]
to get married (ab. woman)	casar-se (vr)	[ka'zarsi]
to get married (ab. man)	casar-se (vr)	[ka'zarsi]
wedding	casamento (m)	[kaza'mẽtu]

golden wedding anniversary	bodas (f pl) de ouro aniversário (m)	['bodas de 'oru] [aniver'sarju]
lover (masc.)	amante (m)	[a'mãtʃi]
mistress (lover)	amante (f)	[a'mãtʃi]
adultery	adultério (m), traição (f)	[aduw'tɛrju], [traj'sãw]
to cheat on ... (commit adultery)	cometer adultério	[kome'ter aduw'tɛrju]
jealous (adj)	ciumento	[sju'mẽtɹ]
to be jealous	ser ciumento, -a	[ser sju'mẽtu, -a]
divorce	divórcio (m)	[dʒi'vɔrsju]
to divorce (vi)	divorciar-se (vr)	[dʒivor'sjarsi]
to quarrel (vi)	brigar (vi)	[bri'gar]
to be reconciled (after an argument)	fazer as pazes	[fa'zer as 'pajzis]
together (adv)	juntos	['ʒũtus]
sex	sexo (m)	['sɛksu]
happiness	felicidade (f)	[felisi'dadʒi]
happy (adj)	feliz	[fe'liz]
misfortune (accident)	infelicidade (f)	[ĩfelisi'dadʒi]
unhappy (adj)	infeliz	[ĩfe'liz]

Character. Feelings. Emotions

58. Feelings. Emotions

feeling (emotion)	sentimento (m)	[sẽtʃi'mẽtu]
feelings	sentimentos (m pl)	[sẽtʃi'mẽtus]
to feel (vt)	sentir (vt)	[sẽ'tʃir]

hunger	fome (f)	['fɔmi]
to be hungry	ter fome	[ter 'fɔmi]
thirst	sede (f)	['sedʒi]
to be thirsty	ter sede	[ter 'sedʒi]
sleepiness	sonolência (f)	[sono'lẽsja]
to feel sleepy	estar sonolento	[is'tar sono'lẽtu]

tiredness	cansaço (m)	[kã'sasu]
tired (adj)	cansado	[kã'sadu]
to get tired	ficar cansado	[fi'kar kã'sadu]

mood (humor)	humor (m)	[u'mor]
boredom	tédio (m)	['tɛdʒju]
to be bored	entediar-se (vr)	[ẽte'dʒjarsi]
seclusion	reclusão (f)	[heklu'zãw]
to seclude oneself	isolar-se (vr)	[izo'larsi]

to worry (make anxious)	preocupar (vt)	[preoku'par]
to be worried	estar preocupado	[is'tar preoku'padu]
worrying (n)	preocupação (f)	[preokupa'sãw]
anxiety	ansiedade (f)	[ãsje'dadʒi]
preoccupied (adj)	preocupado	[preoku'padu]
to be nervous	estar nervoso	[is'tar ner'vozu]
to panic (vi)	entrar em pânico	[ẽ'trar ẽ 'paniku]

hope	esperança (f)	[ispe'rãsa]
to hope (vi, vt)	esperar (vi, vt)	[ispe'rar]

certainty	certeza (f)	[ser'teza]
certain, sure (adj)	certo, seguro de ...	['sɛrtu], [se'guru de]
uncertainty	indecisão (f)	[ĩdesi'zãw]
uncertain (adj)	indeciso	[ĩde'sizu]

drunk (adj)	bêbado	['bebadu]
sober (adj)	sóbrio	['sɔbrju]
weak (adj)	fraco	['fraku]
happy (adj)	feliz	[fe'liz]
to scare (vt)	assustar (vt)	[asus'tar]

fury (madness)	**fúria** (f)	['furja]
rage (fury)	**ira, raiva** (f)	['ira], ['hajva]
depression	**depressão** (f)	[depre'sãw]
discomfort (unease)	**desconforto** (m)	[dʒiskõ'fɔrtu]
comfort	**conforto** (m)	[kõ'fortu]
to regret (be sorry)	**arrepender-se** (vr)	[ahepẽ'dersi]
regret	**arrependimento** (m)	[ahepẽcʒi'mẽtu]
bad luck	**azar** (m), **má sorte** (f)	[a'zar], [ma 'sɔrtʃi]]
sadness	**tristeza** (f)	[tris'teza]
shame (remorse)	**vergonha** (f)	[ver'goɾa]
gladness	**alegria** (f)	[ale'gria]
enthusiasm, zeal	**entusiasmo** (m)	[ẽtu'zjazmu]
enthusiast	**entusiasta** (m)	[ẽtu'zjasta]
to show enthusiasm	**mostrar entusiasmo**	[mos'trar ẽtu'zjazmu]

59. Character. Personality

character	**caráter** (m)	[ka'rater]
character flaw	**falha** (f) **de caráter**	['faʎa de ka'rater]
mind	**mente** (f)	['mẽtʃi]
reason	**razão** (f)	[ha'zãw]
conscience	**consciência** (f)	[kõ'sjẽsja]
habit (custom)	**hábito, costume** (m)	['abitu], [kos'tumi]
ability (talent)	**habilidade** (f)	[abili'dadʒi]
can (e.g., ~ swim)	**saber** (vi)	[sa'ber]
patient (adj)	**paciente**	[pa'sjẽtʃi]
impatient (adj)	**impaciente**	[ĩpa'sjẽtʃi]
curious (inquisitive)	**curioso**	[ku'rjozu]
curiosity	**curiosidade** (f)	[kurjozi'dadʒi]
modesty	**modéstia** (f)	[mo'dɛstu]
modest (adj)	**modesto**	[mo'dɛstu]
immodest (adj)	**imodesto**	[imo'dɛstu]
laziness	**preguiça** (f)	[pre'gisa]
lazy (adj)	**preguiçoso**	[pregi'sozu]
lazy person (masc.)	**preguiçoso** (m)	[pregi'sozu]
cunning (n)	**astúcia** (f)	[as'tusja]
cunning (as adj)	**astuto**	[as'tutɹ]
distrust	**desconfiança** (f)	[dʒiskõ'fjãsa]
distrustful (adj)	**desconfiado**	[dʒiskõ'fjadu]
generosity	**generosidade** (f)	[ʒenerozi'dadʒi]
generous (adj)	**generoso**	[ʒene'rozu]
talented (adj)	**talentoso**	[talẽ'tozu]

talent	talento (m)	[ta'lẽtu]
courageous (adj)	corajoso	[kora'ʒozu]
courage	coragem (f)	[ko'raʒẽ]
honest (adj)	honesto	[o'nɛstu]
honesty	honestidade (f)	[onestʃi'dadʒi]

careful (cautious)	prudente, cuidadoso	[pru'dẽtʃi], [kwida'dozu]
brave (courageous)	valoroso	[valo'rozu]
serious (adj)	sério	['sɛrju]
strict (severe, stern)	severo	[se'vɛru]

decisive (adj)	decidido	[desi'dʒidu]
indecisive (adj)	indeciso	[ĩde'sizu]
shy, timid (adj)	tímido	['tʃimidu]
shyness, timidity	timidez (f)	[tʃimi'dez]

confidence (trust)	confiança (f)	[kõ'fjãsa]
to believe (trust)	confiar (vt)	[kõ'fjar]
trusting (credulous)	crédulo	['krɛdulu]

sincerely (adv)	sinceramente	[sĩsera'mẽtʃi]
sincere (adj)	sincero	[sĩ'sɛru]
sincerity	sinceridade (f)	[sĩseri'dadʒi]
open (person)	aberto	[a'bɛrtu]

calm (adj)	calmo	['kawmu]
frank (sincere)	franco	['frãku]
naïve (adj)	ingênuo	[ĩ'ʒenwu]
absent-minded (adj)	distraído	[dʒistra'idu]
funny (odd)	engraçado	[ẽgra'sadu]

greed, stinginess	ganância (f)	[ga'nãsja]
greedy, stingy (adj)	ganancioso	[ganã'sjozu]
stingy (adj)	avarento, sovina	[avar'ẽtu], [so'vina]
evil (adj)	mal	[maw]
stubborn (adj)	teimoso	[tej'mozu]
unpleasant (adj)	desagradável	[dʒizagra'davew]

selfish person (masc.)	egoísta (m)	[ego'ista]
selfish (adj)	egoísta	[ego'ista]
coward	covarde (m)	[ko'vardʒi]
cowardly (adj)	covarde	[ko'vardʒi]

60. Sleep. Dreams

to sleep (vi)	dormir (vi)	[dor'mir]
sleep, sleeping	sono (m)	['sɔnu]
dream	sonho (m)	['sɔɲu]
to dream (in sleep)	sonhar (vi)	[so'ɲar]
sleepy (adj)	sonolento	[sono'lẽtu]

bed	cama (f)	['kama]
mattress	colchão (m)	[kow'ʃãw]
blanket (comforter)	cobertor (m)	[kuber'tor]
pillow	travesseiro (m)	[trave'sej˞u]
sheet	lençol (m)	[lẽ'sɔw]

insomnia	insônia (f)	[ĩ'sonja]
sleepless (adj)	sem sono	[sẽ 'sɔnu]
sleeping pill	sonífero (m)	[so'niferu]
to take a sleeping pill	tomar um sonífero	[to'mar ũ so'niferu]

to feel sleepy	estar sonolento	[is'tar sono'lẽtu]
to yawn (vi)	bocejar (vi)	[buse'ʒar]
to go to bed	ir para a cama	[ir 'para a 'kama]
to make up the bed	fazer a cama	[fa'zer a kama]
to fall asleep	adormecer (vi)	[adorme'ser]

nightmare	pesadelo (m)	[peza'deIu]
snore, snoring	ronco (m)	['hõku]
to snore (vi)	roncar (vi)	[hõ'kar]

alarm clock	despertador (m)	[dʒisperta'dor]
to wake (vt)	acordar, despertar (vt)	[akor'dar], [dʒisper'tar]
to wake up	acordar (vi)	[akor'dar]
to get up (vi)	levantar-se (vr)	[levã'tarsi]
to wash up (wash face)	lavar-se (vr)	[la'varsi]

61. Humour. Laughter. Gladness

humor (wit, fun)	humor (m)	[u'mor]
sense of humor	senso (m) de humor	['sẽsu də u'mor]
to enjoy oneself	divertir-se (vr)	[dʒiver'tʃirsi]
cheerful (merry)	alegre	[a'lɛgri]
merriment (gaiety)	alegria, diversão (f)	[ale'gria], [dʒiver'sãw]

smile	sorriso (m)	[so'hizu]
to smile (vi)	sorrir (vi)	[so'hir]
to start laughing	começar a rir	[kome'sar a hir]
to laugh (vi)	rir (vi)	[hir]
laugh, laughter	riso (m)	['hizu]

anecdote	anedota (f)	[ane'dɔta]
funny (anecdote, etc.)	engraçado	[ẽgra'sadu]
funny (odd)	ridículo, cômico	[hi'dʒikulu], ['komiku]

to joke (vi)	brincar (vi)	[brĩ'kar]
joke (verbal)	piada (f)	['pjada]
joy (emotion)	alegria (f)	[ale'gria]
to rejoice (vi)	regozijar-se (vr)	[hegozi'ʒarsi]
joyful (adj)	alegre	[a'lɛgri]

62. Discussion, conversation. Part 1

communication	comunicação (f)	[komunika'sãw]
to communicate	comunicar-se (vr)	[komuni'karse]
conversation	conversa (f)	[kõ'vɛrsa]
dialog	diálogo (m)	['dʒjalogu]
discussion (discourse)	discussão (f)	[dʒisku'sãw]
dispute (debate)	debate (m)	[de'batʃi]
to dispute, debate	debater (vt)	[deba'ter]
interlocutor	interlocutor (m)	[ĩterloku'tor]
topic (theme)	tema (m)	['tɛma]
point of view	ponto (m) de vista	['põtu de 'vista]
opinion (point of view)	opinião (f)	[opi'njãw]
speech (talk)	discurso (m)	[dʒis'kursu]
discussion (of report, etc.)	discussão (f)	[dʒisku'sãw]
to discuss (vt)	discutir (vt)	[dʒisku'tʃir]
talk (conversation)	conversa (f)	[kõ'vɛrsa]
to talk (to chat)	conversar (vi)	[kõver'sar]
meeting (encounter)	reunião (f)	[heu'njãw]
to meet (vi, vt)	encontrar-se (vr)	[ẽkõ'trarsi]
proverb	provérbio (m)	[pro'vɛrbju]
saying	ditado, provérbio (m)	[dʒi'tadu], [pro'vɛrbju]
riddle (poser)	adivinha (f)	[adʒi'viɲa]
to pose a riddle	dizer uma adivinha	[dʒi'zer 'uma adʒi'viɲu]
password	senha (f)	['seɲa]
secret	segredo (m)	[se'gredu]
oath (vow)	juramento (m)	[ʒura'mẽtu]
to swear (an oath)	jurar (vi)	[ʒu'rar]
promise	promessa (f)	[pro'mɛsa]
to promise (vt)	prometer (vt)	[prome'ter]
advice (counsel)	conselho (m)	[kõ'seʎu]
to advise (vt)	aconselhar (vt)	[akõse'ʎar]
to follow one's advice	seguir o conselho	[se'gir u kõ'seʎu]
to listen to ... (obey)	escutar (vt)	[isku'tar]
news	novidade, notícia (f)	[novi'dadʒi], [no'tʃisja]
sensation (news)	sensação (f)	[sẽsa'sãw]
information (report)	informação (f)	[ĩforma'sãw]
conclusion (decision)	conclusão (f)	[kõklu'zãw]
voice	voz (f)	[vɔz]
compliment	elogio (m)	[elo'ʒiu]
kind (nice)	amável, querido	[a'mavew], [ke'ridu]
word	palavra (f)	[pa'lavra]
phrase	frase (f)	['frazi]

answer	resposta (f)	[hes'pɔsta]
truth	verdade (f)	[ver'dadʒi]
lie	mentira (f)	[mẽ'tʃira]

thought	pensamento (m)	[pẽsa'mẽtu]
idea (inspiration)	ideia (f)	[i'dɛja]
fantasy	fantasia (f)	[fãta'zia]

63. Discussion, conversation. Part 2

respected (adj)	estimado, respeitado	[istʃi'madu], [hespej'tadu]
to respect (vt)	respeitar (vt)	[hespej tar]
respect	respeito (m)	[hes'pe tu]
Dear ... (letter)	Estimado ..., Caro ...	[istʃi'madu], ['karu]

to introduce (sb to sb)	apresentar (vt)	[aprezẽ'tar]
to make acquaintance	conhecer (vt)	[koɲe'sɐr]
intention	intenção (f)	[ĩtẽ'sãw]
to intend (have in mind)	tencionar (vt)	[tẽsjo'nar]
wish	desejo (m)	[de'zeʒu]
to wish (~ good luck)	desejar (vt)	[deze'ʒar]

surprise (astonishment)	surpresa (f)	[sur'preza]
to surprise (amaze)	surpreender (vt)	[surprjẽ'der]
to be surprised	surpreender-se (vr)	[surprjẽ'dersi]

to give (vt)	dar (vt)	[dar]
to take (get hold of)	pegar (vt)	[pe'gar]
to give back	devolver (vt)	[devow'ver]
to return (give back)	retornar (vt)	[hetor'nar]

to apologize (vi)	desculpar-se (vr)	[dʒiskuw'parsi]
apology	desculpa (f)	[dʒis'kuwpa]
to forgive (vt)	perdoar (vt)	[per'dwar]

to talk (speak)	falar (vi)	[fa'lar]
to listen (vi)	escutar (vt)	[isku'tar]
to hear out	ouvir até o fim	[o'vir a'tɛ u fĩ]
to understand (vt)	entender (vt)	[ẽtẽ'dɛr]

to show (to display)	mostrar (vt)	[mos'trar]
to look at ...	olhar para ...	[ɔ'ʎar 'para]
to call (yell for sb)	chamar (vt)	[ʃa'mar]
to distract (disturb)	perturbar, distrair (vt)	[pertur'bar], [dʒistra'ir]
to disturb (vt)	perturbar (vt)	[pertur'bar]
to pass (to hand sth)	entregar (vt)	[ẽtre'gar]

demand (request)	pedido (m)	[pe'dʒidu]
to request (ask)	pedir (vt)	[pe'dʒ r]
demand (firm request)	exigência (f)	[ezi'ʒẽsja]

to demand (request firmly)	exigir (vt)	[ezi'ʒir]
to tease (call names)	insultar (vt)	[ĩsuw'tar]
to mock (make fun of)	zombar (vt)	[zõ'bar]
mockery, derision	zombaria (f)	[zõba'ria]
nickname	alcunha (f), apelido (m)	[aw'kuɲa], [ape'lidu]

insinuation	insinuação (f)	[ĩsinwa'sãw]
to insinuate (imply)	insinuar (vt)	[ĩsi'nwar]
to mean (vt)	querer dizer	[ke'rer dʒi'zer]

description	descrição (f)	[dʒiskri'sãw]
to describe (vt)	descrever (vt)	[dʒiskre'ver]
praise (compliments)	elogio (m)	[elo'ʒiu]
to praise (vt)	elogiar (vt)	[elo'ʒjar]

disappointment	desapontamento (m)	[dʒizapõta'mẽtu]
to disappoint (vt)	desapontar (vt)	[dʒizapõ'tar]
to be disappointed	desapontar-se (vr)	[dʒizapõ'tarsi]

supposition	suposição (f)	[supozi'sãw]
to suppose (assume)	supor (vt)	[su'por]
warning (caution)	advertência (f)	[adʒiver'tẽsja]
to warn (vt)	advertir (vt)	[adʒiver'tʃir]

64. Discussion, conversation. Part 3

| to talk into (convince) | convencer (vt) | [kõvẽ'ser] |
| to calm down (vt) | acalmar (vt) | [akaw'mar] |

silence (~ is golden)	silêncio (m)	[si'lẽsju]
to be silent (not speaking)	ficar em silêncio	[fi'kar ẽ si'lẽsju]
to whisper (vi, vt)	sussurrar (vi, vt)	[susu'har]
whisper	sussurro (m)	[su'suhu]

| frankly, sincerely (adv) | francamente | [frãka'mẽtʃi] |
| in my opinion ... | na minha opinião ... | [na 'miɲa opi'njãw] |

detail (of the story)	detalhe (m)	[de'taʎi]
detailed (adj)	detalhado	[deta'ʎadu]
in detail (adv)	detalhadamente	[detaʎada'mẽtʃi]

| hint, clue | dica (f) | ['dʒika] |
| to give a hint | dar uma dica | [dar 'uma 'dʒika] |

look (glance)	olhar (m)	[ɔ'ʎar]
to have a look	dar uma olhada	[dar 'uma o'ʎada]
fixed (look)	fixo	['fiksu]
to blink (vi)	piscar (vi)	[pis'kar]
to wink (vi)	piscar (vt)	[pis'kar]
to nod (in assent)	acenar com a cabeça	[ase'nar kõ a ka'besa]

sigh	suspiro (m)	[sus'piɾʟ]
to sigh (vi)	suspirar (vi)	[suspi'rɛr]
to shudder (vi)	estremecer (vi)	[istreme'ser]
gesture	gesto (m)	['ʒɛstu]
to touch (one's arm, etc.)	tocar (vt)	[to'kar]
to seize (e.g., ~ by the arm)	agarrar (vt)	[aga'har]
to tap (on the shoulder)	bater de leve	[ba'ter ce 'lɛvi]

Look out!	Cuidado!	[kwi'dadu]
Really?	Sério?	['sɛrju]
Are you sure?	Tem certeza?	[tẽj ser'teza]
Good luck!	Boa sorte!	['boa 'sɔrtʃi]
I see!	Entendi!	[ẽtẽ'dʒi]
What a pity!	Que pena!	[ki 'pena]

65. Agreement. Refusal

consent	consentimento (m)	[kõsẽtʃi mẽtu]
to consent (vi)	consentir (vi)	[kõsẽ'tʃr]
approval	aprovação (f)	[aprova'sãw]
to approve (vt)	aprovar (vt)	[apro'var]
refusal	recusa (f)	[he'kuza]
to refuse (vi, vt)	negar-se a ...	[ne'garsi]

Great!	Ótimo!	['ɔtʃimu]
All right!	Tudo bem!	['tudu bẽj]
Okay! (I agree)	Está bem! De acordo!	[is'ta bẽj], [de a'kordu]

forbidden (adj)	proibido	[proi'bidu]
it's forbidden	é proibido	[ɛ proi'bidu]
it's impossible	é impossível	[ɛ ĩpo'sivew]
incorrect (adj)	incorreto	[ĩko'hɛːu]

to reject (~ a demand)	rejeitar (vt)	[heʒej'tar]
to support (cause, idea)	apoiar (vt)	[apo'jar]
to accept (~ an apology)	aceitar (vt)	[asej'tar]

to confirm (vt)	confirmar (vt)	[kõfir'mar]
confirmation	confirmação (f)	[kõfirma'sãw]
permission	permissão (f)	[permi'sãw]
to permit (vt)	permitir (vt)	[permi'tʃir]
decision	decisão (f)	[desi'zãw]
to say nothing (hold one's tongue)	não dizer nada	['nãw dʒi'zer 'nada]

condition (term)	condição (f)	[kõdʒi'sãw]
excuse (pretext)	pretexto (m)	[pre'tɛstu]
praise (compliments)	elogio (m)	[elo'ʒiu]
to praise (vt)	elogiar (vt)	[elo'ʒjar]

66. Success. Good luck. Failure

success	êxito, sucesso (m)	['ezitu], [su'sɛsu]
successfully (adv)	com êxito	[kõ 'ezitu]
successful (adj)	bem sucedido	[bẽj suse'dʒidu]
luck (good luck)	sorte (f)	['sɔrtʃi]
Good luck!	Boa sorte!	['boa 'sɔrtʃi]
lucky (e.g., ~ day)	de sorte	[de 'sɔrtʃi]
lucky (fortunate)	sortudo, felizardo	[sor'tudu], [feli'zardu]
failure	fracasso (m)	[fra'kasu]
misfortune	pouca sorte (f)	['poka 'sɔrtʃi]
bad luck	azar (m), má sorte (f)	[a'zar], [ma 'sɔrtʃi]]
unsuccessful (adj)	mal sucedido	[maw suse'dʒidu]
catastrophe	catástrofe (f)	[ka'tastrofi]
pride	orgulho (m)	[or'guʎu]
proud (adj)	orgulhoso	[orgu'ʎozu]
to be proud	estar orgulhoso	[is'tar orgu'ʎozu]
winner	vencedor (m)	[vẽse'dor]
to win (vi)	vencer (vi, vt)	[vẽ'ser]
to lose (not win)	perder (vt)	[per'der]
try	tentativa (f)	[tẽta'tʃiva]
to try (vi)	tentar (vt)	[tẽ'tar]
chance (opportunity)	chance (m)	['ʃãsi]

67. Quarrels. Negative emotions

shout (scream)	grito (m)	['gritu]
to shout (vi)	gritar (vi)	[gri'tar]
to start to cry out	começar a gritar	[kome'sar a gri'tar]
quarrel	discussão (f)	[dʒisku'sãw]
to quarrel (vi)	brigar (vi)	[bri'gar]
fight (squabble)	escândalo (m)	[is'kãdalu]
to make a scene	criar escândalo	[krjar is'kãdalu]
conflict	conflito (m)	[kõ'flitu]
misunderstanding	mal-entendido (m)	[mal ẽtẽ'dʒidu]
insult	insulto (m)	[ĩ'suwtu]
to insult (vt)	insultar (vt)	[ĩsuw'tar]
insulted (adj)	insultado	[ĩsuw'tadu]
resentment	ofensa (f)	[ɔ'fẽsa]
to offend (vt)	ofender (vt)	[ofẽ'der]
to take offense	ofender-se (vr)	[ofẽ'dersi]
indignation	indignação (f)	[ĩdʒigna'sãw]
to be indignant	indignar-se (vr)	[ĩdʒig'narsi]

complaint	queixa (f)	['kejʃa]
to complain (vi, vt)	queixar-se (vr)	[kej'ʃarsi]
apology	desculpa (f)	[dʒis'kuwpa]
to apologize (vi)	desculpar-se (vr)	[dʒiskuw'parsi]
to beg pardon	pedir perdão	[pe'dʒir per'dãw]
criticism	crítica (f)	['kritʃika]
to criticize (vt)	criticar (vt)	[kritʃi'kar]
accusation (charge)	acusação (f)	[akuza'sãw]
to accuse (vt)	acusar (vt)	[aku'zar]
revenge	vingança (f)	[vĩ'gãsa]
to avenge (get revenge)	vingar (vt)	[vĩ'gar]
to pay back	vingar-se (vr)	[vĩ'garsi]
disdain	desprezo (m)	[dʒis'prezu]
to despise (vt)	desprezar (vt)	[dʒispre'zar]
hatred, hate	ódio (m)	['ɔdʒju]
to hate (vt)	odiar (vt)	[o'dʒjar]
nervous (adj)	nervoso	[ner'vozu]
to be nervous	estar nervoso	[is'tar ner'vozu]
angry (mad)	zangado	[zã'gadʊ]
to make angry	zangar (vt)	[zã'gar]
humiliation	humilhação (f)	[umiʎa'sãw]
to humiliate (vt)	humilhar (vt)	[umi'ʎar]
to humiliate oneself	humilhar-se (vr)	[umi'ʎarsi]
shock	choque (m)	['ʃɔki]
to shock (vt)	chocar (vt)	[ʃo'kar]
trouble (e.g., serious ~)	aborrecimento (m)	[abohesi'mẽtu]
unpleasant (adj)	desagradável	[dʒizagra'davew]
fear (dread)	medo (m)	['medu]
terrible (storm, heat)	terrível	[te'hivew]
scary (e.g., ~ story)	assustador	[asusta'dor]
horror	horror (m)	[o'hor]
awful (crime, news)	horrível, terrível	[o'hivew], [te'hivew]
to begin to tremble	começar a tremer	[kome'sar a tre'mer]
to cry (weep)	chorar (vi)	[ʃo'rar]
to start crying	começar a chorar	[kome'sar a ʃo'rar]
tear	lágrima (f)	['lagrima]
fault	falta (f)	['fawta]
guilt (feeling)	culpa (f)	['kuwpa]
dishonor (disgrace)	desonra (f)	[dʒi'zõha]
protest	protesto (m)	[pro'tɛstu]
stress	estresse (m)	[is'trɛsi]

73

to disturb (vt)	perturbar (vt)	[pertur'bar]
to be furious	zangar-se com ...	[zã'garsi kõ]
mad, angry (adj)	zangado	[zã'gadu]
to end (~ a relationship)	terminar (vt)	[termi'nar]
to swear (at sb)	praguejar	[prage'ʒar]

to scare (become afraid)	assustar-se	[asus'tarsi]
to hit (strike with hand)	golpear (vt)	[gow'pjar]
to fight (street fight, etc.)	brigar (vi)	[bri'gar]

to settle (a conflict)	resolver (vt)	[hezow'ver]
discontented (adj)	descontente	[dʒiskõ'tẽtʃi]
furious (adj)	furioso	[fu'rjozu]

| It's not good! | Não está bem! | ['nãw is'ta bẽj] |
| It's bad! | É ruim! | [ɛ hu'ĩ] |

Medicine

68. Diseases

sickness	doença (f)	[do'ēsa]
to be sick	estar doente	[is'tar do'ētʃi]
health	saude (f)	[sa'udʒi]
runny nose (coryza)	nariz (m) escorrendo	[na'riz isko'hēdu]
tonsillitis	amigdalite (f)	[amigda'litʃi]
cold (illness)	resfriado (m)	[hes'frjadu]
to catch a cold	ficar resfriado	[fi'kar hes'frjadu]
bronchitis	bronquite (f)	[brõ'kitʃ]
pneumonia	pneumonia (f)	[pnewmo'nia]
flu, influenza	gripe (f)	['gripi]
nearsighted (adj)	míope	['miopi]
farsighted (adj)	presbita	[pres'bita]
strabismus (crossed eyes)	estrabismo (m)	[istra'bizmu]
cross-eyed (adj)	estrábico, vesgo	[is'trabiku], ['vezgu]
cataract	catarata (f)	[kata'rata]
glaucoma	glaucoma (m)	[glaw'koma]
stroke	AVC (m), apoplexia (f)	[ave'se], [apople'ksia]
heart attack	ataque (m) cardíaco	[a'taki kar'dʒiaku]
myocardial infarction	enfarte (m) do miocárdio	[ē'fartʃi du mjo'kardʒiu]
paralysis	paralisia (f)	[parali'zia]
to paralyze (vt)	paralisar (vt)	[parali'zar]
allergy	alergia (f)	[aler'ʒia]
asthma	asma (f)	['azma]
diabetes	diabetes (f)	[dʒja'bɛtʃis]
toothache	dor (f) de dente	[dor de 'dētʃi]
caries	cárie (f)	['kari]
diarrhea	diarreia (f)	[dʒja'hɛja]
constipation	prisão (f) de ventre	[pri'zãw de 'vētri]
stomach upset	desarranjo (m) intestinal	[dʒiza'hãʒu ĩtestʃi'naw]
food poisoning	intoxicação (f) alimentar	[ĩtoksika'sãw alimē'tar]
to get food poisoning	intoxicar-se	[ĩtoksi'karsi]
arthritis	artrite (f)	[ar'tritʃi]
rickets	raquitismo (m)	[haki'tʃizmu]
rheumatism	reumatismo (m)	[hewma'tʃizmu]

atherosclerosis	arteriosclerose (f)	[arterjoskle'rɔzi]
gastritis	gastrite (f)	[gas'tritʃi]
appendicitis	apendicite (f)	[apēdʒi'sitʃi]
cholecystitis	colecistite (f)	[kulesi'stʃitʃi]
ulcer	úlcera (f)	['uwsera]

measles	sarampo (m)	[sa'rãpu]
rubella (German measles)	rubéola (f)	[hu'bɛola]
jaundice	icterícia (f)	[ikte'risja]
hepatitis	hepatite (f)	[epa'tʃitʃi]

schizophrenia	esquizofrenia (f)	[iskizofre'nia]
rabies (hydrophobia)	raiva (f)	['hajva]
neurosis	neurose (f)	[new'rɔzi]
concussion	contusão (f) cerebral	[kõtu'zãw sere'braw]

cancer	câncer (m)	['kãser]
sclerosis	esclerose (f)	[iskle'rɔzi]
multiple sclerosis	esclerose (f) múltipla	[iskle'rɔzi 'muwtʃipla]

alcoholism	alcoolismo (m)	[awko'lizmu]
alcoholic (n)	alcoólico (m)	[aw'kɔliku]
syphilis	sífilis (f)	['sifilis]
AIDS	AIDS (f)	['ajdʒs]

tumor	tumor (m)	[tu'mor]
malignant (adj)	maligno	[ma'lignu]
benign (adj)	benigno	[be'nignu]

fever	febre (f)	['fɛbri]
malaria	malária (f)	[ma'larja]
gangrene	gangrena (f)	[gã'grena]
seasickness	enjoo (m)	[ē'ʒou]
epilepsy	epilepsia (f)	[epile'psia]

epidemic	epidemia (f)	[epide'mia]
typhus	tifo (m)	['tʃifu]
tuberculosis	tuberculose (f)	[tuberku'lɔzi]
cholera	cólera (f)	['kɔlera]
plague (bubonic ~)	peste (f) bubônica	['pɛstʃi bu'bonika]

69. Symptoms. Treatments. Part 1

symptom	sintoma (m)	[sĩ'tɔma]
temperature	temperatura (f)	[tẽpera'tura]
high temperature (fever)	febre (f)	['fɛbri]
pulse (heartbeat)	pulso (m)	['puwsu]

dizziness (vertigo)	vertigem (f)	[ver'tʃiʒẽ]
hot (adj)	quente	['kẽtʃi]

| shivering | calafrio (m) | [kala'friu] |
| pale (e.g., ~ face) | pálido | ['palidu] |

cough	tosse (f)	['tɔsi]
to cough (vi)	tossir (vi)	[to'sir]
to sneeze (vi)	espirrar (vi)	[ispi'har]
faint	desmaio (m)	[dʒiz'maju]
to faint (vi)	desmaiar (vi)	[dʒizma'jar]

bruise (hématome)	mancha (f) preta	['mãʃa 'preta]
bump (lump)	galo (m)	['galu]
to bang (bump)	machucar-se (vr)	[maʃu'karsi]
contusion (bruise)	contusão (f)	[kõtu'zãw]
to get a bruise	machucar-se (vr)	[maʃu'karsi]

to limp (vi)	mancar (vi)	[mã'kar]
dislocation	deslocamento (f)	[dʒizloka'mẽtu]
to dislocate (vt)	deslocar (vt)	[dʒizlo'kar]
fracture	fratura (f)	[fra'tura]
to have a fracture	fraturar (vt)	[fratu'rar]

cut (e.g., paper ~)	corte (m)	['kɔrtʃi]
to cut oneself	cortar-se (vr)	[kor'tarsi]
bleeding	hemorragia (f)	[emoha'ʒia]

| burn (injury) | queimadura (f) | [kejma'dura] |
| to get burned | queimar-se (vr) | [kej'marsi] |

to prick (vt)	picar (vt)	[pi'kar]
to prick oneself	picar-se (vr)	[pi'karsi]
to injure (vt)	lesionar (vt)	[lezjo'nar]
injury	lesão (m)	[le'zãw]
wound	ferida (f), ferimento (m)	[fe'rida], [feri'mẽtu]
trauma	trauma (m)	['trawma]

to be delirious	delirar (vi)	[deli'rar]
to stutter (vi)	gaguejar (vi)	[gage'ʒar]
sunstroke	insolação (f)	[insola'sãw]

70. Symptoms. Treatments. Part 2

| pain, ache | dor (f) | [dor] |
| splinter (in foot, etc.) | farpa (f) | ['farpa] |

sweat (perspiration)	suor (m)	[swɔr]
to sweat (perspire)	suar (vi)	[swar]
vomiting	vômito (m)	['vomitu]
convulsions	convulsões (f pl)	[kõvuw'sõjs]
pregnant (adj)	grávida	['gravida]
to be born	nascer (vi)	[na'ser]

delivery, labor	parto (m)	['partu]
to deliver (~ a baby)	dar à luz	[dar a luz]
abortion	aborto (m)	[a'bortu]

breathing, respiration	respiração (f)	[hespira'sãw]
in-breath (inhalation)	inspiração (f)	[ĩspira'sãw]
out-breath (exhalation)	expiração (f)	[ispira'sãw]
to exhale (breathe out)	expirar (vi)	[ispi'rar]
to inhale (vi)	inspirar (vi)	[ĩspi'rar]

disabled person	inválido (m)	[ĩ'validu]
cripple	aleijado (m)	[alej'ʒadu]
drug addict	drogado (m)	[dro'gadu]

deaf (adj)	surdo	['surdu]
mute (adj)	mudo	['mudu]
deaf mute (adj)	surdo-mudo	['surdu-'mudu]

mad, insane (adj)	louco, insano	['loku], [ĩ'sanu]
madman (demented person)	louco (m)	['loku]
madwoman	louca (f)	['loka]
to go insane	ficar louco	[fi'kar 'loku]

gene	gene (m)	['ʒɛni]
immunity	imunidade (f)	[imuni'dadʒi]
hereditary (adj)	hereditário	[eredʒi'tarju]
congenital (adj)	congênito	[kõ'ʒenitu]

virus	vírus (m)	['virus]
microbe	micróbio (m)	[mi'krɔbju]
bacterium	bactéria (f)	[bak'tɛrja]
infection	infecção (f)	[ĩfek'sãw]

71. Symptoms. Treatments. Part 3

| hospital | hospital (m) | [ospi'taw] |
| patient | paciente (m) | [pa'sjẽtʃi] |

diagnosis	diagnóstico (m)	[dʒjag'nɔstʃiku]
cure	cura (f)	['kura]
medical treatment	tratamento (m) médico	[trata'mẽtu 'mɛdʒiku]
to get treatment	curar-se (vr)	[ku'rarsi]
to treat (~ a patient)	tratar (vt)	[tra'tar]
to nurse (look after)	cuidar (vt)	[kwi'dar]
care (nursing ~)	cuidado (m)	[kwi'dadu]

operation, surgery	operação (f)	[opera'sãw]
to bandage (head, limb)	enfaixar (vt)	[ẽfaj'ʃar]
bandaging	enfaixamento (m)	[bã'daʒãj]

vaccination	vacinação (f)	[vasina'sãw]
to vaccinate (vt)	vacinar (vt)	[vasi'nar]
injection, shot	injeção (f)	[inʒe'sãw]
to give an injection	dar uma injeção	[dar 'uma inʒe'sãw]

attack	ataque (m)	[a'taki]
amputation	amputação (f)	[ãputa'sãw]
to amputate (vt)	amputar (vt)	[ãpu'tar]
coma	coma (f)	['kɔma]
to be in a coma	estar em coma	[is'tar ẽ 'kɔma]
intensive care	rearimação (f)	[hianima'sãw]

to recover (~ from flu)	recuperar-se (vr)	[hekupe'rarsi]
condition (patient's ~)	estado (m)	[i'stadu]
consciousness	consciência (f)	[kõ'sjẽsja]
memory (faculty)	memória (f)	[me'mɔrja]

to pull out (tooth)	tirar (vt)	[tʃi'rar]
filling	obturação (f)	[obitura'sãw]
to fill (a tooth)	obturar (vt)	[obitu'rar]

| hypnosis | hipnose (f) | [ip'nɔzi] |
| to hypnotize (vt) | hipnotizar (vt) | [ipnotʃi'zar] |

72. Doctors

doctor	médico (m)	['mɛdʒiku]
nurse	enfermeira (f)	[ẽfer'mejra]
personal doctor	médico (m) pessoal	['mɛdʒiku pe'swaw]

dentist	dentista (m)	[dẽ'tʃista]
eye doctor	oculista (m)	[oku'lista]
internist	terapeuta (m)	[tera'pewta]
surgeon	cirurgião (m)	[sirur'ʒjãw]

psychiatrist	psiquiatra (m)	[psi'kjatra]
pediatrician	pediatra (m)	[pe'dʒjatra]
psychologist	psicólogo (m)	[psi'kɔlogu]
gynecologist	ginecologista (m)	[ʒinekolo'ʒista]
cardiologist	cardiologista (m)	[kardʒjclo'ʒista]

73. Medicine. Drugs. Accessories

medicine, drug	medicamento (m)	[medʒika'mẽtu]
remedy	remédio (m)	[he'mɛdʒju]
to prescribe (vt)	receitar (vt)	[hesej'tar]
prescription	receita (f)	[he'sejta]
tablet, pill	comprimido (m)	[kõpri'midu]

ointment	unguento (m)	[ũ'gwẽtu]
ampule	ampola (f)	[ã'pola]
mixture, solution	solução, preparado (m)	[solu'sãw], [prepa'radu]
syrup	xarope (m)	[ʃa'rɔpi]
capsule	cápsula (f)	['kapsula]
powder	pó (m)	[pɔ]

gauze bandage	atadura (f)	[ata'dura]
cotton wool	algodão (m)	[awgo'dãw]
iodine	iodo (m)	['jodu]

Band-Aid	curativo (m) adesivo	[kura'tivu ade'zivu]
eyedropper	conta-gotas (m)	['kõta 'gotas]
thermometer	termômetro (m)	[ter'mometru]
syringe	seringa (f)	[se'rĩga]

wheelchair	cadeira (f) de rodas	[ka'dejra de 'hɔdas]
crutches	muletas (f pl)	[mu'letas]

painkiller	analgésico (m)	[anaw'ʒɛziku]
laxative	laxante (m)	[la'ʃãtʃi]
spirits (ethanol)	álcool (m)	['awkɔw]
medicinal herbs	ervas (f pl) medicinais	['ɛrvas medʒisi'najs]
herbal (~ tea)	de ervas	[de 'ɛrvas]

74. Smoking. Tobacco products

tobacco	tabaco (m)	[ta'baku]
cigarette	cigarro (m)	[si'gahu]
cigar	charuto (m)	[ʃa'rutu]
pipe	cachimbo (m)	[ka'ʃĩbu]
pack (of cigarettes)	maço (m)	['masu]

matches	fósforos (m pl)	['fosforus]
matchbox	caixa (f) de fósforos	['kaɪʃa de 'fosforus]
lighter	isqueiro (m)	[is'kejru]
ashtray	cinzeiro (m)	[sĩ'zejru]
cigarette case	cigarreira (f)	[siga'hejra]

cigarette holder	piteira (f)	[pi'tejra]
filter (cigarette tip)	filtro (m)	['fiwtru]

to smoke (vi, vt)	fumar (vi, vt)	[fu'mar]
to light a cigarette	acender um cigarro	[asẽ'der ũ si'gahu]
smoking	tabagismo (m)	[taba'ʒiʒmu]
smoker	fumante (m)	[fu'mãtʃi]

stub, butt (of cigarette)	bituca (f)	[bi'tuka]
smoke, fumes	fumaça (f)	[fu'masa]
ash	cinza (f)	['sĩza]

HUMAN HABITAT

City

75. City. Life in the city

city, town	**cidade** (f)	[si'dadʒi]
capital city	**capital** (f)	[kapi'taw]
village	**aldeia** (f)	[aw'deja]
city map	**mapa** (m) **da cidade**	['mapa da si'dadʒi]
downtown	**centro** (m) **da cidade**	['sẽtru da si'dadʒi]
suburb	**subúrbio** (m)	[su'burbju]
suburban (adj)	**suburbano**	[subur'banu]
outskirts	**periferia** (f)	[perife'ria]
environs (suburbs)	**arredores** (m pl)	[ahe'doris]
city block	**quarteirão** (m)	[kwartej'rãw]
residential block (area)	**quarteirão** (m) **residencial**	[kwartej'rãw hezidẽ'sjaw]
traffic	**tráfego** (m)	['trafegu]
traffic lights	**semáforo** (m)	[se'maɾoru]
public transportation	**transporte** (m) **público**	[trãs'portʃi 'publiku]
intersection	**cruzamento** (m)	[kruza'mẽtu]
crosswalk	**faixa** (f)	['fajʃa]
pedestrian underpass	**túnel** (m)	['tunew]
to cross (~ the street)	**cruzar, atravessar** (vt)	[kru'zar], [atrave'sar]
pedestrian	**pedestre** (m)	[pe'dɛstri]
sidewalk	**calçada** (f)	[kaw'sada]
bridge	**ponte** (f)	['põtʃi]
embankment (river walk)	**margem** (f) **do rio**	['marʒẽ du 'hiu]
fountain	**fonte** (f)	['fõtʃi]
allée (garden walkway)	**alameda** (f)	[ala'meda]
park	**parque** (m)	['parki]
boulevard	**bulevar** (m)	[bule'var]
square	**praça** (f)	['prasa]
avenue (wide street)	**avenida** (f)	[ave'nida]
street	**rua** (f)	['hua]
side street	**travessa** (f)	[tra'vɛsa]
dead end	**beco** (m) **sem saída**	['beku sẽ sa'ida]
house	**casa** (f)	['kaza]
building	**edifício, prédio** (m)	[edʒi'fisju], ['prɛdʒju]

skyscraper	arranha-céu (m)	[aˈhaɲa-sɛw]
facade	fachada (f)	[faˈʃada]
roof	telhado (m)	[teˈʎadu]
window	janela (f)	[ʒaˈnɛla]
arch	arco (m)	[ˈarku]
column	coluna (f)	[koˈluna]
corner	esquina (f)	[isˈkina]

store window	vitrine (f)	[viˈtrini]
signboard (store sign, etc.)	letreiro (m)	[leˈtrejru]
poster (e.g., playbill)	cartaz (m)	[karˈtaz]
advertising poster	cartaz (m) publicitário	[karˈtaz publisiˈtarju]
billboard	painel (m) publicitário	[pajˈnɛw publisiˈtarju]

garbage, trash	lixo (m)	[ˈliʃu]
trash can (public ~)	lixeira (f)	[liˈʃejra]
to litter (vi)	jogar lixo na rua	[ʒoˈgar ˈliʃu na ˈhua]
garbage dump	aterro (m) sanitário	[aˈtehu saniˈtarju]

phone booth	orelhão (m)	[oreˈʎãw]
lamppost	poste (m) de luz	[ˈpɔstʃi de luz]
bench (park ~)	banco (m)	[ˈbãku]

police officer	polícia (m)	[poˈlisja]
police	polícia (f)	[poˈlisja]
beggar	mendigo, pedinte (m)	[mẽˈdʒigu], [peˈdʒĩtʃi]
homeless (n)	desabrigado (m)	[dʒizabriˈgadu]

76. Urban institutions

store	loja (f)	[ˈlɔʒa]
drugstore, pharmacy	drogaria (f)	[drogaˈria]
eyeglass store	ótica (f)	[ˈɔtʃika]
shopping mall	centro (m) comercial	[ˈsẽtru komerˈsjaw]
supermarket	supermercado (m)	[supermerˈkadu]

bakery	padaria (f)	[padaˈria]
baker	padeiro (m)	[paˈdejru]
pastry shop	pastelaria (f)	[pastelaˈria]
grocery store	mercearia (f)	[mersjaˈria]
butcher shop	açougue (m)	[aˈsogi]

| produce store | fruteira (f) | [fruˈtejra] |
| market | mercado (m) | [merˈkadu] |

coffee house	cafeteria (f)	[kafeteˈria]
restaurant	restaurante (m)	[hestawˈrãtʃi]
pub, bar	bar (m)	[bar]
pizzeria	pizzaria (f)	[pitsaˈria]
hair salon	salão (m) de cabeleireiro	[saˈlãw de kabelejˈrejru]

post office	agência (f) dos correios	[a'ʒẽsja dus ko'hejus]
dry cleaners	lavanderia (f)	[lavãde'ria]
photo studio	estúdio (m) fotográfico	[is'tudʒu foto'grafiku]
shoe store	sapataria (f)	[sapata'ria]
bookstore	livraria (f)	[livra'ria]
sporting goods store	loja (f) de artigos esportivos	['loʒa de ar'tʃigus ispor'tʃivus]
clothes repair shop	costureira (m)	[kostu'rejra]
formal wear rental	aluguel (m) de roupa	[alu'gɛw de 'hopa]
video rental store	videolocadora (f)	['vidʒju·loka'dɔra]
circus	circo (m)	['sirku]
zoo	jardim (m) zoológico	[ʒar'dʒĩ zo'lɔʒiku]
movie theater	cinema (m)	[si'nɛma]
museum	museu (m)	[mu'zew]
library	biblioteca (f)	[bibljo'tɛka]
theater	teatro (m)	['tʃjatru]
opera (opera house)	ópera (f)	['ɔpera]
nightclub	boate (f)	['bwatʃi]
casino	cassino (m)	[ka'sinʊ]
mosque	mesquita (f)	[mes'kita]
synagogue	sinagoga (f)	[sina'gɔga]
cathedral	catedral (f)	[kate'draw]
temple	templo (m)	['tẽplu]
church	igreja (f)	[i'greʒa]
college	faculdade (f)	[fakuw'dadʒi]
university	universidade (f)	[universi'dadʒi]
school	escola (f)	[is'kola]
prefecture	prefeitura (f)	[prefej'tura]
city hall	câmara (f) municipal	['kamara munisi'paw]
hotel	hotel (m)	[o'tɛw]
bank	banco (m)	['bãku]
embassy	embaixada (f)	[ẽbaj'ʃada]
travel agency	agência (f) de viagens	[a'ʒẽsja de 'vjaʒẽs]
information office	agência (f) de informações	[a'ʒẽsja de ĩforma'sõjs]
currency exchange	casa (f) de câmbio	['kaza de 'kãbju]
subway	metrô (m)	[me'trɔ]
hospital	hospital (m)	[ospi'taw]
gas station	posto (m) de gasolina	['postu de gazo'lina]
parking lot	parque (m) de estacionamento	['parki de istasjona'mẽtu]

83

77. Urban transportation

bus	ônibus (m)	['onibus]
streetcar	bonde (m) elétrico	['bõdʒi e'lɛtriku]
trolley bus	trólebus (m)	['trɔlebus]
route (of bus, etc.)	rota (f), itinerário (m)	['hɔta], [itʃine'rarju]
number (e.g., bus ~)	número (m)	['numeru]
to go by ...	ir de ...	[ir de]
to get on (~ the bus)	entrar no ...	[ẽ'trar nu]
to get off ...	descer do ...	[de'ser du]
stop (e.g., bus ~)	parada (f)	[pa'rada]
next stop	próxima parada (f)	['prɔsima pa'rada]
terminus	terminal (m)	[termi'naw]
schedule	horário (m)	[o'rarju]
to wait (vt)	esperar (vt)	[ispe'rar]
ticket	passagem (f)	[pa'saʒẽ]
fare	tarifa (f)	[ta'rifa]
cashier (ticket seller)	bilheteiro (m)	[biʎe'tejru]
ticket inspection	controle (m) de passagens	[kõ'troli de pa'saʒãjʃ]
ticket inspector	revisor (m)	[hevi'zor]
to be late (for ...)	atrasar-se (vr)	[atra'zarsi]
to miss (~ the train, etc.)	perder (vt)	[per'der]
to be in a hurry	estar com pressa	[is'tar kõ 'prɛsa]
taxi, cab	táxi (m)	['taksi]
taxi driver	taxista (m)	[tak'sista]
by taxi	de táxi	[de 'taksi]
taxi stand	ponto (m) de táxis	['põtu de 'taksis]
to call a taxi	chamar um táxi	[ʃa'mar ũ 'taksi]
to take a taxi	pegar um táxi	[pe'gar ũ 'taksi]
traffic	tráfego (m)	['trafegu]
traffic jam	engarrafamento (m)	[ẽgahafa'mẽtu]
rush hour	horas (f pl) de pico	['ɔras de 'piku]
to park (vi)	estacionar (vi)	[istasjo'nar]
to park (vt)	estacionar (vt)	[istasjo'nar]
parking lot	parque (m) de estacionamento	['parki de istasjona'mẽtu]
subway	metrô (m)	[me'tro]
station	estação (f)	[ista'sãw]
to take the subway	ir de metrô	[ir de me'tro]
train	trem (m)	[trẽj]
train station	estação (f) de trem	[ista'sãw de trẽj]

78. Sightseeing

monument	monumento (m)	[monu'mẽtu]
fortress	fortaleza (f)	[forta'leza]
palace	palácio (m)	[pa'lasju]
castle	castelo (m)	[kas'tɛlu]
tower	torre (f)	['tohi]
mausoleum	mausoléu (m)	[mawzo'lɛw]
architecture	arquitetura (f)	[arkite'tuˑa]
medieval (adj)	medieval	[medʒje'vaw]
ancient (adj)	antigo	[ã'tʃigu]
national (adj)	nacional	[nasjo'naw]
famous (monument, etc.)	famoso	[fa'mozu]
tourist	turista (m)	[tu'rista]
guide (person)	guia (m)	['gia]
excursion, sightseeing tour	excursão (f)	[iskur'sãw]
to show (vt)	mostrar (vt)	[mos'trar]
to tell (vt)	contar (vt)	[kõ'tar]
to find (vt)	encontrar (vt)	[ẽkõ'trar]
to get lost (lose one's way)	perder-se (vr)	[per'dersi]
map (e.g., subway ~)	mapa (m)	['mapa]
map (e.g., city ~)	mapa (m)	['mapa]
souvenir, gift	lembrança (f), presente (m)	[lẽ'brãsa], [pre'zẽtʃi]
gift shop	loja (f) de presentes	['lɔʒa de pre'zẽtʃis]
to take pictures	tirar fotos	[tʃi'rar 'fɔtus]
to have one's picture taken	fotografar-se (vr)	[fotogra'farse]

79. Shopping

to buy (purchase)	comprar (vt)	[kõ'prar]
purchase	compra (f)	['kõpra]
to go shopping	fazer compras	[fa'zer 'kõpras]
shopping	compras (f pl)	['kõpras]
to be open (ab. store)	estar aberta	[is'tar a'bɛrta]
to be closed	estar fechada	[is'tar fe'ʃada]
footwear, shoes	calçado (m)	[kaw'sadu]
clothes, clothing	roupa (f)	['hopa]
cosmetics	cosméticos (m pl)	[koz'mɛtʃikus]
food products	alimentos (m pl)	[ali'mẽtus]
gift, present	presente (m)	[pre'zẽtʃi]
salesman	vendedor (m)	[vẽde'dor]
saleswoman	vendedora (f)	[vẽde'dora]

check out, cash desk	caixa (f)	['kaɪʃa]
mirror	espelho (m)	[is'peʎu]
counter (store ~)	balcão (m)	[baw'kãw]
fitting room	provador (m)	[prɔva'dor]

to try on	provar (vt)	[pro'var]
to fit (ab. dress, etc.)	servir (vi)	[ser'vir]
to like (I like ...)	gostar (vt)	[gos'tar]

price	preço (m)	['presu]
price tag	etiqueta (f) de preço	[etʃi'keta de 'presu]
to cost (vt)	custar (vt)	[kus'tar]
How much?	Quanto?	['kwãtu]
discount	desconto (m)	[dʒis'kõtu]

inexpensive (adj)	não caro	['nãw 'karu]
cheap (adj)	barato	[ba'ratu]
expensive (adj)	caro	['karu]
It's expensive	É caro	[ɛ 'karu]

rental (n)	aluguel (m)	[alu'gɛw]
to rent (~ a tuxedo)	alugar (vt)	[alu'gar]
credit (trade credit)	crédito (m)	['krɛdʒitu]
on credit (adv)	a crédito	[a 'krɛdʒitu]

80. Money

money	dinheiro (m)	[dʒi'ɲejru]
currency exchange	câmbio (m)	['kãbju]
exchange rate	taxa (f) de câmbio	['taʃa de 'kãbju]
ATM	caixa (m) eletrônico	['kaɪʃa ele'troniku]
coin	moeda (f)	['mwɛda]

| dollar | dólar (m) | ['dɔlar] |
| euro | euro (m) | ['ewru] |

lira	lira (f)	['lira]
Deutschmark	marco (m)	['marku]
franc	franco (m)	['frãku]
pound sterling	libra (f) esterlina	['libra ister'linu]
yen	iene (m)	['jɛni]

debt	dívida (f)	['dʒivida]
debtor	devedor (m)	[deve'dor]
to lend (money)	emprestar (vt)	[ẽpres'tar]
to borrow (vi, vt)	pedir emprestado	[pe'dʒir ẽpres'tadu]

bank	banco (m)	['bãku]
account	conta (f)	['kõta]
to deposit (vt)	depositar (vt)	[depozi'tar]

to deposit into the account	depositar na conta	[depozi'tar na 'kõta]
to withdraw (vt)	sacar (vt)	[sa'kar]

credit card	cartão (m) de crédito	[kar'tãw de 'krɛdʒitu]
cash	dinheiro (m) vivo	[dʒi'ɲejru 'vivu]
check	cheque (m)	['ʃɛki]
to write a check	passar um cheque	[pa'sar ũ 'ʃɛki]
checkbook	talão (m) de cheques	[ta'lãw de 'ʃɛkis]

wallet	carteira (f)	[kar'tejra]
change purse	niqueleira (f)	[nike'lej‑a]
safe	cofre (m)	['kɔfri]

heir	herdeiro (m)	[er'dejru]
inheritance	herança (f)	[e'rãsa]
fortune (wealth)	fortuna (f)	[for'tuna]

lease	arrendamento (m)	[ahẽda'mẽtu]
rent (money)	aluguel (m)	[alu'gɛw]
to rent (sth from sb)	alugar (vt)	[alu'gar]

price	preço (m)	['presu]
cost	custo (m)	['kustu]
sum	soma (f)	['sɔma]

to spend (vt)	gastar (vt)	[gas'tar]
expenses	gastos (m pl)	['gastus]
to economize (vi, vt)	economizar (vi)	[ekonomi'zar]
economical	econômico	[eko'nomiku]

to pay (vi, vt)	pagar (vt)	[pa'gar]
payment	pagamento (m)	[paga'mẽtu]
change (give the ~)	troco (m)	['troku]

tax	imposto (m)	[ĩ'postu]
fine	multa (f)	['muwta]
to fine (vt)	multar (vt)	[muw'tar]

81. Post. Postal service

post office	agência (f) dos correios	[a'ʒẽs̟a dus ko'hejus]
mail (letters, etc.)	correio (m)	[ko'heju]
mailman	carteiro (m)	[kar'tejru]
opening hours	horário (m)	[o'rarju]

letter	carta (f)	['karta]
registered letter	carta (f) registada	['karta heʒis'tada]
postcard	cartão (m) postal	[kar'tãw pos'taw]
telegram	telegrama (m)	[tele'grama]
package (parcel)	encomenda (f)	[ẽko'mẽda]

money transfer	transferência (f) de dinheiro	[trãsfe'rẽsja de dʒi'ɲejru]
to receive (vt)	receber (vt)	[hese'ber]
to send (vt)	enviar (vt)	[ẽ'vjar]
sending	envio (m)	[ẽ'viu]
address	endereço (m)	[ẽde'resu]
ZIP code	código (m) postal	['kɔdʒigu pos'taw]
sender	remetente (m)	[heme'tẽtʃi]
receiver	destinatário (m)	[destʃina'tarju]
name (first name)	nome (m)	['nɔmi]
surname (last name)	sobrenome (m)	[sobri'nɔmi]
postage rate	tarifa (f)	[ta'rifa]
standard (adj)	ordinário	[ordʒi'narju]
economical (adj)	econômico	[eko'nomiku]
weight	peso (m)	['pezu]
to weigh (~ letters)	pesar (vt)	[pe'zar]
envelope	envelope (m)	[ẽve'lɔpi]
postage stamp	selo (m) postal	['selu pos'taw]
to stamp an envelope	colar o selo	[ko'lar u 'selu]

Dwelling. House. Home

82. House. Dwelling

house	casa (f)	['kaza]
at home (adv)	em casa	[ẽ 'kaza]
yard	pátio (m), quintal (f)	['patʃu], [kĩ'taw]
fence (iron ~)	cerca, grade (f)	['sɛrka], ['gradʒi]
brick (n)	tijolo (m)	[tʃi'ʒolu]
brick (as adj)	de tijolos	[de tʃi'ʒolus]
stone (n)	pedra (f)	['pɛdra]
stone (as adj)	de pedra	[de 'pɛdra]
concrete (n)	concreto (m)	[kõ'krɛtu]
concrete (as adj)	concreto	[kõ'krɛtɹ]
new (new-built)	novo	['novu]
old (adj)	velho	['vɛʎu]
ramshackle	decrépito	[de'krɛpitu]
modern (adj)	moderno	[mo'dɛrnu]
multistory (adj)	de vários andares	[de 'varjus ã'daris]
tall (~ building)	alto	['awtu]
floor, story	andar (m)	[ã'dar]
single-story (adj)	de um andar	[de ũ ã'dar]
1st floor	térreo (m)	['tɛhju]
top floor	andar (m) de cima	[ã'dar de 'sima]
roof	telhado (m)	[te'ʎadɹ]
chimney	chaminé (f)	[ʃami'nɛ]
roof tiles	telha (f)	['teʎa]
tiled (adj)	de telha	[de 'teʎa]
attic (storage place)	sótão (m)	['sɔtãw]
window	janela (f)	[ʒa'nɛla]
glass	vidro (m)	['vidru]
window ledge	parapeito (m)	[para'pejtu]
shutters	persianas (f pl)	[per'sjanas]
wall	parede (f)	[pa'redʒi]
balcony	varanda (f)	[va'rãda]
downspout	calha (f)	['kaʎa]
upstairs (to be ~)	em cima	[ẽ 'sima]
to go upstairs	subir (vi)	[su'bir]

| to come down (the stairs) | descer (vi) | [de'ser] |
| to move (to new premises) | mudar-se (vr) | [mu'darsi] |

83. House. Entrance. Lift

entrance	entrada (f)	[ẽ'trada]
stairs (stairway)	escada (f)	[is'kada]
steps	degraus (m pl)	[de'graws]
banister	corrimão (m)	[kohi'mãw]
lobby (hotel ~)	hall (m) de entrada	[hɔw de ẽ'trada]

mailbox	caixa (f) de correio	['kaɪʃa de ko'heju]
garbage can	lixeira (f)	[li'ʃejra]
trash chute	calha (f) de lixo	['kaʎa de 'liʃu]

elevator	elevador (m)	[eleva'dor]
freight elevator	elevador (m) de carga	[eleva'dor de 'karga]
elevator cage	cabine (f)	[ka'bini]
to take the elevator	pegar o elevador	[pe'gar u eleva'dor]

apartment	apartamento (m)	[aparta'mẽtu]
residents (~ of a building)	residentes (pl)	[hezi'dẽtʃis]
neighbor (masc.)	vizinho (m)	[vi'ziɲu]
neighbor (fem.)	vizinha (f)	[vi'ziɲa]
neighbors	vizinhos (pl)	[vi'ziɲus]

84. House. Doors. Locks

door	porta (f)	['pɔrta]
gate (vehicle ~)	portão (m)	[por'tãw]
handle, doorknob	maçaneta (f)	[masa'neta]
to unlock (unbolt)	destrancar (vt)	[dʒistrã'kar]
to open (vt)	abrir (vt)	[a'brir]
to close (vt)	fechar (vt)	[fe'ʃar]

key	chave (f)	['ʃavi]
bunch (of keys)	molho (m)	['moʎu]
to creak (door, etc.)	ranger (vi)	[hã'ʒer]
creak	rangido (m)	[hã'ʒidu]
hinge (door ~)	dobradiça (f)	[dobra'dʒisa]
doormat	capacho (m)	[ka'paʃu]

door lock	fechadura (f)	[feʃa'dura]
keyhole	buraco (m) da fechadura	[bu'raku da feʃa'dura]
crossbar (sliding bar)	barra (f)	['baha]
door latch	fecho (m)	['feʃu]
padlock	cadeado (m)	[ka'dʒiadu]
to ring (~ the door bell)	tocar (vt)	[to'kar]

ringing (sound)	**toque** (m)	['tɔki]
doorbell	**campainha** (f)	[kampa'iɲa]
doorbell button	**botão** (m)	[bo'tãw]
knock (at the door)	**batida** (f)	[ba'tʃida]
to knock (vi)	**bater** (vi)	[ba'ter]

code	**código** (m)	['kɔdʒigu]
combination lock	**fechadura** (f) **de código**	[feʃa'dura de 'kɔdʒigu]
intercom	**interfone** (m)	[ĩter'fɔni]
number (on the door)	**número** (m)	['numeru]
doorplate	**placa** (f) **de porta**	['plaka de 'pɔrta]
peephole	**olho** (m) **mágico**	['oʎu 'maʒiku]

85. Country house

village	**aldeia** (f)	[aw'deja]
vegetable garden	**horta** (f)	['ɔrta]
fence	**cerca** (f)	['serka]
picket fence	**cerca** (f) **de piquete**	['sɛrka de pi'ketʃi]
wicket gate	**portão** (f) **do jardim**	[por'tãw du ʒar'dʒĩ]

granary	**celeiro** (m)	[se'lejru]
root cellar	**adega** (f)	[a'dɛga]
shed (garden ~)	**galpão, barracão** (m)	[gaw'pãw], [baha'kãw]
water well	**poço** (m)	['posu]

stove (wood-fired ~)	**fogão** (m)	[fo'gãw]
to stoke the stove	**atiçar o fogo**	[atʃi'sar ɹ 'fogu]
firewood	**lenha** (f)	['lɛɲa]
log (firewood)	**lenha** (f)	['lɛɲa]

veranda	**varanda** (f)	[va'rãda]
deck (terrace)	**alpendre** (m)	[aw'pẽdri]
stoop (front steps)	**degraus** (m pl) **de entrada**	[de'graws de ẽ'trada]
swing (hanging seat)	**balanço** (m)	[ba'lãsu]

86. Castle. Palace

castle	**castelo** (m)	[kas'tɛlu]
palace	**palácio** (m)	[pa'lasju]
fortress	**fortaleza** (f)	[forta'leza]

wall (round castle)	**muralha** (f)	[mu'raʎa]
tower	**torre** (f)	['tohi]
keep, donjon	**calabouço** (m)	[kala'bosu]

portcullis	**grade** (f) **levadiça**	['gradʒi leva'dʒisa]
underground passage	**passagem** (f) **subterrânea**	[pa'saʒẽ subite'hanja]

moat	**fosso** (m)	['fosu]
chain	**corrente, cadeia** (f)	[ko'hẽtʃi], [ka'deja]
arrow loop	**seteira** (f)	[se'tejra]
magnificent (adj)	**magnífico**	[mag'nifiku]
majestic (adj)	**majestoso**	[maʒes'tozu]
impregnable (adj)	**inexpugnável**	[inespug'navew]
medieval (adj)	**medieval**	[medʒje'vaw]

87. Apartment

apartment	**apartamento** (m)	[aparta'mẽtu]
room	**quarto, cômodo** (m)	['kwartu], ['komodu]
bedroom	**quarto** (m) **de dormir**	['kwartu de dor'mir]
dining room	**sala** (f) **de jantar**	['sala de ʒã'tar]
living room	**sala** (f) **de estar**	['sala de is'tar]
study (home office)	**escritório** (m)	[iskri'tɔrju]
entry room	**sala** (f) **de entrada**	['sala de ẽ'trada]
bathroom (room with a bath or shower)	**banheiro** (m)	[ba'ɲejru]
half bath	**lavabo** (m)	[la'vabu]
ceiling	**teto** (m)	['tɛtu]
floor	**chão, piso** (m)	['ʃãw], ['pizu]
corner	**canto** (m)	['kãtu]

88. Apartment. Cleaning

to clean (vi, vt)	**arrumar, limpar** (vt)	[ahu'mar], [lĩ'par]
to put away (to stow)	**guardar** (vt)	[gwar'dar]
dust	**pó** (m)	[pɔ]
dusty (adj)	**empoeirado**	[ẽpoej'radu]
to dust (vt)	**tirar o pó**	[tʃi'rar u pɔ]
vacuum cleaner	**aspirador** (m)	[aspira'dor]
to vacuum (vt)	**aspirar** (vt)	[aspi'rar]
to sweep (vi, vt)	**varrer** (vt)	[va'her]
sweepings	**sujeira** (f)	[su'ʒejra]
order	**arrumação, ordem** (f)	[ahuma'sãw], ['ordẽ]
disorder, mess	**desordem** (f)	[dʒi'zordẽ]
mop	**esfregão** (m)	[isfre'gaw]
dust cloth	**pano** (m), **trapo** (m)	['panu], ['trapu]
short broom	**vassoura** (f)	[va'sora]
dustpan	**pá** (f) **de lixo**	[pa de 'liʃu]

89. Furniture. Interior

furniture	mobiliário (m)	[mobi'ljɛrju]
table	mesa (f)	['meza]
chair	cadeira (f)	[ka'dejra]
bed	cama (f)	['kama]
couch, sofa	sofá, divã (m)	[so'fa], [dʒi'vã]
armchair	poltrona (f)	[pow'trɔna]
bookcase	estante (f)	[is'tãtʃi]
shelf	prateleira (f)	[prate'lejra]
wardrobe	guarda-roupas (m)	['gwarda 'hopa]
coat rack (wall-mounted ~)	cabide (m) de parede	[ka'bidʒi de pa'redʒi]
coat stand	cabideiro (m) de pé	[kabi'dejru de pɛ]
bureau, dresser	cômoda (f)	['komoda]
coffee table	mesinha (f) de centro	[me'ziɲa de 'sẽtru]
mirror	espelho (m)	[is'peʎu]
carpet	tapete (m)	[ta'petʃi]
rug, small carpet	tapete (m)	[ta'petʃi]
fireplace	lareira (f)	[la'rejrɛ]
candle	vela (f)	['vɛla]
candlestick	castiçal (m)	[kastʃi'saw]
drapes	cortinas (f pl)	[kor'tʃinas]
wallpaper	papel (m) de parede	[pa'pɛw de pa'redʒi]
blinds (jalousie)	persianas (f pl)	[per'sjanas]
table lamp	luminária (f) de mesa	[lumi'narja de 'meza]
wall lamp (sconce)	luminária (f) de parede	[lumi'narja de pa'redʒi]
floor lamp	abajur (m) de pé	[aba'ʒur de 'pɛ]
chandelier	lustre (m)	['lustri]
leg (of chair, table)	pé (m)	[pɛ]
armrest	braço, descanso (m)	['brasʊ], [dʒis'kãsu]
back (backrest)	costas (f pl)	['kɔstas]
drawer	gaveta (f)	[ga'veta]

90. Bedding

bedclothes	roupa (f) de cama	['hopa de 'kama]
pillow	travesseiro (m)	[trave'sejru]
pillowcase	fronha (f)	['froɲa]
duvet, comforter	cobertor (m)	[kuber'tor]
sheet	lençol (m)	[lẽ'sɔw]
bedspread	colcha (f)	['kowʃa]

91. Kitchen

kitchen	**cozinha** (f)	[ko'ziɲa]
gas	**gás** (m)	[gajs]
gas stove (range)	**fogão** (m) **a gás**	[fo'gãw a gajs]
electric stove	**fogão** (m) **elétrico**	[fo'gãw e'lɛtriku]
oven	**forno** (m)	['fornu]
microwave oven	**forno** (m) **de micro-ondas**	['fornu de mikro'õdas]

refrigerator	**geladeira** (f)	[ʒela'dejra]
freezer	**congelador** (m)	[kõʒela'dor]
dishwasher	**máquina** (f) **de lavar louça**	['makina de la'var 'losa]

meat grinder	**moedor** (m) **de carne**	[moe'dor de 'karni]
juicer	**espremedor** (m)	[espreme'dor]
toaster	**torradeira** (f)	[toha'dejra]
mixer	**batedeira** (f)	[bate'dejra]

coffee machine	**máquina** (f) **de café**	['makina de ka'fɛ]
coffee pot	**cafeteira** (f)	[kafe'tejra]
coffee grinder	**moedor** (m) **de café**	[moe'dor de ka'fɛ]

kettle	**chaleira** (f)	[ʃa'lejra]
teapot	**bule** (m)	['buli]
lid	**tampa** (f)	['tãpa]
tea strainer	**coador** (m) **de chá**	[koa'dor de ʃa]

spoon	**colher** (f)	[ko'ʎer]
teaspoon	**colher** (f) **de chá**	[ko'ʎer de ʃa]
soup spoon	**colher** (f) **de sopa**	[ko'ʎer de 'sopa]
fork	**garfo** (m)	['garfu]
knife	**faca** (f)	['faka]

tableware (dishes)	**louça** (f)	['losa]
plate (dinner ~)	**prato** (m)	['pratu]
saucer	**pires** (m)	['piris]

shot glass	**cálice** (m)	['kalisi]
glass (tumbler)	**copo** (m)	['kɔpu]
cup	**xícara** (f)	['ʃikara]

sugar bowl	**açucareiro** (m)	[asuka'rejru]
salt shaker	**saleiro** (m)	[sa'lejru]
pepper shaker	**pimenteiro** (m)	[pimẽ'tejru]
butter dish	**manteigueira** (f)	[mãtej'gejra]

stock pot (soup pot)	**panela** (f)	[pa'nɛla]
frying pan (skillet)	**frigideira** (f)	[friʒi'dejra]
ladle	**concha** (f)	['kõʃa]
colander	**coador** (m)	[koa'dor]

tray (serving ~)	bandeja (f)	[bã'deʒɐ]
bottle	garrafa (f)	[ga'hafa]
jar (glass)	pote (m) de vidro	['pɔtʃi de 'vidru]
can	lata (f)	['lata]

bottle opener	abridor (m) de garrafa	[abri'dor de ga'hafa]
can opener	abridor (m) de latas	[abri'dor de 'latas]
corkscrew	saca-rolhas (m)	['saka-'hoʎas]
filter	filtro (m)	['fiwtru]
to filter (vt)	filtrar (vt)	[fiw'trar]

| trash, garbage (food waste, etc.) | lixo (m) | ['liʃu] |
| trash can (kitchen ~) | lixeira (f) | [li'ʃejra] |

92. Bathroom

bathroom	banheiro (m)	[ba'ɲejru]
water	água (f)	['agwa]
faucet	torneira (f)	[tor'nejra]
hot water	água (f) quente	['agwa kẽtʃi]
cold water	água (f) fria	['agwa 'fria]

toothpaste	pasta (f) de dente	['pasta de 'dẽtʃi]
to brush one's teeth	escovar os dentes	[isko'var us 'dẽtʃis]
toothbrush	escova (f) de dente	[is'kova de 'dẽtʃi]

to shave (vi)	barbear-se (vr)	[bar'bjarsi]
shaving foam	espuma (f) de barbear	[is'puma de bar'bjar]
razor	gilete (f)	[ʒi'lɛtʃi]

to wash (one's hands, etc.)	lavar (vt)	[la'var]
to take a bath	tomar banho	[to'mar baɲu]
shower	chuveiro (m), ducha (f)	[ʃu'vejru], ['duʃa]
to take a shower	tomar uma ducha	[to'mar 'uma 'duʃa]

bathtub	banheira (f)	[ba'ɲejra]
toilet (toilet bowl)	vaso (m) sanitário	['vazu sani'tarju]
sink (washbasin)	pia (f)	['pia]

| soap | sabonete (m) | [sabo'netʃi] |
| soap dish | saboneteira (f) | [sabone'tejra] |

sponge	esponja (f)	[is'põʒa]
shampoo	xampu (m)	[ʃã'pu]
towel	toalha (f)	[to'aʎa]
bathrobe	roupão (m) de banho	[ho'pãw de 'baɲu]

| laundry (laundering) | lavagem (f) | [la'vaʒẽ] |
| washing machine | lavadora (f) de roupas | [lava'dora de 'hopas] |

| to do the laundry | lavar a roupa | [la'var a 'hopa] |
| laundry detergent | detergente (m) | [deter'ʒẽtʃi] |

93. Household appliances

TV set	televisor (m)	[televi'zor]
tape recorder	gravador (m)	[grava'dor]
VCR (video recorder)	videogravador (m)	['vidʒju·grava'dor]
radio	rádio (m)	['hadʒju]
player (CD, MP3, etc.)	leitor (m)	[lej'tor]

video projector	projetor (m)	[proʒe'tor]
home movie theater	cinema (m) em casa	[si'nɛma ẽ 'kaza]
DVD player	DVD Player (m)	[deve'de 'plejer]
amplifier	amplificador (m)	[ãplifika'dor]
video game console	console (f) de jogos	[kõ'sɔli de 'ʒogus]

video camera	câmera (f) de vídeo	['kamera de 'vidʒju]
camera (photo)	máquina (f) fotográfica	['makina foto'grafika]
digital camera	câmera (f) digital	['kamera dʒiʒi'taw]

vacuum cleaner	aspirador (m)	[aspira'dor]
iron (e.g., steam ~)	ferro (m) de passar	['fɛhu de pa'sar]
ironing board	tábua (f) de passar	['tabwa de pa'sar]

telephone	telefone (m)	[tele'fɔni]
cell phone	celular (m)	[selu'lar]
typewriter	máquina (f) de escrever	['makina de iskre'ver]
sewing machine	máquina (f) de costura	['makina de kos'tura]

microphone	microfone (m)	[mikro'fɔni]
headphones	fone (m) de ouvido	['fɔni de o'vidu]
remote control (TV)	controle remoto (m)	[kõ'troli he'mɔtu]

CD, compact disc	CD (m)	['sede]
cassette, tape	fita (f) cassete	['fita ka'sɛtʃi]
vinyl record	disco (m) de vinil	['dʒisku de vi'niw]

94. Repairs. Renovation

renovations	renovação (f)	[henova'sãw]
to renovate (vt)	renovar (vt), fazer obras	[heno'var], [fa'zer 'ɔbras]
to repair, to fix (vt)	reparar (vt)	[hepa'rar]
to put in order	consertar (vt)	[kõser'tar]
to redo (do again)	refazer (vt)	[hefa'zer]

| paint | tinta (f) | [tʃĩta] |
| to paint (~ a wall) | pintar (vt) | [pĩ'tar] |

house painter	**pintor** (m)	[pĩ'tor]
paintbrush	**pincel** (m)	[pĩ'sɛw]
whitewash	**cal** (f)	[kaw]
to whitewash (vt)	**caiar** (vt)	[kaj'ar]
wallpaper	**papel** (m) **de parede**	[pa'pɛw de pa'reʤi]
to wallpaper (vt)	**colocar papel** **de parede**	[kolo'kar pa'pɛw de pa'reʤi]
varnish	**verniz** (m)	[ver'niz]
to varnish (vt)	**envernizar** (vt)	[ẽverni'zar]

95. Plumbing

water	**água** (f)	['agwa]
hot water	**água** (f) **quente**	['agwa 'kẽtʃi]
cold water	**água** (f) **fria**	['agwa 'fria]
faucet	**torneira** (f)	[tor'nejra]
drop (of water)	**gota** (f)	['gota]
to drip (vi)	**gotejar** (vi)	[gote'ʒar]
to leak (ab. pipe)	**vazar** (vt)	[va'zar]
leak (pipe ~)	**vazamento** (m)	[vaza'mẽtu]
puddle	**poça** (f)	['posa]
pipe	**tubo** (m)	['tubu]
valve (e.g., ball ~)	**válvula** (f)	['vawvula]
to be clogged up	**entupir-se** (vr)	[ẽtu'pirsi]
tools	**ferramentas** (f pl)	[feha'mẽtas]
adjustable wrench	**chave** (f) **inglesa**	['ʃavi ĩ'glɜza]
to unscrew (lid, filter, etc.)	**desenroscar** (vt)	[dezẽhos'kar]
to screw (tighten)	**enroscar** (vt)	[ẽhos'kar]
to unclog (vt)	**desentupir** (vt)	[ʤizẽtu'pir]
plumber	**encanador** (m)	[ẽkana'dor]
basement	**porão** (m)	[po'rãw]
sewerage (system)	**rede** (f) **de esgotos**	['heʤi de iz'gotus]

96. Fire. Conflagration

fire (accident)	**incêndio** (m)	[ĩ'sẽʤu]
flame	**chama** (f)	['ʃama]
spark	**faísca** (f)	[fa'iska]
smoke (from fire)	**fumaça** (f)	[fu'masa]
torch (flaming stick)	**tocha** (f)	['tɔʃa]
campfire	**fogueira** (f)	[fo'gejra]
gas, gasoline	**gasolina** (f)	[gazo'lina]

kerosene (type of fuel)	querosene (m)	[kero'zɛni]
flammable (adj)	inflamável	[ĩfla'mavew]
explosive (adj)	explosivo	[isplo'zivu]
NO SMOKING	PROIBIDO FUMAR!	[proi'bidu fu'mar]

safety	segurança (f)	[segu'rãsa]
danger	perigo (m)	[pe'rigu]
dangerous (adj)	perigoso	[peri'gozu]

to catch fire	incendiar-se (vr)	[ĩsē'dʒjarse]
explosion	explosão (f)	[isplo'zãw]
to set fire	incendiar (vt)	[ĩsē'dʒjar]
arsonist	incendiário (m)	[ĩsē'dʒjarju]
arson	incêndio (m) criminoso	[ĩ'sēdʒju krimi'nozu]

to blaze (vi)	flamejar (vi)	[flame'ʒar]
to burn (be on fire)	queimar (vi)	[kej'mar]
to burn down	queimar tudo (vi)	[kej'mar 'tudu]

to call the fire department	chamar os bombeiros	[ʃa'mar us bõ'bejrus]
firefighter, fireman	bombeiro (m)	[bõ'bejru]
fire truck	caminhão (m) de bombeiros	[kami'nãw de bõ'bejrus]
fire department	corpo (m) de bombeiros	['korpu de bõ'bejrus]
fire truck ladder	escada (f) extensível	[is'kada istē'sivɛl]

fire hose	mangueira (f)	[mã'gejra]
fire extinguisher	extintor (m)	[istĩ'tor]
helmet	capacete (m)	[kapa'setʃi]
siren	sirene (f)	[si'rɛni]

to cry (for help)	gritar (vi)	[gri'tar]
to call for help	chamar por socorro	[ʃa'mar por so'kohu]
rescuer	socorrista (m)	[soko'hista]
to rescue (vt)	salvar, resgatar (vt)	[saw'var], [hezga'tar]

to arrive (vi)	chegar (vi)	[ʃe'gar]
to extinguish (vt)	apagar (vt)	[apa'gar]
water	água (f)	['agwa]
sand	areia (f)	[a'reja]

| ruins (destruction) | ruínas (f pl) | ['hwinas] |
| to collapse (building, etc.) | ruir (vi) | ['hwir] |

| to fall down (vi) | desmoronar (vi) | [dʒizmoro'nar] |
| to cave in (ceiling, floor) | desabar (vi) | [dʒiza'bar] |

| piece of debris | fragmento (m) | [frag'mētu] |
| ash | cinza (f) | ['sĩza] |

| to suffocate (die) | sufocar (vi) | [sufo'kar] |
| to be killed (perish) | perecer (vi) | [pere'ser] |

HUMAN ACTIVITIES

Job. Business. Part 1

97. Banking

bank	barco (m)	['bãku]
branch (of bank, etc.)	balcão (f)	[baw'kãw]
bank clerk, consultant	consultor (m) bancário	[kõsuw'tor bã'karju]
manager (director)	gerente (m)	[ʒe'rẽtʃ]
bank account	conta (f)	['kõta]
account number	número (m) da conta	['numeru da 'kõta]
checking account	conta (f) corrente	['kõta ko'hẽtʃi]
savings account	conta (f) poupança	['kõta po'pãsa]
to open an account	abrir uma conta	[a'brir 'uma 'kõta]
to close the account	fechar uma conta	[fe'ʃar 'uma 'kõta]
to deposit into the account	depositar na conta	[depozi'tar na 'kõta]
to withdraw (vt)	sacar (vt)	[sa'kar]
deposit	depósito (m)	[de'pozitu]
to make a deposit	fazer um depósito	[fa'zer ũ de'pozitu]
wire transfer	transferência (f) bancária	[trãsfe'rẽsja bã'karja]
to wire, to transfer	transferir (vt)	[trãsfe'rir]
sum	soma (f)	['soma]
How much?	Quanto?	['kwãtu]
signature	assinatura (f)	[asina'tura]
to sign (vt)	assinar (vt)	[asi'nar]
credit card	cartão (m) de crédito	[kar'tãw de 'krɛdʒitu]
code (PIN code)	senha (f)	['sɛɲa]
credit card number	número (m) do cartão de crédito	['numeru du kar'tãw de 'krɛdʒitu]
ATM	caixa (m) eletrônico	['kaiʃa ele'troniku]
check	cheque (m)	['ʃɛki]
to write a check	passar um cheque	[pa'sar ũ 'ʃɛki]
checkbook	talão (m) de cheques	[ta'lãw de 'ʃɛkis]
loan (bank ~)	empréstimo (m)	[ẽ'prɛstʃimu]
to apply for a loan	pedir um empréstimo	[pe'dʒir ũ ẽ'prɛstʃimu]

to get a loan	obter empréstimo	[ob'ter ẽ'prɛstʃimu]
to give a loan	dar um empréstimo	[dar ũ ẽ'prɛstʃimu]
guarantee	garantia (f)	[garã'tʃia]

98. Telephone. Phone conversation

telephone	telefone (m)	[tele'fɔni]
cell phone	celular (m)	[selu'lar]
answering machine	secretária (f) eletrônica	[sekre'tarja ele'tronika]

| to call (by phone) | fazer uma chamada | [fa'zer 'uma ʃa'mada] |
| phone call | chamada (f) | [ʃa'mada] |

to dial a number	discar um número	[dʒis'kar ũ 'numeru]
Hello!	Alô!	[a'lo]
to ask (vt)	perguntar (vt)	[pergũ'tar]
to answer (vi, vt)	responder (vt)	[hespõ'der]

to hear (vt)	ouvir (vt)	[o'vir]
well (adv)	bem	[bẽj]
not well (adv)	mal	[maw]
noises (interference)	ruído (m)	['hwidu]

receiver	fone (m)	['fɔni]
to pick up (~ the phone)	pegar o telefone	[pe'gar u tele'fɔni]
to hang up (~ the phone)	desligar (vi)	[dʒizli'gar]

busy (engaged)	ocupado	[oku'padu]
to ring (ab. phone)	tocar (vi)	[to'kar]
telephone book	lista (f) telefônica	['lista tele'fonika]

local (adj)	local	[lo'kaw]
local call	chamada (f) local	[ʃa'mada lo'kaw]
long distance (~ call)	de longa distância	['de 'lõgu dʒis'tãsja]
long-distance call	chamada (f) de longa distância	[ʃa'mada de 'lõgu dʒis'tãsja]
international (adj)	internacional	[ĩternasjo'naw]
international call	chamada (f) internacional	[ʃa'mada ĩternasjo'naw]

99. Cell phone

cell phone	celular (m)	[selu'lar]
display	tela (f)	['tɛla]
button	botão (m)	[bo'tãw]
SIM card	cartão SIM (m)	[kar'tãw sim]

| battery | bateria (f) | [bate'ria] |
| to be dead (battery) | descarregar-se (vr) | [dʒiskahe'garsi] |

charger	carregador (m)	[kahega'dor]
menu	menu (m)	[me'nu]
settings	configurações (f pl)	[kõfigura'sõjs]
tune (melody)	melodia (f)	[melo'dʒia]
to select (vt)	escolher (vt)	[isko'ʎer]

calculator	calculadora (f)	[kawkula'dora]
voice mail	correio (m) de voz	[ko'heju de vɔz]
alarm clock	despertador (m)	[dʒisperta'dor]
contacts	contatos (m pl)	[kõ'tatus]

| SMS (text message) | mensagem (f) de texto | [mẽ'saʒẽ de 'testu] |
| subscriber | assinante (m) | [asi'nãtʃi] |

100. Stationery

| ballpoint pen | careta (f) | [ka'neta] |
| fountain pen | careta (f) tinteiro | [ka'neta tʃi'tejru] |

pencil	lápis (m)	['lapis]
highlighter	marcador (m) de texto	[marka'dor de 'testu]
felt-tip pen	caneta (f) hidrográfica	[ka'neta idro'grafika]

| notepad | bloco (m) de notas | ['blɔku de 'nɔtas] |
| agenda (diary) | agenda (f) | [a'ʒẽda] |

ruler	régua (f)	['hɛgwa]
calculator	calculadora (f)	[kawkula'dora]
eraser	borracha (f)	[bo'haʃa]
thumbtack	alfinete (m)	[awfi'netʃi]
paper clip	clipe (m)	['klipi]

glue	cola (f)	['kɔla]
stapler	grampeador (m)	[grãpja'dor]
hole punch	furador (m) de papel	[fura'dor de pa'pɛw]
pencil sharpener	apontador (m)	[apõta'dor]

Job. Business. Part 2

101. Mass Media

newspaper	jornal (m)	[ʒor'naw]
magazine	revista (f)	[he'vista]
press (printed media)	imprensa (f)	[ĩ'prẽsa]
radio	rádio (m)	['hadʒju]
radio station	estação (f) de rádio	[ista'sãw de 'hadʒju]
television	televisão (f)	[televi'zãw]
presenter, host	apresentador (m)	[aprezẽta'dor]
newscaster	locutor (m)	[loku'tor]
commentator	comentarista (m)	[komẽta'rista]
journalist	jornalista (m)	[ʒorna'lista]
correspondent (reporter)	correspondente (m)	[kohespõ'dẽtʃi]
press photographer	repórter (m) fotográfico	[he'porter foto'grafiku]
reporter	repórter (m)	[he'porter]
editor	redator (m)	[heda'tor]
editor-in-chief	redator-chefe (m)	[heda'tor 'ʃɛfi]
to subscribe (to ...)	assinar a ...	[asi'nar a]
subscription	assinatura (f)	[asina'tura]
subscriber	assinante (m)	[asi'nãtʃi]
to read (vi, vt)	ler (vt)	[ler]
reader	leitor (m)	[lej'tor]
circulation (of newspaper)	tiragem (f)	[tʃi'raʒẽ]
monthly (adj)	mensal	[mẽ'saw]
weekly (adj)	semanal	[sema'naw]
issue (edition)	número (m)	['numeru]
new (~ issue)	recente, novo	[he'sẽtʃi], ['novu]
headline	manchete (f)	[mã'ʃɛtʃi]
short article	pequeno artigo (m)	[pe'kenu ar'tʃigu]
column (regular article)	coluna (f)	[ko'luna]
article	artigo (m)	[ar'tʃigu]
page	página (f)	['paʒina]
reportage, report	reportagem (f)	[hepor'taʒẽ]
event (happening)	evento (m)	[e'vẽtu]
sensation (news)	sensação (f)	[sẽsa'sãw]
scandal	escândalo (m)	[is'kãdalu]
scandalous (adj)	escandaloso	[iskãda'lozu]

great (~ scandal)	**grande**	['grãdʒi]
show (e.g., cooking ~)	**programa** (m)	[pro'grama]
interview	**entrevista** (f)	[ẽtre'vista]
live broadcast	**transmissão** (f) **ao vivo**	[trãzmi'sãw aw 'vivu]
channel	**canal** (m)	[ka'naw]

102. Agriculture

agriculture	**agricultura** (f)	[agrikuw'tura]
peasant (masc.)	**camponês** (m)	[kãpo'nes]
peasant (fem.)	**camponesa** (f)	[kãpo'neza]
farmer	**agricultor, fazendeiro** (m)	[agrikuw'tor], [fazẽ'dejru]
tractor (farm ~)	**trator** (m)	[tra'tor]
combine, harvester	**colheitadeira** (f)	[koʎejta'dejra]
plow	**arado** (m)	[a'radu]
to plow (vi, vt)	**arar** (vt)	[a'rar]
plowland	**campo** (m) **lavrado**	['kãpu la'vradu]
furrow (in field)	**sulco** (m)	[suw'ku]
to sow (vi, vt)	**semear** (vt)	[se'mjar]
seeder	**plantadeira** (f)	[plãta'dejra]
sowing (process)	**semeadura** (f)	[semja'dura]
scythe	**foice** (m)	['fɔjsi]
to mow, to scythe	**cortar com foice**	[kor'tar kõ 'fɔjsi]
spade (tool)	**pá** (f)	[pa]
to till (vt)	**cavar** (vt)	[ka'var]
hoe	**enxada** (f)	[ẽ'ʃada]
to hoe, to weed	**capinar** (vt)	[kapi'nɛr]
weed (plant)	**erva** (f) **daninha**	['ɛrva da'niɲa]
watering can	**regador** (m)	[hega'dor]
to water (plants)	**regar** (vt)	[he'gar]
watering (act)	**rega** (f)	['hɛga]
pitchfork	**forquilha** (f)	[for'kiʎa]
rake	**ancinho** (m)	[ã'siɲu]
fertilizer	**fertilizante** (m)	[fertʃili'zãtʃi]
to fertilize (vt)	**fertilizar** (vt)	[fertʃili'zar]
manure (fertilizer)	**estrume, esterco** (m)	[is'trumi], [is'terku]
field	**campo** (m)	['kãpu]
meadow	**prado** (m)	['pradu]
vegetable garden	**horta** (f)	['ɔrta]
orchard (e.g., apple ~)	**pomar** (m)	[po'mar]

103

to graze (vt)	pastar (vt)	[pas'tar]
herder (herdsman)	pastor (m)	[pas'tor]
pasture	pastagem (f)	[pas'taʒẽ]

| cattle breeding | pecuária (f) | [pe'kwarja] |
| sheep farming | criação (f) de ovelhas | [krja'sãw de o'veʎas] |

plantation	plantação (f)	[plãta'sãw]
row (garden bed ~s)	canteiro (m)	[kã'tejru]
hothouse	estufa (f)	[is'tufa]

| drought (lack of rain) | seca (f) | ['seka] |
| dry (~ summer) | seco | ['seku] |

grain	grão (m)	['grãw]
cereal crops	cereais (m pl)	[se'rjajs]
to harvest, to gather	colher (vt)	[ko'ʎer]

miller (person)	moleiro (m)	[mu'lejru]
mill (e.g., gristmill)	moinho (m)	['mwiɲu]
to grind (grain)	moer (vt)	[mwer]
flour	farinha (f)	[fa'riɲa]
straw	palha (f)	['paʎa]

103. Building. Building process

construction site	canteiro (m) de obras	[kã'tejru de 'ɔbras]
to build (vt)	construir (vt)	[kõs'trwir]
construction worker	construtor (m)	[kõstru'tor]

project	projeto (m)	[pro'ʒɛtu]
architect	arquiteto (m)	[arki'tɛtu]
worker	operário (m)	[ope'rarju]

foundation (of a building)	fundação (f)	[fũda'sãw]
roof	telhado (m)	[te'ʎadu]
foundation pile	estaca (f)	[is'taka]
wall	parede (f)	[pa'redʒi]

| reinforcing bars | barras (f pl) de reforço | ['bahas de he'forsu] |
| scaffolding | andaime (m) | [ã'dajmi] |

concrete	concreto (m)	[kõ'krɛtu]
granite	granito (m)	[gra'nitu]
stone	pedra (f)	['pɛdra]
brick	tijolo (m)	[tʃi'ʒolu]

sand	areia (f)	[a'reja]
cement	cimento (m)	[si'mẽtu]
plaster (for walls)	emboço, reboco (m)	[ẽ'bosu], [he'boku]

to plaster (vt)	**emboçar, rebocar** (vt)	[ēbo'sar], [hebo'kar]
paint	**tinta** (f)	[tʃĩta]
to paint (~ a wall)	**pintar** (vt)	[pĩ'tar]
barrel	**barril** (m)	[ba'hiw]
crane	**grua** (f), **guindaste** (m)	['grua], [gĩ'dastʃi]
to lift, to hoist (vt)	**erguer** (vt)	[er'ger]
to lower (vt)	**baixar** (vt)	[baɪ'ʃar]
bulldozer	**bu dózer** (m)	[buw'dozer]
excavator	**escavadora** (f)	[iskava'dora]
scoop, bucket	**caçamba** (f)	[ka'sãba]
to dig (excavate)	**escavar** (vt)	[iska'vɐr]
hard hat	**capacete** (m) **de proteção**	[kapa'setʃi de prote'sãw]

Professions and occupations

104. Job search. Dismissal

job	**trabalho** (m)	[traˈbaʎu]
staff (work force)	**equipe** (f)	[eˈkipi]
personnel	**pessoal** (m)	[peˈswaw]
career	**carreira** (f)	[kaˈhejra]
prospects (chances)	**perspectivas** (f pl)	[perspekˈtʃivas]
skills (mastery)	**habilidades** (f pl)	[abiliˈdaʤis]
selection (screening)	**seleção** (f)	[seleˈsãw]
employment agency	**agência** (f) **de emprego**	[aˈʒẽsja de ẽˈpregu]
résumé	**currículo** (m)	[kuˈhikulu]
job interview	**entrevista** (f) **de emprego**	[ẽtreˈvista de ẽˈpregu]
vacancy, opening	**vaga** (f)	[ˈvaga]
salary, pay	**salário** (m)	[saˈlarju]
fixed salary	**salário** (m) **fixo**	[saˈlarju ˈfiksu]
pay, compensation	**pagamento** (m)	[pagaˈmẽtu]
position (job)	**cargo** (m)	[ˈkargu]
duty (of employee)	**dever** (m)	[deˈver]
range of duties	**gama** (f) **de deveres**	[ˈgama de deˈveris]
busy (I'm ~)	**ocupado**	[okuˈpadu]
to fire (dismiss)	**despedir, demitir** (vt)	[ʤispeˈdʒir], [demiˈtʃir]
dismissal	**demissão** (f)	[demiˈsãw]
unemployment	**desemprego** (m)	[ʤizẽˈpregu]
unemployed (n)	**desempregado** (m)	[ʤizẽpreˈgadu]
retirement	**aposentadoria** (f)	[apozẽtadoˈria]
to retire (from job)	**aposentar-se** (vr)	[apozẽˈtarsi]

105. Business people

director	**diretor** (m)	[ʤireˈtor]
manager (director)	**gerente** (m)	[ʒeˈrẽtʃi]
boss	**patrão, chefe** (m)	[paˈtrãw], [ˈʃɛfi]
superior	**superior** (m)	[supeˈrjor]
superiors	**superiores** (m pl)	[supeˈrjores]
president	**presidente** (m)	[preziˈdẽtʃi]

chairman	**chairman, presidente** (m)	['tʃɛamen], [prezi'dētʃi]
deputy (substitute)	**substituto** (m)	[substi'tutu]
assistant	**assistente** (m)	[asis'tētʃi]
secretary	**secretário** (m)	[sekre'tarju]
personal assistant	**secretário** (m) **pessoal**	[sekre'tarju pe'swaw]
businessman	**homem** (m) **de negócios**	['ɔmẽ de ne'gɔsjus]
entrepreneur	**empreendedor** (m)	[ẽprjẽde'dor]
founder	**fundador** (m)	[fũda'dor]
to found (vt)	**fundar** (vt)	[fũ'dar]
incorporator	**principiador** (m)	[prĩsipja'dor]
partner	**parceiro, sócio** (m)	[par'sejru], ['sɔsju]
stockholder	**acionista** (m)	[asjo'nista]
millionaire	**milionário** (m)	[miljo'narju]
billionaire	**bilionário** (m)	[biljo'narju]
owner, proprietor	**proprietário** (m)	[proprje'tarju]
landowner	**proprietário** (m) **de terras**	[proprje'tarju de 'tɛhas]
client	**cliente** (m)	['kljētʃi]
regular client	**cliente** (m) **habitual**	['kljētʃi abi'twaw]
buyer (customer)	**comprador** (m)	[kõpra'dor]
visitor	**visitante** (m)	[vizi'tãtʃi]
professional (n)	**profissional** (m)	[profisjo'naw]
expert	**perito** (m)	[pe'ritu]
specialist	**especialista** (m)	[ispesja'lista]
banker	**banqueiro** (m)	[bã'kejru]
broker	**corretor** (m)	[kohe'tor]
cashier, teller	**caixa** (m, f)	['kaɪʃa]
accountant	**contador** (m)	[kõta'dɔr]
security guard	**guarda** (m)	['gwarda]
investor	**investidor** (m)	[ĩvestʃi'dor]
debtor	**devedor** (m)	[deve'dor]
creditor	**credor** (m)	[kre'dor]
borrower	**mutuário** (m)	[mu'twarju]
importer	**importador** (m)	[ĩporta'dor]
exporter	**exportador** (m)	[isporta'dor]
manufacturer	**produtor** (m)	[produ'tor]
distributor	**distribuidor** (m)	[dʒistribwi'dor]
middleman	**intermediário** (m)	[ĩterme'dʒjarju]
consultant	**consultor** (m)	[kõsuw'tor]
sales representative	**representante** (m) **comercial**	[heprezẽ'tãtʃi komer'sjaw]
agent	**agente** (m)	[a'ʒẽtʃi]
insurance agent	**agente** (m) **de seguros**	[a'ʒẽtʃi de se'gurus]

106. Service professions

cook	cozinheiro (m)	[kozi'ɲejru]
chef (kitchen chef)	chefe (m) de cozinha	['ʃɛfi de ko'ziɲa]
baker	padeiro (m)	[pa'dejru]
bartender	barman (m)	[bar'mã]
waiter	garçom (m)	[gar'sõ]
waitress	garçonete (f)	[garso'netʃi]
lawyer, attorney	advogado (m)	[adʒivo'gadu]
lawyer (legal expert)	jurista (m)	[ʒu'rista]
notary public	notário (m)	[no'tarju]
electrician	eletricista (m)	[eletri'sista]
plumber	encanador (m)	[ẽkana'dor]
carpenter	carpinteiro (m)	[karpĩ'tejru]
masseur	massagista (m)	[masa'ʒista]
masseuse	massagista (f)	[masa'ʒista]
doctor	médico (m)	['mɛdʒiku]
taxi driver	taxista (m)	[tak'sista]
driver	condutor, motorista (m)	[kõdu'tor], [moto'rista]
delivery man	entregador (m)	[ẽtrega'dor]
chambermaid	camareira (f)	[kama'rejra]
security guard	guarda (m)	['gwarda]
flight attendant (fem.)	aeromoça (f)	[aero'mosa]
schoolteacher	professor (m)	[profe'sor]
librarian	bibliotecário (m)	[bibljote'karju]
translator	tradutor (m)	[tradu'tor]
interpreter	intérprete (m)	[ĩ'tɛrpretʃi]
guide	guia (m)	['gia]
hairdresser	cabeleireiro (m)	[kabelej'rejru]
mailman	carteiro (m)	[kar'tejru]
salesman (store staff)	vendedor (m)	[vẽde'dor]
gardener	jardineiro (m)	[ʒardʒi'nejru]
domestic servant	criado (m)	['krjadu]
maid (female servant)	criada (f)	['krjada]
cleaner (cleaning lady)	empregada (f) de limpeza	[ẽpre'gada de lĩ'peza]

107. Military professions and ranks

private	soldado (m) raso	[sow'dadu 'hazu]
sergeant	sargento (m)	[sar'ʒẽtu]

| lieutenant | tenente (m) | [te'nẽtʃi] |
| captain | capitão (m) | [kapi'tãw] |

major	major (m)	[ma'ʒɔr]
colonel	coronel (m)	[koro'nɛw]
general	general (m)	[ʒene'raw]
marshal	marechal (m)	[mare'ʃaw]
admiral	almirante (m)	[awmi'rãːʃi]

military (n)	militar (m)	[mili'tar]
soldier	soldado (m)	[sow'dadu]
officer	oficial (m)	[ofi'sjaw]
commander	comandante (m)	[komã'dãtʃi]

border guard	guarda (m) de fronteira	['gwarda de frõ'tejra]
radio operator	operador (m) de rádio	[opera'dɔr de 'hadʒju]
scout (searcher)	explorador (m)	[isplora'dor]
pioneer (sapper)	sapedor-mineiro (m)	[sapa'dɔr-mi'nejru]
marksman	atirador (m)	[atʃira'dɔr]
navigator	navegador (m)	[navega dor]

108. Officials. Priests

| king | rei (m) | [hej] |
| queen | rainha (f) | [ha'iɲa] |

| prince | príncipe (m) | ['prĩsipi] |
| princess | princesa (f) | [prĩ'seza] |

| czar | czar (m) | ['kzar] |
| czarina | czarina (f) | [kza'rina] |

president	presidente (m)	[prezi'dẽtʃi]
Secretary (minister)	min stro (m)	[mi'nistru]
prime minister	primeiro-ministro (m)	[pri'mejru mi'nistru]
senator	senador (m)	[sena'dor]

diplomat	diplomata (m)	[dʒiplo'mata]
consul	cônsul (m)	['kõsuw]
ambassador	embaixador (m)	[ẽbajʃa'dor]
counselor (diplomatic officer)	conselheiro (m)	[kõse'ʎejru]

official, functionary (civil servant)	funcionário (m)	[fũsjo'narju]
prefect	prefeito (m)	[pre'fejtu]
mayor	Presidente (m) da Câmara	[prezi'dẽtʃi da 'kamara]
judge	juiz (m)	[ʒwiz]
prosecutor (e.g., district attorney)	procurador (m)	[prokura'dor]

missionary	missionário (m)	[misjo'narju]
monk	monge (m)	['mõʒi]
abbot	abade (m)	[a'badʒi]
rabbi	rabino (m)	[ha'binu]

vizier	vizir (m)	[vi'zir]
shah	xá (m)	[ʃa]
sheikh	xeique (m)	['ʃɛjki]

109. Agricultural professions

beekeeper	abelheiro (m)	[abi'ʎejru]
herder, shepherd	pastor (m)	[pas'tor]
agronomist	agrônomo (m)	[a'gronomu]
cattle breeder	criador (m) de gado	[krja'dor de 'gadu]
veterinarian	veterinário (m)	[veteri'narju]

farmer	agricultor, fazendeiro (m)	[agrikuw'tor], [fazẽ'dejru]
winemaker	vinicultor (m)	[vinikuw'tor]
zoologist	zoólogo (m)	[zo'ɔlogu]
cowboy	vaqueiro (m)	[va'kejru]

110. Art professions

| actor | ator (m) | [a'tor] |
| actress | atriz (f) | [a'triz] |

| singer (masc.) | cantor (m) | [kã'tor] |
| singer (fem.) | cantora (f) | [kã'tora] |

| dancer (masc.) | bailarino (m) | [bajla'rinu] |
| dancer (fem.) | bailarina (f) | [bajla'rina] |

| performer (masc.) | artista (m) | [ar'tʃista] |
| performer (fem.) | artista (f) | [ar'tʃista] |

musician	músico (m)	['muziku]
pianist	pianista (m)	[pja'nista]
guitar player	guitarrista (m)	[gita'hista]

conductor (orchestra ~)	maestro (m)	[ma'ɛstru]
composer	compositor (m)	[kõpozi'tor]
impresario	empresário (m)	[ẽpre'zarju]

film director	diretor (m) de cinema	[dʒire'tor de si'nɛma]
producer	produtor (m)	[produ'tor]
scriptwriter	roteirista (m)	[hotej'rista]
critic	crítico (m)	['kritʃiku]

writer	escritor (m)	[iskri'tor]
poet	poeta (m)	['pwɛta]
sculptor	escultor (m)	[iskuw'tɔr]
artist (painter)	pintor (m)	[pĩ'tor]

juggler	malabarista (m)	[malaba'rista]
clown	palhaço (m)	[pa'ʎasu]
acrobat	acrobata (m)	[akro'bata]
magician	ilusionista (m)	[iluzjo'nista]

111. Various professions

doctor	médico (m)	['mɛdʒiku]
nurse	enfermeira (f)	[ẽfer'mejra]
psychiatrist	psiquiatra (m)	[psi'kjatra]
dentist	dentista (m)	[dẽ'tʃista]
surgeon	cirurgião (m)	[sirur'ʒjãw]

astronaut	astronauta (m)	[astro'nawta]
astronomer	astrônomo (m)	[as'tronomu]
pilot	piloto (m)	[pi'lotu]

driver (of taxi, etc.)	motorista (m)	[moto'rista]
engineer (train driver)	maquinista (m)	[maki'nista]
mechanic	mecânico (m)	[me'kaniku]

miner	mineiro (m)	[mi'nejru]
worker	operário (m)	[ope'rɛrju]
locksmith	serralheiro (m)	[seha'ʎejru]
joiner (carpenter)	marceneiro (m)	[marse'nejru]
turner (lathe operator)	torneiro (m)	[tor'nejru]
construction worker	construtor (m)	[kõstru'tor]
welder	soldador (m)	[sowda'dor]

professor (title)	professor (m)	[profe'sor]
architect	arquiteto (m)	[arki'tɛtu]
historian	historiador (m)	[istorja'dor]
scientist	cientista (m)	[sjẽ'tʃista]
physicist	físico (m)	['fiziku]
chemist (scientist)	químico (m)	['kimiku]

archeologist	arqueólogo (m)	[ar'kjɔlogu]
geologist	geólogo (m)	[ʒe'ɔlogu]
researcher (scientist)	pesquisador (m)	[peskiza'dor]

| babysitter | babysitter, babá (f) | [bebi'sitter], [ba'ba] |
| teacher, educator | professor (m) | [profe'sor] |

| editor | redator (m) | [heda'tor] |
| editor-in-chief | redator-chefe (m) | [heda'tor 'ʃɛfi] |

111

| correspondent | correspondente (m) | [kohespõ'dẽtʃi] |
| typist (fem.) | datilógrafa (f) | [datʃi'lɔgrafa] |

designer	designer (m)	[dʒi'zajner]
computer expert	perito (m) em informática	[pe'ritu ẽ ĩfur'matika]
programmer	programador (m)	[programa'dor]
engineer (designer)	engenheiro (m)	[ẽʒe'ɲejru]

sailor	marujo (m)	[ma'ruʒu]
seaman	marinheiro (m)	[mari'ɲejru]
rescuer	socorrista (m)	[soko'hista]

fireman	bombeiro (m)	[bõ'bejru]
police officer	polícia (m)	[po'lisja]
watchman	guarda-noturno (m)	['gwarda no'turnu]
detective	detetive (m)	[dete'tʃivi]

customs officer	funcionário (m) da alfândega	[fũsjo'narju da aw'fãdʒiga]
bodyguard	guarda-costas (m)	['gwarda 'kɔstas]
prison guard	guarda (m) prisional	['gwarda prizjo'naw]
inspector	inspetor (m)	[ĩspe'tor]

sportsman	esportista (m)	[ispor'tʃista]
trainer, coach	treinador (m)	[trejna'dor]
butcher	açougueiro (m)	[aso'gejru]
cobbler (shoe repairer)	sapateiro (m)	[sapa'tejru]
merchant	comerciante (m)	[komer'sjãtʃi]
loader (person)	carregador (m)	[kahega'dor]

| fashion designer | estilista (m) | [istʃi'lista] |
| model (fem.) | modelo (f) | [mo'delu] |

112. Occupations. Social status

| schoolboy | estudante (m) | [istu'dãtʃi] |
| student (college ~) | estudante (m) | [istu'dãtʃi] |

philosopher	filósofo (m)	[fi'lɔzofu]
economist	economista (m)	[ekono'mista]
inventor	inventor (m)	[ĩvẽ'tor]

unemployed (n)	desempregado (m)	[dʒizẽpre'gadu]
retiree	aposentado (m)	[apozẽ'tadu]
spy, secret agent	espião (m)	[is'pjãw]

prisoner	preso, prisioneiro (m)	['prezu], [prizjo'nejru]
striker	grevista (m)	[gre'vista]
bureaucrat	burocrata (m)	[buro'krata]
traveler (globetrotter)	viajante (m)	[vja'ʒãtʃi]

gay, homosexual (n)	hom ossexual (m)	[omosek'swaw]
hacker	hacker (m)	['haker]
hippie	hippie (m, f)	['hɪpɪ]

bandit	bandido (m)	[bã'dʒidu]
hit man, killer	assassino (m)	[asa'sinu]
drug addict	drogado (m)	[dro'gadu]
drug dealer	traficante (m)	[trafi'kãtʃi]
prostitute (fem.)	prostituta (f)	[prostʃi'tuta]
pimp	cafetão (m)	[kafe'tãw]

sorcerer	bruxo (m)	['bruʃu]
sorceress (evil ~)	bruxa (f)	['bruʃa]
pirate	pirata (m)	[pi'rata]
slave	escravo (m)	[is'kravu]
samurai	samurai (m)	[samu'raj]
savage (primitive)	selvagem (m)	[sew'vaʒẽ]

Sports

113. Kinds of sports. Sportspersons

sportsman	**esportista** (m)	[ispor'tʃista]
kind of sports	**tipo** (m) **de esporte**	['tʃipu de is'pɔrtʃi]
basketball	**basquete** (m)	[bas'kɛtʃi]
basketball player	**jogador** (m) **de basquete**	[ʒoga'dor de bas'kɛtʃi]
baseball	**beisebol** (m)	[bejsi'bɔw]
baseball player	**jogador** (m) **de beisebol**	[ʒoga'dor de bejsi'bɔw]
soccer	**futebol** (m)	[futʃi'bɔw]
soccer player	**jogador** (m) **de futebol**	[ʒoga'dor de futʃi'bɔw]
goalkeeper	**goleiro** (m)	[go'lejru]
hockey	**hóquei** (m)	['hɔkej]
hockey player	**jogador** (m) **de hóquei**	[ʒoga'dor de 'hɔkej]
volleyball	**vôlei** (m)	['volej]
volleyball player	**jogador** (m) **de vôlei**	[ʒoga'dor de 'volej]
boxing	**boxe** (m)	['bɔksi]
boxer	**boxeador** (m)	[boksja'dor]
wrestling	**luta** (f)	['luta]
wrestler	**lutador** (m)	[luta'dor]
karate	**caratê** (m)	[kara'te]
karate fighter	**carateca** (m)	[kara'teka]
judo	**judô** (m)	[ʒu'do]
judo athlete	**judoca** (m)	[ʒu'dɔka]
tennis	**tênis** (m)	['tenis]
tennis player	**tenista** (m)	[te'nista]
swimming	**natação** (f)	[nata'sãw]
swimmer	**nadador** (m)	[nada'dor]
fencing	**esgrima** (f)	[iz'grima]
fencer	**esgrimista** (m)	[izgri'mista]
chess	**xadrez** (m)	[ʃa'drez]
chess player	**jogador** (m) **de xadrez**	[ʒoga'dor de ʃa'drez]

| alpinism | alpinsmo (m) | [awpi'nizmu] |
| alpinist | alpinsta (m) | [awpi'nista] |

| running | corrida (f) | [ko'hida] |
| runner | corredor (m) | [kohe'dor] |

| athletics | atletismo (m) | [atle'tʃizmu] |
| athlete | atleta (m) | [at'lɛta] |

| horseback riding | hipismo (m) | [i'pizmu] |
| horse rider | cavaleiro (m) | [kava'lejru] |

figure skating	patinação (f) artística	[patʃina'sãw ar'tʃistʃika]
figure skater (masc.)	patinador (m)	[patʃina'dor]
figure skater (fem.)	patinadora (f)	[patʃina'dora]

| powerlifting | halterofilismo (m) | [awterofi'lizmu] |
| powerlifter | halterofilista (m) | [awterofi'lista] |

| car racing | corrida (f) de carros | [ko'hida de 'kahos] |
| racer (driver) | piloto (m) | [pi'lotu] |

| cycling | ciclismo (m) | [si'klizmu] |
| cyclist | ciclista (m) | [si'klista] |

broad jump	salto (m) em distância	['sawtu ẽ dʒis'tãsja]
pole vault	salto (m) com vara	['sawtu kõ 'vara]
jumper	atleta (m) de saltos	[at'lɛta de 'sawtus]

114. Kinds of sports. Miscellaneous

football	futebol (m) americano	[futʃi'bow ameri'kanu]
badminton	badminton (m)	[bad'mĩtɔn]
biathlon	biatlo (m)	[bi'atlu]
billiards	bilhar (m)	[bi'ʎar]

bobsled	bobsled (m)	['bɔbsled]
bodybuilding	musculação (f)	[muskula'sãw]
water polo	polo (m) aquático	['pɔlu a'kwatʃiku]
handball	handebol (m)	[ãde'bɔl]
golf	golfe (m)	['gowfi]

rowing, crew	remo (m)	['hɛmu]
scuba diving	mergulho (m)	[mer'guʎu]
cross-country skiing	corrida (f) de esqui	[ko'hida de is'ki]
table tennis (ping-pong)	tênis (m) de mesa	['tenis de 'meza]

sailing	vela (f)	['vɛla]
rally racing	rali (m)	[ha'li]
rugby	rúgbi (m)	['hugbi]

snowboarding	**snowboard** (m)	[snowbɔrd]
archery	**arco-e-flecha** (m)	['arku l 'flɛʃa]

115. Gym

barbell	**barra** (f)	['baha]
dumbbells	**halteres** (m pl)	[aw'tɛris]
training machine	**aparelho** (m) **de musculação**	[apa'reʎu de muskula'sãw]
exercise bicycle	**bicicleta** (f) **ergométrica**	[bisi'klɛta ergo'mɛtrika]
treadmill	**esteira** (f) **de corrida**	[is'tejra de ko'hida]
horizontal bar	**barra** (f) **fixa**	['baha 'fiksa]
parallel bars	**barras** (f pl) **paralelas**	['bahas para'lɛlas]
vault (vaulting horse)	**cavalo** (m)	[ka'valu]
mat (exercise ~)	**tapete** (m) **de ginástica**	[ta'petʃi de ʒi'nastʃika]
jump rope	**corda** (f) **de saltar**	['kɔrda de saw'tar]
aerobics	**aeróbica** (f)	[ae'rɔbika]
yoga	**ioga, yoga** (f)	['jɔga]

116. Sports. Miscellaneous

Olympic Games	**Jogos** (m pl) **Olímpicos**	['ʒɔgus o'lĩpikus]
winner	**vencedor** (m)	[vẽse'dor]
to be winning	**vencer** (vi)	[vẽ'ser]
to win (vi)	**vencer** (vi, vt)	[vẽ'ser]
leader	**líder** (m)	['lider]
to lead (vi)	**liderar** (vt)	[lide'rar]
first place	**primeiro lugar** (m)	[pri'mejru lu'gar]
second place	**segundo lugar** (m)	[se'gũdu lu'gar]
third place	**terceiro lugar** (m)	[ter'sejru lu'gar]
medal	**medalha** (f)	[me'daʎa]
trophy	**troféu** (m)	[tro'fɛw]
prize cup (trophy)	**taça** (f)	['tasa]
prize (in game)	**prêmio** (m)	['premju]
main prize	**prêmio** (m) **principal**	['premju prĩsi'paw]
record	**recorde** (m)	[he'kɔrdʒi]
to set a record	**estabelecer um recorde**	[istabele'ser ũ he'kɔrdʒi]
final	**final** (m)	[fi'naw]
final (adj)	**final**	[fi'naw]
champion	**campeão** (m)	[kã'pjãw]

championship	campeonato (m)	[kãpjo'natu]
stadium	estádio (m)	[is'tadʒu]
stand (bleachers)	arquibancadas (f pl)	[arkibã'kadas]
fan, supporter	fã, torcedor (m)	[fã], [torse'dor]
opponent, rival	adversário (m)	[adʒiver'sarju]

| start (start line) | partida (f) | [par'tʃida] |
| finish line | linha (f) de chegada | ['liɲa de ʃe'gada] |

| defeat | derrota (f) | [de'hotɛ] |
| to lose (not win) | perder (vt) | [per'der] |

referee	árbitro, juiz (m)	[ar'bitru], [ʒwiz]
jury (judges)	júri (m)	['ʒuri]
score	resultado (m)	[hezuw'tadu]
tie	empate (m)	[ë'patʃi]
to tie (vi)	empatar (vi)	[ëpa'tar]
point	ponto (m)	['põtu]
result (final score)	resultado (m) final	[hezuw'tadu fi'naw]

period	tempo (m)	['tẽpu]
half-time	intervalo (m)	[ĩter'valu]
doping	doping (m)	['dopĩg]
to penalize (vt)	penalizar (vt)	[penali'zar]
to disqualify (vt)	desqualificar (vt)	[dʒiskwalifi'kar]

apparatus	aparelho, aparato (m)	[apa'reʌu], [apa'ratu]
javelin	dardo (m)	['dardu]
shot (metal ball)	peso (m)	['pezu]
ball (snooker, etc.)	bola (f)	['bola]

aim (target)	alvo (m)	['awvu]
target	alvo (m)	['awvu]
to shoot (vi)	disparar, atirar (vi)	[dʒispa'rar], [atʃi'rar]
accurate (~ shot)	preciso	[pre'sizɹ]

trainer, coach	treinador (m)	[trejna'dor]
to train (sb)	treinar (vt)	[trej'nar]
to train (vi)	treinar-se (vr)	[trej'narsi]
training	treino (m)	['trejnu]

gym	academia (f) de ginástica	[akade'mia de ʒi'nastʃika]
exercise (physical)	exercício (m)	[ezer'sisju]
warm-up (athlete ~)	aquecimento (m)	[akesi'mẽtu]

Education

117. School

school	escola (f)	[is'kɔla]
principal (headmaster)	diretor (m) de escola	[dʒire'tor de is'kɔla]
pupil (boy)	aluno (m)	[a'lunu]
pupil (girl)	aluna (f)	[a'luna]
schoolboy	estudante (m)	[istu'dãtʃi]
schoolgirl	estudante (f)	[istu'dãtʃi]
to teach (sb)	ensinar (vt)	[ẽsi'nar]
to learn (language, etc.)	aprender (vt)	[aprẽ'der]
to learn by heart	decorar (vt)	[deko'rar]
to learn (~ to count, etc.)	estudar (vi)	[istu'dar]
to be in school	estar na escola	[is'tar na is'kɔla]
to go to school	ir à escola	[ir a is'kɔla]
alphabet	alfabeto (m)	[awfa'bɛtu]
subject (at school)	disciplina (f)	[dʒisi'plina]
classroom	sala (f) de aula	['sala de 'awla]
lesson	lição, aula (f)	[li'sãw], ['awla]
recess	recreio (m)	[he'kreju]
school bell	toque (m)	['tɔki]
school desk	classe (f)	['klasi]
chalkboard	quadro (m) negro	['kwadru 'negru]
grade	nota (f)	['nɔta]
good grade	boa nota (f)	['boa 'nɔta]
bad grade	nota (f) baixa	['nɔta 'baɪʃa]
to give a grade	dar uma nota	[dar 'uma 'nɔta]
mistake, error	erro (m)	['ehu]
to make mistakes	errar (vi)	[e'har]
to correct (an error)	corrigir (vt)	[kohi'ʒir]
cheat sheet	cola (f)	['kɔla]
homework	dever (m) de casa	[de'ver de 'kaza]
exercise (in education)	exercício (m)	[ezer'sisju]
to be present	estar presente	[is'tar pre'zẽtʃi]
to be absent	estar ausente	[is'tar aw'zẽtʃi]
to miss school	faltar às aulas	[faw'tar as 'awlas]

to punish (vt)	pun r (vt)	[pu'nir]
punishment	pun ção (f)	[puni'sãw]
conduct (behavior)	corr portamento (m)	[kõporta'mẽtu]

report card	boletim (m) escolar	[bole'tʃĩ isko'lar]
pencil	lápis (m)	['lapis]
eraser	borracha (f)	[bo'haʃɐ]
chalk	giz (m)	[ʒiz]
pencil case	porta-lápis (m)	['porta-' apis]

schoolbag	mala, pasta, mochila (f)	['mala], ['pasta], [mo'ʃila]
pen	caneta (f)	[ka'neta]
school notebook	caderno (m)	[ka'dɛrnu]
textbook	livro (m) didático	['livru dʒi'datʃiku]
drafting compass	compasso (m)	[kõ'pasɹ]

to make technical drawings	traçar (vt)	[tra'sar]
technical drawing	desenho (m) técnico	[de'zɛɲɹ 'tɛkniku]

poem	poesia (f)	[poe'zia]
by heart (adv)	de cor	[de korˈ]
to learn by heart	decorar (vt)	[deko'rar]

school vacation	férias (f pl)	['fɛrjas]
to be on vacation	estar de férias	[is'tar de 'fɛrjas]
to spend one's vacation	passar as férias	[pa'sar as 'fɛrjas]

test (written math ~)	teste (m), prova (f)	['tɛstʃi], ['prova]
essay (composition)	redação (f)	[heda'sãw]
dictation	ditado (m)	[dʒi'tadu]
exam (examination)	exame (m), prova (f)	[e'zamĩ], ['prova]
to take an exam	fazer prova	[fa'zer prova]
experiment (e.g., chemistry ~)	experiência (f)	[ispe'rjẽsja]

118. College. University

academy	academia (f)	[akade'mia]
university	universidade (f)	[universi'dadʒi]
faculty (e.g., ~ of Medicine)	faculdade (f)	[fakuw'dadʒi]

student (masc.)	estudante (m)	[istu'dãtʃi]
student (fem.)	estudante (f)	[istu'dãtʃi]
lecturer (teacher)	professor (m)	[profe'sor]

lecture hall, room	auditório (m)	[awdʒi'tɔrju]
graduate	graduado (m)	[gra'dwadu]
diploma	diploma (m)	[dʒip'lɔma]

dissertation	tese (f)	['tɛzi]
study (report)	estudo (m)	[is'tudu]
laboratory	laboratório (m)	[labora'tɔrju]

lecture	palestra (f)	[pa'lɛstra]
coursemate	colega (m) de curso	[ko'lɛga de 'kursu]
scholarship	bolsa (f) de estudos	['bowsa de is'tudus]
academic degree	grau (m) acadêmico	['graw aka'demiku]

119. Sciences. Disciplines

mathematics	matemática (f)	[mate'matʃika]
algebra	álgebra (f)	['awʒebra]
geometry	geometria (f)	[ʒeome'tria]

astronomy	astronomia (f)	[astrono'mia]
biology	biologia (f)	[bjolo'ʒia]
geography	geografia (f)	[ʒeogra'fia]
geology	geologia (f)	[ʒeolo'ʒia]
history	história (f)	[is'tɔrja]

medicine	medicina (f)	[medʒi'sina]
pedagogy	pedagogia (f)	[pedago'ʒia]
law	direito (m)	[dʒi'rejtu]

physics	física (f)	['fizika]
chemistry	química (f)	['kimika]
philosophy	filosofia (f)	[filozo'fia]
psychology	psicologia (f)	[psikolo'ʒia]

120. Writing system. Orthography

grammar	gramática (f)	[gra'matʃika]
vocabulary	vocabulário (m)	[vokabu'larju]
phonetics	fonética (f)	[fo'nɛtʃika]

noun	substantivo (m)	[substã'tʃivu]
adjective	adjetivo (m)	[adʒe'tʃivu]
verb	verbo (m)	['vɛrbu]
adverb	advérbio (m)	[adʒi'vɛrbju]

pronoun	pronome (m)	[pro'nɔmi]
interjection	interjeição (f)	[ĩterʒej'sãw]
preposition	preposição (f)	[prepozi'sãw]

root	raiz (f)	[ha'iz]
ending	terminação (f)	[termina'sãw]
prefix	prefixo (m)	[pre'fiksu]

syllable	**sílaba** (f)	['silaba]
suffix	**sufixo** (m)	[su'fiksu]
stress mark	**acento** (m)	[a'sẽtu]
apostrophe	**apóstrofo** (m)	[a'pɔstrofu]
period, dot	**ponto** (m)	['põtu]
comma	**vírgula** (f)	['virgula]
semicolon	**ponto e vírgula** (m)	['põtu e 'virgula]
colon	**dois pontos** (m pl)	['dojs 'põtus]
ellipsis	**reticências** (f pl)	[hetʃi'sẽsˌas]
question mark	**ponto** (m) **de interrogação**	['põtu de ĩtehoga'sãw]
exclamation point	**ponto** (m) **de exclamação**	['põtu de isklama'sãw]
quotation marks	**aspas** (f pl)	['aspas]
in quotation marks	**entre aspas**	[ẽtri 'aspas]
parenthesis	**parênteses** (m pl)	[pa'rẽtez s]
in parenthesis	**entre parênteses**	[ẽtri pa'rẽtezis]
hyphen	**hífen** (m)	['ifẽ]
dash	**travessão** (m)	[trave'sãw]
space (between words)	**espaço** (m)	[is'pasu]
letter	**letra** (f)	['letra]
capital letter	**letra** (f) **maiúscula**	['letra ma'juskula]
vowel (n)	**vogal** (f)	[vo'gaw]
consonant (n)	**consoante** (f)	[kõso'ãtʃi]
sentence	**frase** (f)	['frazi]
subject	**sujeito** (m)	[su'ʒejtu]
predicate	**predicado** (m)	[predʒi'kadu]
line	**linha** (f)	['liɲa]
on a new line	**em uma nova linha**	[ẽ 'uma 'nɔva 'liɲa]
paragraph	**parágrafo** (m)	[pa'ragrafu]
word	**palavra** (f)	[pa'lavra]
group of words	**grupo** (m) **de palavras**	['grupu de pa'lavras]
expression	**expressão** (f)	[ispre'sãw]
synonym	**sinônimo** (m)	[si'nonimu]
antonym	**antônimo** (m)	[ã'tonimu]
rule	**regra** (f)	['hɛgra]
exception	**exceção** (f)	[ese'sãw]
correct (adj)	**correto**	[ko'hɛtu]
conjugation	**conjugação** (f)	[kõʒuga'sãw]
declension	**declinação** (f)	[deklina'sãw]
nominal case	**caso** (m)	['kazu]
question	**pergunta** (f)	[per'gũta]

| to underline (vt) | sublinhar (vt) | [subli'ɲar] |
| dotted line | linha (f) pontilhada | ['liɲa põtʃi'ʎada] |

121. Foreign languages

language	língua (f)	['lĩgwa]
foreign (adj)	estrangeiro	[istrã'ʒejru]
foreign language	língua (f) estrangeira	['lĩgwa istrã'ʒejra]
to study (vt)	estudar (vt)	[istu'dar]
to learn (language, etc.)	aprender (vt)	[aprẽ'der]

to read (vi, vt)	ler (vt)	[ler]
to speak (vi, vt)	falar (vi)	[fa'lar]
to understand (vt)	entender (vt)	[ẽtẽ'der]
to write (vt)	escrever (vt)	[iskre'ver]

fast (adv)	rapidamente	[hapida'mẽtʃi]
slowly (adv)	lentamente	[lẽta'mẽtʃi]
fluently (adv)	fluentemente	[fluẽte'mẽtʃi]

rules	regras (f pl)	['hɛgras]
grammar	gramática (f)	[gra'matʃika]
vocabulary	vocabulário (m)	[vokabu'larju]
phonetics	fonética (f)	[fo'nɛtʃika]

textbook	livro (m) didático	['livru dʒi'datʃiku]
dictionary	dicionário (m)	[dʒisjo'narju]
teach-yourself book	manual (m) autodidático	[ma'nwaw awtodʒi'datʃiku]
phrasebook	guia (m) de conversação	['gia de kõversa'sãw]

cassette, tape	fita (f) cassete	['fita ka'sɛtʃi]
videotape	videoteipe (m)	[vidʒju'tejpi]
CD, compact disc	CD, disco (m) compacto	['sede], ['dʒisku kõ'paktu]
DVD	DVD (m)	[deve'de]

alphabet	alfabeto (m)	[awfa'bɛtu]
to spell (vt)	soletrar (vt)	[sole'trar]
pronunciation	pronúncia (f)	[pro'nũsja]

accent	sotaque (m)	[so'taki]
with an accent	com sotaque	[kõ so'taki]
without an accent	sem sotaque	[sẽ so'taki]

| word | palavra (f) | [pa'lavra] |
| meaning | sentido (m) | [sẽ'tʃidu] |

course (e.g., a French ~)	curso (m)	['kursu]
to sign up	inscrever-se (vr)	[ĩskre'verse]
teacher	professor (m)	[profe'sor]
translation (process)	tradução (f)	[tradu'sãw]

translation (text, etc.)	tradução (f)	[tradu'sãw]
translator	tradutor (m)	[tradu'tor]
interpreter	intérprete (m)	[ĩ'tɛrpretʃi]

| polyglot | poliglota (m) | [pɔli'glɔta] |
| memory | memória (f) | [me'mɔrja] |

122. Fairy tale characters

Santa Claus	Papai Noel (m)	[pa'paj nɔ'ɛl]
Cinderella	Cinderela (f)	[sĩde'rɛla]
mermaid	sereia (f)	[se'reja]
Neptune	Netuno (m)	[ne'tunu]

magician, wizard	bruxo, feiticeiro (m)	['bruʃu], [fejtʃi'sejru]
fairy	fada (f)	['fada]
magic (adj)	mágico	['maʒikʋ]
magic wand	varinha (f) mágica	[va'riɲa 'maʒika]

fairy tale	conto (m) de fadas	['kõtu de 'fadas]
miracle	milagre (m)	[mi'lagri]
dwarf	anão (m)	[a'nãw]
to turn into …	transformar-se em …	[trãsfor'marsi ẽ]

ghost	fantasma (m)	[fã'tazma]
phantom	fantasma (m)	[fã'tazma]
monster	monstro (m)	['mõstru]
dragon	dragão (m)	[dra'gãw]
giant	gigante (m)	[ʒi'gãtʃi]

123. Zodiac Signs

Aries	Áries (f)	['aris]
Taurus	Touro (m)	['toru]
Gemini	Gêmeos (m pl)	['ʒemjus]
Cancer	Câncer (m)	['kãser]
Leo	Leão (m)	[le'ãw]
Virgo	Virgem (f)	['virʒẽ]

Libra	Libra (f)	['libra]
Scorpio	Escorpião (m)	[iskorpi'ãw]
Sagittarius	Sagitário (m)	[saʒi'tarju]
Capricorn	Capricórnio (m)	[kapri'kɔrnju]
Aquarius	Aquário (m)	[a'kwarju]
Pisces	Peixes (pl)	['pejʃis]

| character | caráter (m) | [ka'rater] |
| character traits | traços (m pl) do caráter | ['trasus du ka'rater] |

behavior	comportamento (m)	[kõporta'mẽtu]
to tell fortunes	prever a sorte	[pre'ver a 'sɔrtʃi]
fortune-teller	adivinha (f)	[adʒi'viɲa]
horoscope	horóscopo (m)	[o'rɔskopu]

Arts

124. Theater

theater	teatro (m)	['tʃatru]
opera	ópera (f)	['ɔpera]
operetta	opereta (f)	[ope'reta]
ballet	balé (m)	[ba'lɛ]

theater poster	cartaz (m)	[kar'taz]
troupe	companhia (f)	[kõpa'ɲia
(theatrical company)	de teatro	de 'tʃatru]
tour	turnê (f)	[tur'ne]
to be on tour	estar em turnê	[is'tar ẽ tur'ne]
to rehearse (vi, vt)	ensaiar (vt)	[ẽsa'jar]
rehearsal	ensaio (m)	[ẽ'saju]
repertoire	repertório (m)	[heper'tɔrju]

performance	apresentação (f)	[aprezẽta'sãw]
theatrical show	espetáculo (m)	[ispe'takulu]
play	peça (f)	['pɛsa]

ticket	entrada (m)	[ẽ'trada]
box office (ticket booth)	bilheteira (f)	[biʎe'tejra]
lobby, foyer	hall (m)	[hɔw]
coat check (cloakroom)	vestiário (m)	[ves'tʃjarju]
coat check tag	senha (f) numerada	['sɛɲa nume'rada]
binoculars	binóculo (m)	[bi'nɔkulu]
usher	lanterninha (m, f)	[lãter'niɲa]

orchestra seats	plateia (f)	[pla'tɛja]
balcony	balcão (m)	[baw'kãw]
dress circle	primeiro balcão (m)	[pri'mejru baw'kãw]
box	camarote (m)	[kama'rɔtʃi]
row	fila (f)	['fila]
seat	assento (m)	[a'sẽtu]

audience	público (m)	['publiku]
spectator	espectador (m)	[ispekta'dor]
to clap (vi, vt)	aplaudir (vt)	[aplaw'dʒir]
applause	aplauso (m)	[a'plawzu]
ovation	ovação (f)	[ova'sãw]

stage	palco (m)	['pawku]
curtain	cortina (f)	[kor'tʃina]
scenery	cenário (m)	[se'narju]

backstage	bastidores (m pl)	[bastʃi'doris]
scene (e.g., the last ~)	cena (f)	['sɛna]
act	ato (m)	['atu]
intermission	intervalo (m)	[ĩter'valu]

125. Cinema

| actor | ator (m) | [a'tor] |
| actress | atriz (f) | [a'triz] |

movies (industry)	cinema (m)	[si'nɛma]
movie	filme (m)	['fiwmi]
episode	episódio (m)	[epi'zɔdʒu]

detective movie	filme (m) policial	['fiwmi poli'sjaw]
action movie	filme (m) de ação	['fiwmi de a'sãw]
adventure movie	filme (m) de aventuras	['fiwmi de avẽ'turas]
sci-fi movie	filme (m) de ficção científica	['fiwmi de fik'sãw sjẽ'tʃifika]
horror movie	filme (m) de horror	['fiwmi de o'hor]

comedy movie	comédia (f)	[ko'mɛdʒja]
melodrama	melodrama (m)	[melo'drama]
drama	drama (m)	['drama]

fictional movie	filme (m) de ficção	['fiwmi de fik'sãw]
documentary	documentário (m)	[dokumẽ'tarju]
cartoon	desenho (m) animado	[de'zɛɲu ani'madu]
silent movies	cinema (m) mudo	[si'nɛma 'mudu]

role (part)	papel (m)	[pa'pɛw]
leading role	papel (m) principal	[pa'pɛw prĩsi'paw]
to play (vi, vt)	representar (vt)	[heprezẽ'tar]

movie star	estrela (f) de cinema	[is'trela de si'nɛma]
well-known (adj)	conhecido	[koɲe'sidu]
famous (adj)	famoso	[fa'mozu]
popular (adj)	popular	[popu'lar]

script (screenplay)	roteiro (m)	[ho'tejru]
scriptwriter	roteirista (m)	[hotej'rista]
movie director	diretor (m) de cinema	[dʒire'tor de si'nɛma]
producer	produtor (m)	[produ'tor]
assistant	assistente (m)	[asis'tẽtʃi]
cameraman	diretor (m) de fotografia	[dʒire'tor de fotogra'fia]
stuntman	dublê (m)	[du'ble]
double (stand-in)	dublê (m) de corpo	[du'ble de korpu]

| to shoot a movie | filmar (vt) | [fiw'mar] |
| audition, screen test | audição (f) | [awdʒi'sãw] |

shooting	filmagem (f)	[fiw'maʒẽ]
movie crew	equipe (f) de filmagem	[e'kipi dɛ fiw'maʒẽ]
movie set	set (m) de filmagem	['sɛtʃi de fiw'maʒẽ]
camera	câmera (f)	['kamera]

movie theater	cinema (m)	[si'nɛma]
screen (e.g., big ~)	tela (f)	['tɛla]
to show a movie	exibir um filme	[ezi'bir ũ 'fiwmi]

soundtrack	trilha (f) sonora	['triʎa so'nɔra]
special effects	efeitos (m pl) especiais	[e'fejtus ispe'sjajs]
subtitles	legendas (f pl)	[le'ʒẽdas]
credits	crédito (m)	['krɛdʒitu]
translation	tradução (f)	[tradu'sãw]

126. Painting

art	arte (f)	['artʃi]
fine arts	belas-artes (f pl)	[bɛlaz 'artʃis]
art gallery	galeria (f) de arte	[gale'ria de 'artʃi]
art exhibition	exibição (f) de arte	[ezibi'sãw de 'artʃi]

painting (art)	pintura (f)	[pĩ'tura]
graphic art	arte (f) gráfica	['artʃis 'grafikas]
abstract art	arte (f) abstrata	['artʃi abs'trata]
impressionism	impressionismo (m)	[ĩpresjo'nizmu]

picture (painting)	pintura (f), quadro (m)	[pĩ'tura], ['kwadru]
drawing	desenho (m)	[de'zɛɲu]
poster	pôster (m)	['poster]

illustration (picture)	ilustração (f)	[ilustra'sãw]
miniature	miniatura (f)	[minja'tura]
copy (of painting, etc.)	cópia (f)	['kɔpja]
reproduction	reprodução (f)	[heprodu'sãw]

mosaic	mosaico (m)	[mo'zajku]
stained glass window	vitral (m)	[vi'traw]
fresco	afresco (m)	[a'fresku]
engraving	gravura (f)	[gra'vura]

bust (sculpture)	busto (m)	['bustu]
sculpture	escultura (f)	[iskuw'tura]
statue	estátua (f)	[is'tatwa]
plaster of Paris	gesso (m)	['ʒesu]
plaster (as adj)	em gesso	[ẽ 'ʒesu]

portrait	retrato (m)	[he'tratu]
self-portrait	autorretrato (m)	[awtohe'tratu]
landscape painting	paisagem (f)	[paj'zaʒẽ]

still life	natureza (f) morta	[natu'reza 'mɔrta]
caricature	caricatura (f)	[karika'tura]
sketch	esboço (m)	[iz'bosu]

paint	tinta (f)	[tʃĩta]
watercolor paint	aquarela (f)	[akwa'rɛla]
oil (paint)	tinta (f) a óleo	[tʃĩta a 'ɔlju]
pencil	lápis (m)	['lapis]
India ink	tinta (f) nanquim	[tʃĩta nã'kĩ]
charcoal	carvão (m)	[kar'vãw]

| to draw (vi, vt) | desenhar (vt) | [deze'ɲar] |
| to paint (vi, vt) | pintar (vt) | [pĩ'tar] |

to pose (vi)	posar (vi)	[po'zar]
artist's model (masc.)	modelo (m)	[mo'delu]
artist's model (fem.)	modelo (f)	[mo'delu]

artist (painter)	pintor (m)	[pĩ'tor]
work of art	obra (f)	['ɔbra]
masterpiece	obra-prima (f)	['ɔbra 'prima]
studio (artist's workroom)	estúdio (m)	[is'tudʒu]

canvas (cloth)	tela (f)	['tɛla]
easel	cavalete (m)	[kava'letʃi]
palette	paleta (f)	[pa'leta]

frame (picture ~, etc.)	moldura (f)	[mow'dura]
restoration	restauração (f)	[hestawra'sãw]
to restore (vt)	restaurar (vt)	[hestaw'rar]

127. Literature & Poetry

literature	literatura (f)	[litera'tura]
author (writer)	autor (m)	[aw'tor]
pseudonym	pseudônimo (m)	[psew'donimu]

book	livro (m)	['livru]
volume	volume (m)	[vo'lumi]
table of contents	índice (m)	['ĩdʒisi]
page	página (f)	['paʒina]
main character	protagonista (m)	[protago'nista]
autograph	autógrafo (m)	[aw'tɔgrafu]

short story	conto (m)	['kõtu]
story (novella)	novela (f)	[no'vɛla]
novel	romance (m)	[ho'mãsi]
work (writing)	obra (f)	['ɔbra]
fable	fábula (m)	['fabula]
detective novel	romance (m) policial	[ho'mãsi poli'sjaw]

poem (verse)	verso (m)	['vɛrsu]
poetry	poesia (f)	[poe'ziɐ]
poem (epic, ballad)	poema (m)	['pwema]
poet	poeta (m)	['pwɛta]

fiction	ficção (f)	[fik'sãw]
science fiction	ficção (f) científica	[fik'sãw sjẽ'tʃifika]
adventures	aventuras (f pl)	[avẽ'turas]
educational literature	literatura (f) didática	[litera'tura dʒi'datʃika]
children's literature	literatura (f) infantil	[litera'tura ĩfã'tʃiw]

128. Circus

circus	circo (m)	['sirku]
traveling circus	circo (m) ambulante	['sirku ãbu'lãtʃi]
program	programa (m)	[pro'grama]
performance	apresentação (f)	[aprezẽta'sãw]

| act (circus ~) | número (m) | ['numeru] |
| circus ring | picadeiro (f) | [pika'dejru] |

| pantomime (act) | pantomima (f) | [pãto'mima] |
| clown | palhaço (m) | [pa'ʎasu] |

acrobat	acrobata (m)	[akro'bata]
acrobatics	acrobacia (f)	[akroba'sia]
gymnast	ginasta (m)	[ʒi'nasta]
acrobatic gymnastics	ginástica (f)	[ʒi'nastʃika]
somersault	salto (m) mortal	['sawtu mor'taw]
athlete (strongman)	homem (m) forte	['omẽ 'fortʃi]
tamer (e.g., lion ~)	domador (m)	[doma'dor]
rider (circus horse ~)	cavaleiro (m) equilibrista	[kava'lejru ekili'brista]
assistant	assistente (m)	[asis'tẽtʃi]

stunt	truque (m)	['truki]
magic trick	truque (m) de mágica	['truki de 'maʒika]
conjurer, magician	ilusionista (m)	[iluzjo'nista]

juggler	malabarista (m)	[malaba'rista]
to juggle (vi, vt)	fazer malabarismos	[fa'zer malaba'rizmus]
animal trainer	adestrador (m)	[adestra'dor]
animal training	adestramento (m)	[adestra'mẽtu]
to train (animals)	adestrar (vt)	[ades'trar]

129. Music. Pop music

| music | música (f) | ['muzika] |
| musician | músico (m) | ['muziku] |

musical instrument	**instrumento** (m) **musical**	[ĩstru'mẽtu muzi'kaw]
to play ...	**tocar ...**	[to'kar]
guitar	**guitarra** (f)	[gi'taha]
violin	**violino** (m)	[vjo'linu]
cello	**violoncelo** (m)	[vjolõ'sɛlu]
double bass	**contrabaixo** (m)	[kõtra'baɪʃu]
harp	**harpa** (f)	['arpa]
piano	**piano** (m)	['pjanu]
grand piano	**piano** (m) **de cauda**	['pjanu de 'kawda]
organ	**órgão** (m)	['ɔrgãw]
wind instruments	**instrumentos** (m pl) **de sopro**	[ĩstru'mẽtus de 'sopru]
oboe	**oboé** (m)	[o'bwɛ]
saxophone	**saxofone** (m)	[sakso'fɔni]
clarinet	**clarinete** (m)	[klari'netʃi]
flute	**flauta** (f)	['flawta]
trumpet	**trompete** (m)	[trõ'pɛte]
accordion	**acordeão** (m)	[akor'dʒjãw]
drum	**tambor** (m)	[tã'bor]
duo	**dueto** (m)	['dwetu]
trio	**trio** (m)	['triu]
quartet	**quarteto** (m)	[kwar'tetu]
choir	**coro** (m)	['koru]
orchestra	**orquestra** (f)	[or'kɛstra]
pop music	**música** (f) **pop**	['muzika 'pɔpi]
rock music	**música** (f) **rock**	['muzika 'hɔki]
rock group	**grupo** (m) **de rock**	['grupu de 'hɔki]
jazz	**jazz** (m)	[dʒɛz]
idol	**ídolo** (m)	['idolu]
admirer, fan	**fã, admirador** (m)	[fã], [adʒimira'dor]
concert	**concerto** (m)	[kõ'sertu]
symphony	**sinfonia** (f)	[sĩfo'nia]
composition	**composição** (f)	[kõpozi'sãw]
to compose (write)	**compor** (vt)	[kõ'por]
singing (n)	**canto** (m)	['kãtu]
song	**canção** (f)	[kã'sãw]
tune (melody)	**melodia** (f)	[melo'dʒia]
rhythm	**ritmo** (m)	['hitʃmu]
blues	**blues** (m)	[bluz]
sheet music	**notas** (f pl)	['nɔtas]
baton	**batuta** (f)	[ba'tuta]
bow	**arco** (m)	['arku]

| string | **corda** (f) | ['kɔrda] |
| case (e.g., guitar ~) | **estojo** (m) | [is'toʒu] |

Rest. Entertainment. Travel

130. Trip. Travel

tourism, travel	turismo (m)	[tu'rizmu]
tourist	turista (m)	[tu'rista]
trip, voyage	viagem (f)	['vjaʒẽ]
adventure	aventura (f)	[avẽ'tura]
trip, journey	viagem (f)	['vjaʒẽ]
vacation	férias (f pl)	['fɛrjas]
to be on vacation	estar de férias	[is'tar de 'fɛrjas]
rest	descanso (m)	[dʒis'kãsu]
train	trem (m)	[trẽj]
by train	de trem	[de trẽj]
airplane	avião (m)	[a'vjãw]
by airplane	de avião	[de a'vjãw]
by car	de carro	[de 'kaho]
by ship	de navio	[de na'viu]
luggage	bagagem (f)	[ba'gaʒẽ]
suitcase	mala (f)	['mala]
luggage cart	carrinho (m)	[ka'hiɲu]
passport	passaporte (m)	[pasa'pɔrtʃi]
visa	visto (m)	['vistu]
ticket	passagem (f)	[pa'saʒẽ]
air ticket	passagem (f) aérea	[pa'saʒẽ a'erja]
guidebook	guia (m) de viagem	['gia de vi'aʒẽ]
map (tourist ~)	mapa (m)	['mapa]
area (rural ~)	área (f)	['arja]
place, site	lugar (m)	[lu'gar]
exotica (n)	exotismo (m)	[ezo'tʃizmu]
exotic (adj)	exótico	[e'zɔtʃiku]
amazing (adj)	surpreendente	[surprjẽ'dẽtʃi]
group	grupo (m)	['grupu]
excursion, sightseeing tour	excursão (f)	[iskur'sãw]
guide (person)	guia (m)	['gia]

131. Hotel

hotel	**hotel** (m)	[o'tɛw]
motel	**mote** (m)	[mo'tɛw]
three-star (~ hotel)	**três estrelas**	['tres is'trɛlas]
five-star	**cinco estrelas**	['sĩku is'trelas]
to stay (in a hotel, etc.)	**ficar** (vi, vt)	[fi'kar]
room	**quarto** (m)	['kwartu]
single room	**quarto** (m) **individual**	['kwartu ĩdʒivi'dwaw]
double room	**quarto** (m) **duplo**	['kwartu 'duplu]
to book a room	**reservar um quarto**	[hezer'var ũ 'kwartu]
half board	**meia pensão** (f)	['meja pẽ'sãw]
full board	**pensão** (f) **completa**	[pẽ'sãw kõ'plɛta]
with bath	**com banheira**	[kõ ba'ɲejra]
with shower	**com chuveiro**	[kõ ʃu'vejru]
satellite television	**televisão** (m) **por satélite**	[televi'zãw por sa'tɛlitʃi]
air-conditioner	**ar** (m) **condicionado**	[ar kõdʒisjo'nadu]
towel	**toalha** (f)	[to'aʎa]
key	**chave** (f)	['ʃavi]
administrator	**administrador** (m)	[adʒiministra'dor]
chambermaid	**camareira** (f)	[kama'rejra]
porter, bellboy	**bagageiro** (m)	[baga'ʒejru]
doorman	**porteiro** (m)	[por'tejru]
restaurant	**restaurante** (m)	[hestaw'rãtʃi]
pub, bar	**bar** (m)	[bar]
breakfast	**café** (m) **da manhã**	[ka'fɛ da ma'ɲã]
dinner	**jantar** (m)	[ʒã'tar]
buffet	**bufê** (m)	[bu'fe]
lobby	**saguão** (m)	[sa'gwãw]
elevator	**elevador** (m)	[eleva'dor]
DO NOT DISTURB	**NÃO PERTURBE**	['nãw per'turbi]
NO SMOKING	**PROIBIDO FUMAR!**	[proi'bidu fu'mar]

132. Books. Reading

book	**livro** (m)	['livru]
author	**autor** (m)	[aw'tor]
writer	**escritor** (m)	[iskri'tor]
to write (~ a book)	**escrever** (vt)	[iskre'ver]
reader	**leitor** (m)	[lej'tor]
to read (vi, vt)	**ler** (vt)	[ler]

reading (activity)	leitura (f)	[lej'tura]
silently (to oneself)	para si	['para si]
aloud (adv)	em voz alta	[ẽ vɔz 'awta]

to publish (vt)	publicar (vt)	[publi'kar]
publishing (process)	publicação (f)	[publika'sãw]
publisher	editor (m)	[edʒi'tor]
publishing house	editora (f)	[edʒi'tora]

to come out (be released)	sair (vi)	[sa'ir]
release (of a book)	lançamento (m)	[lãsa'mẽtu]
print run	tiragem (f)	[tʃi'raʒẽ]

bookstore	livraria (f)	[livra'ria]
library	biblioteca (f)	[bibljo'tɛka]

story (novella)	novela (f)	[no'vɛla]
short story	conto (m)	['kõtu]
novel	romance (m)	[ho'mãsi]
detective novel	romance (m) policial	[ho'mãsi poli'sjaw]

memoirs	memórias (f pl)	[me'mɔrias]
legend	lenda (f)	['lẽda]
myth	mito (m)	['mitu]

poetry, poems	poesia (f)	[poe'zia]
autobiography	autobiografia (f)	[awtobjogra'fia]
selected works	obras (f pl) escolhidas	['ɔbraʃ isko'ʎidas]
science fiction	ficção (f) científica	[fik'sãw sjẽ'tʃifika]

title	título (m)	['tʃitulu]
introduction	introdução (f)	[ĩtrodu'sãw]
title page	folha (f) de rosto	['foʎa de 'hostu]

chapter	capítulo (m)	[ka'pitulu]
extract	excerto (m)	[e'sɛrtu]
episode	episódio (m)	[epi'zɔdʒu]

plot (storyline)	enredo (m)	[ẽ'hedu]
contents	conteúdo (m)	[kõte'udu]
table of contents	índice (m)	['indʒisi]
main character	protagonista (m)	[protago'nista]

volume	volume (m)	[vo'lumi]
cover	capa (f)	['kapa]
binding	encadernação (f)	[ẽkaderna'sãw]
bookmark	marcador (m) de página	[marka'dor de 'paʒina]
page	página (f)	['paʒina]
to page through	folhear (vt)	[fo'ʎjar]
margins	margem (f)	['marʒẽ]
annotation	anotação (f)	[anota'sãw]
(marginal note, etc.)		

footnote	nota (f) de rodapé	['nota də hoda'pɛ]
text	texto (m)	['testu]
type, font	forte (f)	['fõtʃi]
misprint, typo	falha (f) de impressão	['faʎa də impre'sãw]

translation	tradução (f)	[tradu'sãw]
to translate (vt)	traduzir (vt)	[tradu'zir]
original (n)	original (m)	[oriʒi'naw]

famous (adj)	famoso	[fa'mozu]
unknown (not famous)	desconhecido	[dʒiskoɲe'sidu]
interesting (adj)	interessante	[ĩtere'sãtʃi]
bestseller	best-seller (m)	[bɛst'sɛler]

dictionary	dicionário (m)	[dʒisjo'narju]
textbook	livro (m) didático	['livru dʒ 'datʃiku]
encyclopedia	enciclopédia (f)	[ẽsiklo'pɛdʒja]

133. Hunting. Fishing

hunting	caça (f)	['kasa]
to hunt (vi, vt)	caçar (vi)	[ka'sar]
hunter	caçador (m)	[kasa'dor]

to shoot (vi)	disparar, atirar (vi)	[dʒispa'rar], [atʃi'rar]
rifle	rifle (m)	['hifli]
bullet (shell)	cartucho (m)	[kar'tuʃu]
shot (lead balls)	chumbo (m) de caça	['ʃũbu de 'kasa]

steel trap	armadilha (f)	arma'dʒiʎa]
snare (for birds, etc.)	armadilha (f)	arma'dʒiʎa]
to fall into the steel trap	cair na armadilha	[ka'ir na arma'dʒiʎa]
to lay a steel trap	pôr a armadilha	['por a arma'dʒiʎa]

poacher	caçador (m) furtivo	[kasa'dor fur'tʃivu]
game (in hunting)	caça (f)	['kasa]
hound dog	cão (m) de caça	['kãw de 'kasa]
safari	safári (m)	[sa'fari]
mounted animal	animal (m) empalhado	[ani'maw ẽpa'ʎadu]

fisherman, angler	pescador (m)	[peska'dor]
fishing (angling)	pesca (f)	['pɛska]
to fish (vi)	pescar (vt)	[pes'kar]

fishing rod	vara (f) de pesca	['vara de 'ɔɛska]
fishing line	linha (f) de pesca	['liɲa de 'pɛska]
hook	anzol (m)	[ã'zɔw]
float, bobber	boia (f), flutuador (m)	['bɔja], [flutwa'dor]
bait	isca (f)	['iska]
to cast a line	lançar a linha	[lã'sar a 'liɲa]

to bite (ab. fish)	**morder** (vt)	[mor'der]
catch (of fish)	**pesca** (f)	['pɛska]
ice-hole	**buraco** (m) **no gelo**	[bu'raku nu 'ʒelu]

fishing net	**rede** (f)	['hedʒi]
boat	**barco** (m)	['barku]
to net (to fish with a net)	**pescar com rede**	[pes'kar kõ 'hedʒi]
to cast[throw] the net	**lançar a rede**	[lã'sar a 'hedʒi]
to haul the net in	**puxar a rede**	[pu'ʃar a 'hedʒi]
to fall into the net	**cair na rede**	[ka'ir na 'hedʒi]

whaler (person)	**baleeiro** (m)	[bale'ejro]
whaleboat	**baleeira** (f)	[bale'ejra]
harpoon	**arpão** (m)	[ar'pãw]

134. Games. Billiards

billiards	**bilhar** (m)	[bi'ʎar]
billiard room, hall	**sala** (f) **de bilhar**	['sala de bi'ʎar]
ball (snooker, etc.)	**bola** (f) **de bilhar**	['bɔla de bi'ʎar]

to pocket a ball	**embolsar uma bola**	[ẽbow'sar 'uma 'bɔla]
cue	**taco** (m)	['taku]
pocket	**caçapa** (f)	[ka'sapa]

135. Games. Playing cards

diamonds	**ouros** (m pl)	['orus]
spades	**espadas** (f pl)	[is'padas]
hearts	**copas** (f pl)	['kɔpas]
clubs	**paus** (m pl)	['paws]

ace	**ás** (m)	[ajs]
king	**rei** (m)	[hej]
queen	**dama** (f), **rainha** (f)	['dama], [ha'iɲa]
jack, knave	**valete** (m)	[va'lɛtʃi]

playing card	**carta** (f) **de jogar**	['karta de ʒo'gar]
cards	**cartas** (f pl)	['kartas]

trump	**trunfo** (m)	['trũfu]
deck of cards	**baralho** (m)	[ba'raʎu]

point	**ponto** (m)	['põtu]
to deal (vi, vt)	**dar, distribuir** (vt)	[dar], [dʒistri'bwir]
to shuffle (cards)	**embaralhar** (vt)	[ẽbara'ʎar]
lead, turn (n)	**vez, jogada** (f)	[vez], [ʒo'gada]
cardsharp	**trapaceiro** (m)	[trapa'sejru]

136. Rest. Games. Miscellaneous

to stroll (vi, vt)	passear (vi)	[pa'sjar]
stroll (leisurely walk)	passeio (m)	[pa'seju]
car ride	viagem (f) de carro	['vjaʒẽ de 'kaho]
adventure	aventura (f)	[avẽ'tura]
picnic	piquenique (m)	[piki'niki]
game (chess, etc.)	jogo (m)	['ʒogu]
player	jogador (m)	[ʒoga'dor]
game (one ~ of chess)	partida (f)	[par'tʃida]
collector (e.g., philatelist)	colecionador (m)	[kolesjona'dor]
to collect (stamps, etc.)	colecionar (vt)	[kolesjo'nar]
collection	coleção (f)	[kole'sãw]
crossword puzzle	palavras (f pl) cruzadas	[pa'lavras kru'zadas]
racetrack	hipódromo (m)	[i'pɔdromu]
(horse racing venue)		
disco (discotheque)	discoteca (f)	[dʒisko'tɛka]
sauna	sauna (f)	['sawna]
lottery	loteria (f)	[lote'ria]
camping trip	campismo (m)	[kã'pizmu]
camp	acampamento (m)	[akãpa'mẽtu]
tent (for camping)	barraca (f)	[ba'haka]
compass	bússola (f)	['busola]
camper	campista (m)	[kã'pista]
to watch (movie, etc.)	ver (vt), assistir à ...	[ver], [asis'tʃir a]
viewer	telespectador (m)	[telespekta'dor]
TV show (TV program)	programa (m) de TV	[pro'grama de te've]

137. Photography

camera (photo)	máquina (f) fotográfica	['makina foto'grafika]
photo, picture	foto, fotografia (f)	['fɔtu], [fotogra'fia]
photographer	fotógrafo (m)	[fo'tɔgrafu]
photo studio	estúdio (m) fotográfico	[is'tudʒu foto'grafiku]
photo album	álbum (m) de fotografias	['awbũ de fotogra'fias]
camera lens	lente (f) fotográfica	['lẽtʃi foto'grafika]
telephoto lens	lente (f) teleobjetiva	['lẽtʃi teleobʒe'tʃiva]
filter	filtro (m)	['fiwtru]
lens	lente (f)	['lẽtʃi]
optics (high-quality ~)	ótica (f)	['ɔtʃika]
diaphragm (aperture)	abertura (f)	[aber'tura]

| exposure time (shutter speed) | exposição (f) | [ispozi'sãw] |
| viewfinder | visor (m) | [vi'zor] |

digital camera	câmera (f) digital	['kamera ʤiʒi'taw]
tripod	tripé (m)	[tri'pɛ]
flash	flash (m)	[flaʃ]

to photograph (vt)	fotografar (vt)	[fotogra'far]
to take pictures	tirar fotos	[tʃi'rar 'fɔtus]
to have one's picture taken	fotografar-se (vr)	[fotogra'farse]

focus	foco (m)	['fɔku]
to focus	focar (vt)	[fo'kar]
sharp, in focus (adj)	nítido	['nitʃidu]
sharpness	nitidez (f)	[nitʃi'dez]

| contrast | contraste (m) | [kõ'trastʃi] |
| contrast (as adj) | contrastante | [kõtras'tãtʃi] |

picture (photo)	retrato (m)	[he'tratu]
negative (n)	negativo (m)	[nega'tʃivu]
film (a roll of ~)	filme (m)	['fiwmi]
frame (still)	fotograma (m)	[foto'grama]
to print (photos)	imprimir (vt)	[ĩpri'mir]

138. Beach. Swimming

beach	praia (f)	['praja]
sand	areia (f)	[a'reja]
deserted (beach)	deserto	[de'zɛrtu]

suntan	bronzeado (m)	[brõ'zjadu]
to get a tan	bronzear-se (vr)	[brõ'zjarsi]
tan (adj)	bronzeado	[brõ'zjadu]
sunscreen	protetor (m) solar	[prute'tor so'lar]

bikini	biquíni (m)	[bi'kini]
bathing suit	maiô (m)	[ma'jo]
swim trunks	calção (m) de banho	[kaw'sãw de 'baɲu]

swimming pool	piscina (f)	[pi'sina]
to swim (vi)	nadar (vi)	[na'dar]
shower	chuveiro (m), ducha (f)	[ʃu'vejru], ['duʃa]
to change (one's clothes)	mudar, trocar (vt)	[mu'dar], [tro'kar]
towel	toalha (f)	[to'aʎa]

boat	barco (m)	['barku]
motorboat	lancha (f)	['lãʃa]
water ski	esqui (m) aquático	[is'ki a'kwatʃiku]

paddle boat	barco (m) de pedais	['barku de pe'dajs]
surfing	surfe (m)	['surfi]
surfer	surfista (m)	[sur'fista]

scuba set	equipamento (m) de mergulho	[ekipa'mẽtu de mer'guʎu]
flippers (swim fins)	pé (m pl) de pato	[pɛ de 'patu]
mask (diving ~)	máscara (f)	['maskara]
diver	mergulhador (m)	[merguʎa'dor]
to dive (vi)	mergulhar (vi)	[mergu'ʎar]
underwater (adv)	debaixo d'água	[de'baɪʃu 'dagwa]

beach umbrella	guarda-sol (m)	['gwarda 'sɔw]
sunbed (lounger)	espreguiçadeira (f)	[ispregisa'dejra]
sunglasses	óculos (m pl) de sol	['ɔkulus de 'sɔw]
air mattress	colchão (m) de ar	[kow'ʃãw de 'ar]

| to play (amuse oneself) | brincar (vi) | [brĩ'kar] |
| to go for a swim | ir nadar | [ir na'dar] |

beach ball	bola (f) de praia	['bɔla de 'praja]
to inflate (vt)	encher (vt)	[ẽ'ʃer]
inflatable, air (adj)	inflável	[ĩ'flavew]

wave	onda (f)	['õda]
buoy (line of ~s)	boia (f)	['bɔja]
to drown (ab. person)	afogar-se (vr)	[afo'garse]

to save, to rescue	salvar (vt)	[saw'var]
life vest	colete (m) salva-vidas	[ko'letʃi 'sawva 'vidas]
to observe, to watch	observar (vt)	[obser'var]
lifeguard	salva-vidas (m)	[sawva-'vidas]

TECHNICAL EQUIPMENT. TRANSPORTATION

Technical equipment

139. Computer

computer	computador (m)	[kõputaˈdor]
notebook, laptop	computador (m) portátil	[kõputaˈdɔr porˈtatʃiw]
to turn on	ligar (vt)	[liˈgar]
to turn off	desligar (vt)	[dʒizliˈgar]
keyboard	teclado (m)	[tɛkˈladu]
key	tecla (f)	[ˈtɛkla]
mouse	mouse (m)	[ˈmawz]
mouse pad	tapete (m) para mouse	[taˈpetʃi ˈpara ˈmawz]
button	botão (m)	[boˈtãw]
cursor	cursor (m)	[kurˈsor]
monitor	monitor (m)	[moniˈtor]
screen	tela (f)	[ˈtɛla]
hard disk	disco (m) rígido	[ˈdʒisku ˈhiʒidu]
hard disk capacity	capacidade (f) do disco rígido	[kapasiˈdadʒi du ˈdʒisku ˈhiʒidu]
memory	memória (f)	[meˈmɔrja]
random access memory	memória RAM (f)	[meˈmɔrja ram]
file	arquivo (m)	[arˈkivu]
folder	pasta (f)	[ˈpasta]
to open (vt)	abrir (vt)	[aˈbrir]
to close (vt)	fechar (vt)	[feˈʃar]
to save (vt)	salvar (vt)	[sawˈvar]
to delete (vt)	deletar (vt)	[deleˈtar]
to copy (vt)	copiar (vt)	[koˈpjar]
to sort (vt)	ordenar (vt)	[ordeˈnar]
to transfer (copy)	copiar (vt)	[koˈpjar]
program	programa (m)	[proˈgrama]
software	software (m)	[sofˈtwer]
programmer	programador (m)	[programaˈdor]
to program (vt)	programar (vt)	[prograˈmar]
hacker	hacker (m)	[ˈhaker]

password	senha (f)	['sɛɲa]
virus	vírus (m)	['virus]
to find, to detect	detectar (vt)	[detek'tar]

| byte | byte (m) | ['bajtʃi] |
| megabyte | megabyte (m) | [mega'bajtʃi] |

| data | dados (m pl) | ['dadus] |
| database | base (f) de dados | ['bazi de 'dadus] |

cable (USB, etc.)	cabo (m)	['kabu]
to disconnect (vt)	desconectar (vt)	[dezkonek'tar]
to connect (sth to sth)	conectar (vt)	[konek'tar]

140. Internet. E-mail

Internet	internet (f)	[iter'nɛtʃi]
browser	browser (m)	['brawzer]
search engine	motor (m) de busca	[mo'tor ce 'buska]
provider	provedor (m)	[prove'dor]

webmaster	webmaster (m)	[web'master]
website	website (m)	[websajt]
webpage	página web (f)	['paʒina webi]

| address (e-mail ~) | endereço (m) | [ede'resu] |
| address book | livro (m) de endereços | ['livru de ede'resus] |

mailbox	caixa (f) de correio	['kaɪʃa de ko'heju]
mail	correio (m)	[ko'heju]
full (adj)	cheia	['ʃeja]

| message | mensagem (f) | [mē'saʒē] |
| incoming messages | mensagens (f pl) recebidas | [mē'saʒēs hese'bidas] |

outgoing messages	mensagens (f pl) enviadas	[mē'saʒēs ē'vjadas]
sender	remetente (m)	[heme'tētʃi]
to send (vt)	enviar (vt)	[ē'vjar]
sending (of mail)	envio (m)	[ē'viu]

| receiver | destinatário (m) | [destʃina'tarju] |
| to receive (vt) | receber (vt) | [hese'ber] |

| correspondence | correspondência (f) | [kohespő'dēsja] |
| to correspond (vi) | corresponder-se (vr) | [kohespő'dersi] |

file	arquivo (m)	[ar'kivu]
to download (vt)	fazer o download, baixar (vt)	[fa'zer u dawn'load], [baj'ʃar]
to create (vt)	criar (vt)	[krjar]

| to delete (vt) | deletar (vt) | [dele'tar] |
| deleted (adj) | deletado | [dele'tadu] |

connection (ADSL, etc.)	conexão (f)	[konek'sãw]
speed	velocidade (f)	[velosi'dadʒi]
modem	modem (m)	['modẽ]
access	acesso (m)	[a'sɛsu]
port (e.g., input ~)	porta (f)	['pɔrta]

| connection (make a ~) | conexão (f) | [konek'sãw] |
| to connect to ... (vi) | conectar (vi) | [konek'tar] |

| to select (vt) | escolher (vt) | [isko'ʎer] |
| to search (for ...) | buscar (vt) | [bus'kar] |

Transportation

141. Airplane

airplane	**avião** (m)	[a'vjãw]
air ticket	**passagem** (f) **aérea**	[pa'saʒẽ a'erja]
airline	**companhia** (f) **aérea**	[kõpa'ɲa a'erja]
airport	**aeroporto** (m)	[aero'portu]
supersonic (adj)	**supersônico**	[super'soniku]
captain	**comandante** (m) **do avião**	[komã'cãtʃi du a'vjãw]
crew	**tripulação** (f)	[tripula'sãw]
pilot	**piloto** (m)	[pi'lotu]
flight attendant (fem.)	**aeromoça** (f)	[aero'mosa]
navigator	**copiloto** (m)	[kopi'lotu]
wings	**asas** (f pl)	['azas]
tail	**cauda** (f)	['kawda]
cockpit	**cabine** (f)	[ka'bini]
engine	**motor** (m)	[mo'tor]
undercarriage (landing gear)	**trem** (m) **de pouso**	[trẽj de 'pozu]
turbine	**turbina** (f)	[tur'bina]
propeller	**hélice** (f)	['ɛlisi]
black box	**caixa-preta** (f)	['kaɪʃa 'preta]
yoke (control column)	**coluna** (f) **de controle**	[ko'luna de kõ'troli]
fuel	**combustível** (m)	[kõbus'tʃivew]
safety card	**instruções** (f pl) **de segurança**	[ĩstru'sõjs de segu'rãsa]
oxygen mask	**máscara** (f) **de oxigênio**	['maskara de oksi'ʒenju]
uniform	**uniforme** (m)	[uni'formi]
life vest	**colete** (m) **salva-vidas**	[ko'letʃi 'sawva 'vidas]
parachute	**paraquedas** (m)	[para'kɛdas]
takeoff	**decolagem** (f)	[deko'laʒẽ]
to take off (vi)	**descolar** (vi)	[dʒisko'lar]
runway	**pista** (f) **de decolagem**	['pista de deko'laʒẽ]
visibility	**visibilidade** (f)	[vizibili'dadʒi]
flight (act of flying)	**voo** (m)	['vou]
altitude	**altura** (f)	[aw'turɛ]
air pocket	**poço** (m) **de ar**	['posu ce 'ar]
seat	**assento** (m)	[a'sẽtu]
headphones	**fone** (m) **de ouvido**	['fɔni de o'vidu]

folding tray (tray table)	mesa (f) retrátil	['meza he'tratʃiw]
airplane window	janela (f)	[ʒa'nɛla]
aisle	corredor (m)	[kohe'dor]

142. Train

train	trem (m)	[trẽj]
commuter train	trem (m) elétrico	[trẽj e'lɛtriku]
express train	trem (m)	[trẽj]
diesel locomotive	locomotiva (f) diesel	[lokomo'tʃiva 'dʒizew]
steam locomotive	locomotiva (f) a vapor	[lokomo'tʃiva a va'por]

| passenger car | vagão (f) de passageiros | [va'gãw de pasa'ʒejrus] |
| dining car | vagão-restaurante (m) | [va'gãw-hestaw'rãtʃi] |

rails	carris (m pl)	[ka'his]
railroad	estrada (f) de ferro	[is'trada de 'fɛhu]
railway tie	travessa (f)	[tra'vɛsa]

platform (railway ~)	plataforma (f)	[plata'fɔrma]
track (~ 1, 2, etc.)	linha (f)	['liɲa]
semaphore	semáforo (m)	[se'maforu]
station	estação (f)	[ista'sãw]

engineer (train driver)	maquinista (m)	[maki'nista]
porter (of luggage)	bagageiro (m)	[baga'ʒejru]
car attendant	hospedeiro, -a (m, f)	[ospe'dejru, -a]
passenger	passageiro (m)	[pasa'ʒejru]
conductor (ticket inspector)	revisor (m)	[hevi'zor]

| corridor (in train) | corredor (m) | [kohe'dor] |
| emergency brake | freio (m) de emergência | ['freju de imer'ʒẽsja] |

compartment	compartimento (m)	[kõpartʃi'mẽtu]
berth	cama (f)	['kama]
upper berth	cama (f) de cima	['kama de 'sima]
lower berth	cama (f) de baixo	['kama de 'baɪʃu]
bed linen, bedding	roupa (f) de cama	['hopa de 'kama]

ticket	passagem (f)	[pa'saʒẽ]
schedule	horário (m)	[o'rarju]
information display	painel (m) de informação	[paj'nɛw de ĩforma'sãw]

to leave, to depart	partir (vt)	[par'tʃir]
departure (of train)	partida (f)	[par'tʃida]
to arrive (ab. train)	chegar (vi)	[ʃe'gar]
arrival	chegada (f)	[ʃe'gada]
to arrive by train	chegar de trem	[ʃe'gar de trẽj]
to get on the train	pegar o trem	[pe'gar u trẽj]

to get off the train	des:er de trem	[de'ser de trẽj]
train wreck	acicente (m) ferroviário	[asi'dẽtʃi feho'vjarju]
to derail (vi)	des:arrilar (vi)	[dʒiskahi'ʎar]
steam locomotive	locomotiva (f) a vapor	[lokomo'tʃiva a va'por]
stoker, fireman	fogu sta (m)	[fo'gista]
firebox	fornalha (f)	[for'naʎa]
coal	carvão (m)	[kar'vãw̃]

143. Ship

ship	navio (m)	[na'viu]
vessel	embarcação (f)	[ẽbarka'sãw̃]
steamship	barco (m) a vapor	['barku a va'por]
riverboat	barco (m) fluvial	['barku flu'vjaw]
cruise ship	transatlântico (m)	[trãzat'lãtʃiku]
cruiser	cruzeiro (m)	[kru'zejru]
yacht	iate (m)	['jatʃi]
tugboat	rebocador (m)	[heboka'dor]
barge	barcaça (f)	[bar'kasa]
ferry	ferry (m), balsa (f)	['fɛʀi], ['balsa]
sailing ship	veleiro (m)	[ve'lejru]
brigantine	bergantim (m)	[behgã'tʃ]
ice breaker	quebra-gelo (m)	['kɛbra 'ʒelu]
submarine	submarino (m)	[subma'rinu]
boat (flat-bottomed ~)	bote, barco (m)	['botʃi], ['barku]
dinghy (lifeboat)	baleeira (f)	[bale'ejrɛ]
lifeboat	bote (m) salva-vidas	['botʃi 'savva 'vidas]
motorboat	lancha (f)	['lãʃa]
captain	capitão (m)	[kapi'tãw̃]
seaman	marinheiro (m)	[mari'ɲejru]
sailor	marujo (m)	[ma'ruʒu]
crew	tripulação (f)	[tripula'sãw̃]
boatswain	contramestre (m)	[kõtra'mɛstri]
ship's boy	grumete (m)	[gru'mɛtʃi]
cook	cozinheiro (m) de bordo	[kozi'ɲejru de 'bordu]
ship's doctor	médico (m) de bordo	['mɛdʒiku de 'bordu]
deck	convés (m)	[kõ'vɛs]
mast	mastro (m)	['mastru]
sail	vela (f)	['vɛla]
hold	porão (m)	[po'rãw̃]
bow (prow)	proa (f)	['proa]

stern	popa (f)	['popa]
oar	remo (m)	['hɛmu]
screw propeller	hélice (f)	['ɛlisi]

cabin	cabine (m)	[ka'bini]
wardroom	sala (f) dos oficiais	['sala dus ofi'sjajs]
engine room	sala (f) das máquinas	['sala das 'makinas]
bridge	ponte (m) de comando	['põtʃi de ko'mãdu]
radio room	sala (f) de comunicações	['sala de komunika'sõjs]

| wave (radio) | onda (f) | ['õda] |
| logbook | diário (m) de bordo | ['dʒjarju de 'bordu] |

spyglass	luneta (f)	[lu'neta]
bell	sino (m)	['sinu]
flag	bandeira (f)	[bã'dejra]

| hawser (mooring ~) | cabo (m) | ['kabu] |
| knot (bowline, etc.) | nó (m) | [nɔ] |

| deckrails | corrimão (m) | [kohi'mãw] |
| gangway | prancha (f) de embarque | ['prãʃa de ẽ'barki] |

| anchor | âncora (f) | ['ãkora] |
| to weigh anchor | recolher a âncora | [heko'ʎer a 'ãkora] |

| to drop anchor | jogar a âncora | [ʒo'gar a 'ãkora] |
| anchor chain | amarra (f) | [a'maha] |

| port (harbor) | porto (m) | ['portu] |
| quay, wharf | cais, amarradouro (m) | [kajs], [amaha'doru] |

| to berth (moor) | atracar (vi) | [atra'kar] |
| to cast off | desatracar (vi) | [dʒizatra'kar] |

| trip, voyage | viagem (f) | ['vjaʒẽ] |
| cruise (sea trip) | cruzeiro (m) | [kru'zejru] |

| course (route) | rumo (m) | ['humu] |
| route (itinerary) | itinerário (m) | [itʃine'rarju] |

fairway	canal (m) de navegação	[ka'naw de navega'sãw]
(safe water channel)		
shallows	banco (m) de areia	['bãku de a'reja]
to run aground	encalhar (vt)	[ẽka'ʎar]

storm	tempestade (f)	[tẽpes'tadʒi]
signal	sinal (m)	[si'naw]
to sink (vi)	afundar-se (vr)	[afũ'darse]
Man overboard!	Homem ao mar!	['ɔmẽ aw mah]
SOS (distress signal)	SOS	[ɛseo'ɛsi]
ring buoy	boia (f) salva-vidas	['bɔja 'sawva 'vidas]

144. Airport

airport	aeroporto (m)	[aero'pɔrtu]
airplane	avião (m)	[a'vjãw]
airline	companhia (f) aérea	[kõpa'ɾia a'erja]
air traffic controller	controlador (m) de tráfego aéreo	[kõtrola'dor de 'trafəgu a'erju]
departure	partida (f)	[par'tʃica]
arrival	chegada (f)	[ʃe'gada]
to arrive (by plane)	chegar (vi)	[ʃe'gar]
departure time	hora (f) de partida	['ɔra de par'tʃida]
arrival time	hora (f) de chegada	['ɔra de ʃe'gada]
to be delayed	estar atrasado	[is'tar atra'zadu]
flight delay	atraso (m) de voo	[a'trazu de 'vou]
information board	painel (m) de informação	[paj'nɛw de ĩforma'sãw]
information	informação (f)	[ĩformɐ'sãw]
to announce (vt)	anunciar (vt)	[anũ'sjar]
flight (e.g., next ~)	voo (m)	['vou]
customs	alfândega (f)	[aw'fãdʒiga]
customs officer	funcionário (m) da alfândega	[fũsjo'narju da aw'fãdʒiga]
customs declaration	declaração (f) alfandegária	[deklara'sãw awfãde'garja]
to fill out (vt)	preencher (vt)	[preẽ'ʃər]
to fill out the declaration	preencher a declaração	[preẽ'ʃər a deklara'sãw]
passport control	controle (m) de passaporte	[kõ'tro i de pasa'pɔrtʃi]
luggage	bagagem (f)	[ba'gaʒẽ]
hand luggage	bagagem (f) de mão	[ba'gaʒẽ de 'mãw]
luggage cart	carrinho (m)	[ka'hiɾu]
landing	pouso (m)	['pozu]
landing strip	pista (f) de pouso	['pista de 'pozu]
to land (vi)	aterrissar (vi)	[atehi'sar]
airstair (passenger stair)	escada (f) de avião	[is'kaca de a'vjãw]
check-in	check-in (m)	[ʃɛ'kin]
check-in counter	balcão (m) do check-in	[baw'kãw du ʃɛ'kin]
to check-in (vi)	fazer o check-in	[fa'zer u ʃɛ'kin]
boarding pass	cartão (m) de embarque	[kar'tãw de ẽ'barki]
departure gate	portão (m) de embarque	[por'tãw de ẽ'barki]
transit	trânsito (m)	['trãzitu]
to wait (vt)	esperar (vt)	[ispe'rar]

departure lounge	sala (f) de espera	['sala de is'pɛra]
to see off	despedir-se de ...	[dʒispe'dʒirsi de]
to say goodbye	despedir-se (vr)	[dʒispe'dʒirsi]

145. Bicycle. Motorcycle

bicycle	bicicleta (f)	[bisi'klɛta]
scooter	lambreta (f)	[lã'breta]
motorcycle, bike	moto (f)	['mɔtu]

to go by bicycle	ir de bicicleta	[ir de bisi'klɛta]
handlebars	guidão (m)	[gi'dãw]
pedal	pedal (m)	[pe'daw]
brakes	freios (m pl)	['frejus]
bicycle seat (saddle)	banco, selim (m)	['bãku], [se'lĩ]

pump	bomba (f)	['bõba]
luggage rack	bagageiro (m) de teto	[baga'ʒejru de tɛtu]
front lamp	lanterna (f)	[lã'tɛrna]
helmet	capacete (m)	[kapa'setʃi]

wheel	roda (f)	['hɔda]
fender	para-choque (m)	[para'ʃɔki]
rim	aro (m)	['aru]
spoke	raio (m)	['haju]

Cars

146. Types of cars

automobile, car	carro, automóvel (m)	['kaho], [awto'mɔvew]
sports car	carro (m) esportivo	['kaho ispor'tʃivu]
limousine	limusine (f)	[limu'zini]
off-road vehicle	todo o terreno (m)	['todu u te'hɛnu]
convertible (n)	conversível (m)	[kõver'sivew]
minibus	minibus (m)	['minibus]
ambulance	ambulância (f)	[ãbu'lãsja]
snowplow	limpa-neve (m)	['lĩpa 'nɛvi]
truck	caminhão (m)	[kami'ɲãw]
tanker truck	caminhão-tanque (m)	[kami'ɲãw-'tãki]
van (small truck)	perua, van (f)	[pe'rua], [van]
road tractor (trailer truck)	caminhão-trator (m)	[kami'ɲãw-tra'tor]
trailer	reboque (m)	[he'bɔki]
comfortable (adj)	confortável	[kõfor'tavew]
used (adj)	usado	[u'zadʊ]

147. Cars. Bodywork

hood	capô (m)	[ka'po]
fender	para-choque (m)	[para'ʃɔki]
roof	teto (m)	['tɛtu]
windshield	para-brisa (m)	[para'briza]
rear-view mirror	retrovisor (m)	[hetrovi'zor]
windshield washer	esguicho (m)	[iʃ'giʃu]
windshield wipers	limpadores (m) de para-brisas	[lĩpa'dores de para'brizas]
side window	vidro (m) lateral	['vidru late'raw]
window lift (power window)	elevador (m) do vidro	[eleva'dor du 'vidru]
antenna	antena (f)	[ã'tɛna]
sunroof	teto (m) solar	['tɛtu sɔ'lar]
bumper	para-choque (m)	[para'ʃɔki]
trunk	porta-malas (f)	[pɔrta-'malas]
roof luggage rack	bagageira (f)	[baga'ʒejra]

door	**porta** (f)	['pɔrta]
door handle	**maçaneta** (f)	[masa'neta]
door lock	**fechadura** (f)	[feʃa'dura]

license plate	**placa** (f)	['plaka]
muffler	**silenciador** (m)	[silẽsja'dor]
gas tank	**tanque** (m) **de gasolina**	['tãki de gazo'lina]
tailpipe	**tubo** (m) **de exaustão**	['tubu de ezaw'stãw]

gas, accelerator	**acelerador** (m)	[aselera'dor]
pedal	**pedal** (m)	[pe'daw]
gas pedal	**pedal** (m) **do acelerador**	[pe'daw du aselera'dor]

brake	**freio** (m)	['freju]
brake pedal	**pedal** (m) **do freio**	[pe'daw du 'freju]
to brake (use the brake)	**frear** (vt)	[fre'ar]
parking brake	**freio** (m) **de mão**	['freju de mãw]

clutch	**embreagem** (f)	[ẽb'rjaʒẽ]
clutch pedal	**pedal** (m) **da embreagem**	[pe'daw da ẽb'rjaʒẽ]
clutch disc	**disco** (m) **de embreagem**	['dʒisku de ẽb'rjaʒẽ]
shock absorber	**amortecedor** (m)	[amortese'dor]

wheel	**roda** (f)	['hɔda]
spare tire	**pneu** (m) **estepe**	['pnew is'tɛpi]
tire	**pneu** (m)	['pnew]
hubcap	**calota** (f)	[ka'lɔta]

driving wheels	**rodas** (f pl) **motrizes**	['hɔdas muo'trizis]
front-wheel drive (as adj)	**de tração dianteira**	[de tra'sãw dʒjã'tejra]
rear-wheel drive (as adj)	**de tração traseira**	[de tra'sãw tra'zejra]
all-wheel drive (as adj)	**de tração às 4 rodas**	[de tra'sãw as 'kwatru 'hɔdas]

| gearbox | **caixa** (f) **de mudanças** | ['kaɪʃa de mu'dãsas] |
| automatic (adj) | **automático** | [awto'matʃiku] |

| mechanical (adj) | **mecânico** | [me'kaniku] |
| gear shift | **alavanca** (f) **de câmbio** | [ala'vãka de 'kãbju] |

| headlight | **farol** (m) | [fa'rɔw] |
| headlights | **faróis** (m pl) | [fa'rɔis] |

low beam	**farol** (m) **baixo**	[fa'rɔw 'baɪʃu]
high beam	**farol** (m) **alto**	[fa'rɔw 'altu]
brake light	**luzes** (f pl) **de parada**	['luzes de pa'rada]

parking lights	**luzes** (f pl) **de posição**	['luzes de pozi'sãw]
hazard lights	**luzes** (f pl) **de emergência**	['luzes de emer'ʒesia]
fog lights	**faróis** (m pl) **de neblina**	[fa'rɔis de ne'blina]
turn signal	**pisca-pisca** (m)	[piska-'piska]
back-up light	**luz** (f) **de marcha ré**	[luz de 'marʃa hɛ]

148. Cars. Passenger compartment

car inside (interior)	interior (m) do carro	[ĩte'rjor du 'kaho]
leather (as adj)	de couro	[de 'koru]
velour (as adj)	de veludo	[de ve'ludu]
upholstery	estofamento (m)	[istofa'mẽtu]
instrument (gage)	indicador (m)	[ĩdʒika'dor]
dashboard	painel (m)	[paj'nɛw]
speedometer	velocímetro (m)	[velo'simetru]
needle (pointer)	ponteiro (m)	[põ'tejru]
odometer	hocômetro, odômetro (m)	[o'dometru]
indicator (sensor)	indicador (m)	[ĩdʒika'dor]
level	nível (m)	['nivew]
warning light	luz (f) de aviso	[luz de a'vizu]
steering wheel	volante (m)	[vo'lãtʃi]
horn	buzina (f)	[bu'zina]
button	botão (m)	[bo'tãw]
switch	interruptor (m)	[ĩtehup'tor]
seat	assento (m)	[a'sẽtu]
backrest	costas (f pl) do assento	['kostas du a'sẽtu]
headrest	cabeceira (f)	[kabe'sejra]
seat belt	cinto (m) de segurança	['sĩtu de segu'rãsa]
to fasten the belt	apertar o cinto	[aper'tar u 'sĩtu]
adjustment (of seats)	ajuste (m)	[a'ʒustʃi]
airbag	airbag (m)	[ɛr'bɛgi]
air-conditioner	ar (m) condicionado	[ar kõdʒisjo'nadu]
radio	rádio (m)	['hadʒju]
CD player	leitor (m) de CD	[lej'tor de 'sede]
to turn on	ligar (vt)	[li'gar]
antenna	antena (f)	[ã'tɛna]
glove box	porta-luvas (m)	['porta-'uvas]
ashtray	cinzeiro (m)	[sĩ'zejru]

149. Cars. Engine

engine, motor	motor (m)	[mo'tor]
diesel (as adj)	a diesel	[a 'dʒizew]
gasoline (as adj)	a gasolina	[a gazo'lina]
engine volume	cilindrada (f)	[silĩ'drada]
power	potência (f)	[po'tẽsja]
horsepower	cavalo (m) de potência	[ka'valu de po'tẽsja]
piston	pistão (m)	[pis'tãw]

cylinder	cilindro (m)	[si'lĩdru]
valve	válvula (f)	['vawvula]

injector	injetor (m)	[ĩʒɛ'tor]
generator (alternator)	gerador (m)	[ʒera'dor]
carburetor	carburador (m)	[karbura'dor]
motor oil	óleo (m) de motor	['ɔlju de mo'tor]

radiator	radiador (m)	[hadʒja'dor]
coolant	líquido (m) de arrefecimento	['likidu de ahefesi'mẽtu]
cooling fan	ventilador (m)	[vẽtʃila'dor]

battery (accumulator)	bateria (f)	[bate'ria]
starter	dispositivo (m) de arranque	[dʒispozi'tʃivu de a'hãki]
ignition	ignição (f)	[igni'sãw]
spark plug	vela (f) de ignição	['vɛla de igni'sãw]

terminal (of battery)	terminal (m)	[termi'naw]
positive terminal	terminal (m) positivo	[termi'naw pozi'tʃivu]
negative terminal	terminal (m) negativo	[termi'naw nega'tʃivu]
fuse	fusível (m)	[fu'zivew]

air filter	filtro (m) de ar	['fiwtru de ar]
oil filter	filtro (m) de óleo	['fiwtru de 'ɔlju]
fuel filter	filtro (m) de combustível	['fiwtru de kõbus'tʃivew]

150. Cars. Crash. Repair

car crash	acidente (m) de carro	[asi'dẽtʃi de 'kaho]
traffic accident	acidente (m) rodoviário	[asi'dẽtʃi hodo'vjarju]
to crash (into the wall, etc.)	bater ...	[ba'ter]
to get smashed up	sofrer um acidente	[so'frer ũ asi'dẽtʃi]
damage	dano (m)	['danu]
intact (unscathed)	intato	[ĩ'tatu]

breakdown	pane (f)	['pani]
to break down (vi)	avariar (vi)	[ava'rjar]
towrope	cabo (m) de reboque	['kabu de he'bɔki]

puncture	furo (m)	['furu]
to be flat	estar furado	[is'tar fu'radu]
to pump up	encher (vt)	[ẽ'ʃer]
pressure	pressão (f)	[pre'sãw]
to check (to examine)	verificar (vt)	[verifi'kar]

repair	reparo (m)	[he'paru]
auto repair shop	oficina (f) automotiva	[ɔfi'sina awtɔmo'tʃiva]

spare part	peça (f) de reposição	['pɛsa de hepozi'sãw]
part	peça (f)	['pɛsa]
bolt (with nut)	parafuso (m)	[para'fuzu]
screw (fastener)	parafuso (m)	[para'fuzu]
nut	porca (f)	['porka]
washer	arruela (f)	[a'hwɛla]
bearing (e.g., ball ~)	rolamento (m)	[hola'mẽtu]
tube	tubo (m)	['tubu]
gasket (head ~)	junta, gaxeta (f)	['ʒũta], [ga'ʃɛta]
cable, wire	fio, cabo (m)	['fiu], ['kabu]
jack	macaco (m)	[ma'kaku]
wrench	chave de boca	['ʃavi de 'boka]
hammer	martelo (m)	[mar'tɛlu]
pump	bomba (f)	['bõba]
screwdriver	chave (f) de fenda	['ʃavi de 'fẽda]
fire extinguisher	extintor (m)	[istĩ'tor]
warning triangle	triângulo (m) de emergência	['trjãgulu de imer'ʒẽsja]
to stall (vi)	morrer (vi)	[mo'her]
stall (n)	paragem (f)	[pa'raʒẽ]
to be broken	estar quebrado	[is'tar ke'bradu]
to overheat (vi)	superaquecer-se (vr)	[superake'sersi]
to be clogged up	entupir-se (vr)	[ẽtu'pirsi]
to freeze up (pipes, etc.)	congelar-se (vr)	[kõʒe'larsi]
to burst (vi, ab. tube)	rebentar (vi)	[hebẽ'tar]
pressure	pressão (f)	[pre'sãw]
level	nível (m)	['nivew]
slack (~ belt)	frouxo	['froʃu]
dent	batida (f)	[ba'tʃida]
knocking noise (engine)	ruído (m)	['hwidu]
crack	fissura (f)	[fi'sura]
scratch	arranhão (m)	[aha'ɲãw]

151. Cars. Road

road	estrada (f)	[is'trada]
highway	autoestrada (f)	[awtois'trada]
freeway	rodovia (f)	[hodo'via]
direction (way)	direção (f)	[dʒire'sãw]
distance	distância (f)	[dʒis'tãsja]
bridge	ponte (f)	['põtʃi]
parking lot	parque (m) de estacionamento	['parki de istasjona'mẽtu]
square	praça (f)	['prasa]

| interchange | nó (m) rodoviário | [nɔ hodo'vjarju] |
| tunnel | túnel (m) | ['tunew] |

gas station	posto (m) de gasolina	['pɔstu de gazo'lina]
parking lot	parque (m) de estacionamento	['parki de istasjona'mẽtu]
gas pump (fuel dispenser)	bomba (f) de gasolina	['bõba de gazo'lina]
auto repair shop	oficina (f) automotiva	[ɔfi'sina awtɔmo'tʃiva]
to get gas (to fill up)	abastecer (vt)	[abaste'ser]
fuel	combustível (m)	[kõbus'tʃivew]
jerrycan	galão (m) de gasolina	[ga'lãw de gazo'lina]

asphalt	asfalto (m)	[as'fawtu]
road markings	marcação (f) de estradas	[marka'sãw de is'tradas]
curb	meio-fio (m)	['meju-'fiu]
guardrail	guard-rail (m)	[gward-'hejl]
ditch	valeta (f)	[va'leta]
roadside (shoulder)	acostamento (m)	[akosta'mẽtu]
lamppost	poste (m) de luz	['pɔstʃi de luz]

to drive (a car)	dirigir (vt)	[dʒiri'ʒir]
to turn (e.g., ~ left)	virar (vi)	[vi'rar]
to make a U-turn	dar retorno	[dar he'tornu]
reverse (~ gear)	ré (f)	[hɛ]

to honk (vi)	buzinar (vi)	[buzi'nar]
honk (sound)	buzina (f)	[bu'zina]
to get stuck (in the mud, etc.)	atolar-se (vr)	[ato'larsi]
to spin the wheels	patinar (vi)	[patʃi'nar]
to cut, to turn off (vt)	desligar (vt)	[dʒizli'gar]

speed	velocidade (f)	[velosi'dadʒi]
to exceed the speed limit	exceder a velocidade	[ese'der a velosi'dadʒi]
to give a ticket	multar (vt)	[muw'tar]
traffic lights	semáforo (m)	[se'maforu]
driver's license	carteira (f) de motorista	[kar'tejra de moto'rista]

grade crossing	passagem (f) de nível	[pa'saʒẽ de 'nivew]
intersection	cruzamento (m)	[kruza'mẽtu]
crosswalk	faixa (f)	['fajʃa]
bend, curve	curva (f)	['kurva]
pedestrian zone	zona (f) de pedestres	['zɔna de pe'dɛstris]

PEOPLE. LIFE EVENTS

Life events

152. Holidays. Event

celebration, holiday	festa (f)	['fɛsta]
national day	feriado (m) nacional	[fe'rjadu nasjo'naw]
public holiday	feriado (m)	[fe'rjadu]
to commemorate (vt)	festejar (vt)	[feste'ʒar]
event (happening)	evento (m)	[e'vẽtu]
event (organized activity)	evento (m)	[e'vẽtu]
banquet (party)	banquete (m)	[bã'ketʃi]
reception (formal party)	recepção (f)	[hesep'sãw]
feast	festim (m)	[fes'tʃĩ]
anniversary	aniversário (m)	[aniver'sarju]
jubilee	jubileu (m)	[ʒubi'lew]
to celebrate (vt)	celebrar (vt)	[sele'brar]
New Year	Ano (m) Novo	['anu 'novu]
Happy New Year!	Feliz Ano Novo!	[fe'liz 'anu 'novu]
Santa Claus	Papai Noel (m)	[pa'paj nɔ'ɛl]
Christmas	Natal (m)	[na'taw]
Merry Christmas!	Feliz Natal!	[fe'liz na'taw]
Christmas tree	árvore (f) de Natal	['arvor de na'taw]
fireworks (fireworks show)	fogos (m pl) de artifício	['fogus de artʃi'fisju]
wedding	casamento (m)	[kaza'mẽtu]
groom	novo (m)	['nojvu]
bride	nova (f)	['nojva]
to invite (vt)	convidar (vt)	[kõvi'dar]
invitation card	convite (m)	[kõ'vitʃi]
guest	convidado (m)	[kõvi'cadu]
to visit	visitar (vt)	[vizi'tar]
(~ your parents, etc.)		
to meet the guests	receber os convidados	[hese'ber us kõvi'dadus]
gift, present	presente (m)	[pre'zẽtʃi]
to give (sth as present)	oferecer, dar (vt)	[ofere ser], [dar]
to receive gifts	receber presentes	[hese'ber pre'zẽtʃis]

bouquet (of flowers)	buquê (m) de flores	[bu'ke de 'floris]
congratulations	felicitações (f pl)	[felisita'sõjs]
to congratulate (vt)	felicitar (vt)	[felisi'tar]

greeting card	cartão (m) de parabéns	[kar'tãw de para'bẽjs]
to send a postcard	enviar um cartão postal	[ẽ'vjar ũ kart'ãw pos'taw]
to get a postcard	receber um cartão postal	[hese'ber ũ kart'ãw pos'taw]

toast	brinde (m)	['brĩdʒi]
to offer (a drink, etc.)	oferecer (vt)	[ofere'ser]
champagne	champanhe (m)	[ʃã'paɲi]

to enjoy oneself	divertir-se (vr)	[dʒiver'tʃirsi]
merriment (gaiety)	diversão (f)	[dʒiver'sãw]
joy (emotion)	alegria (f)	[ale'gria]

| dance | dança (f) | ['dãsa] |
| to dance (vi, vt) | dançar (vi) | [dã'sar] |

| waltz | valsa (f) | ['vawsa] |
| tango | tango (m) | ['tãgu] |

153. Funerals. Burial

cemetery	cemitério (m)	[semi'tɛrju]
grave, tomb	sepultura (f), túmulo (m)	[sepuw'tura], ['tumulu]
cross	cruz (f)	[kruz]
gravestone	lápide (f)	['lapidʒi]
fence	cerca (f)	['serka]
chapel	capela (f)	[ka'pɛla]

death	morte (f)	['mortʃi]
to die (vi)	morrer (vi)	[mo'her]
the deceased	defunto (m)	[de'fũtu]
mourning	luto (m)	['lutu]

to bury (vt)	enterrar, sepultar (vt)	[ẽte'har], [sepuw'tar]
funeral home	casa (f) funerária	['kaza fune'raria]
funeral	funeral (m)	[fune'raw]

wreath	coroa (f) de flores	[ko'roa de 'floris]
casket, coffin	caixão (m)	[kaɪ'ʃãw]
hearse	carro (m) funerário	['kaho fune'rarju]
shroud	mortalha (f)	[mor'taʎa]
funeral procession	procissão (f) funerária	[prosi'sãw fune'rarja]
funerary urn	urna (f) funerária	['urna fune'rarja]
crematory	crematório (m)	[krema'tɔrju]
obituary	obituário (m), necrologia (f)	[obi'twarju], [nekrolo'ʒia]

to cry (weep)	**chorar** (vi)	[ʃo'rar]
to sob (vi)	**soluçar** (vi)	[solu'sar]

154. War. Soldiers

platoon	**pelotão** (m)	[pelo'tãw]
company	**companhia** (f)	[kõpa'ɲia]
regiment	**regimento** (m)	[heʒi'mẽtu]
army	**exército** (m)	[e'zɛrsitu]
division	**divisão** (f)	[dʒivi'zãw]
section, squad	**esquadrão** (m)	[iskwa'drãw]
host (army)	**hoste** (f)	['ɔste]
soldier	**soldado** (m)	[sow'dadu]
officer	**oficial** (m)	[ofi'sjaw]
private	**soldado** (m) **raso**	[sow'dadu 'hazu]
sergeant	**sargento** (m)	[sar'ʒẽtu]
lieutenant	**tenente** (m)	[te'nẽtʃi]
captain	**capitão** (m)	[kapi'tãw]
major	**major** (m)	[ma'ʒɔr]
colonel	**coronel** (m)	[koro'nɛw]
general	**general** (m)	[ʒene'raw]
sailor	**marujo** (m)	[ma'ruʒu]
captain	**capitão** (m)	[kapi'tãw]
boatswain	**contramestre** (m)	[kõtra'mɛstri]
artilleryman	**artilheiro** (m)	[artʃi'ʎejɾu]
paratrooper	**soldado** (m) **paraquedista**	[sow'dadu parake'dʒista]
pilot	**piloto** (m)	[pi'lotu]
navigator	**navegador** (m)	[navegɐ'dor]
mechanic	**mecânico** (m)	[me'kaniku]
pioneer (sapper)	**sapador-mineiro** (m)	[sapa'dor-mi'nejru]
parachutist	**paraquedista** (m)	[parake'dʒista]
reconnaissance scout	**explorador** (m)	[isplora'dor]
sniper	**atirador** (m) **de tocaia**	[atʃira'dor de to'kaja]
patrol (group)	**patrulha** (f)	[pa'truʎa]
to patrol (vt)	**patrulhar** (vt)	[patru'ʎar]
sentry, guard	**sentinela** (f)	[sẽtʃi'nɛla]
warrior	**guerreiro** (m)	[ge'hejɾu]
patriot	**patriota** (m)	[pa'trjɔta]
hero	**herói** (m)	[e'rɔj]
heroine	**heroína** (f)	[ero'ina]
traitor	**traidor** (m)	[traj'dor]
to betray (vt)	**trair** (vt)	[tra'ir]

| deserter | desertor (m) | [dezer'tor] |
| to desert (vi) | desertar (vt) | [deser'tar] |

mercenary	mercenário (m)	[merse'narju]
recruit	recruta (m)	[he'kruta]
volunteer	voluntário (m)	[volũ'tarju]

dead (n)	morto (m)	['mortu]
wounded (n)	ferido (m)	[fe'ridu]
prisoner of war	prisioneiro (m) de guerra	[prizjo'nejru de 'gɛha]

155. War. Military actions. Part 1

war	guerra (f)	['gɛha]
to be at war	guerrear (vt)	[ge'hjar]
civil war	guerra (f) civil	['gɛha si'viw]

treacherously (adv)	perfidamente	[perfida'mẽt∫i]
declaration of war	declaração (f) de guerra	[deklara'sãw de 'gɛha]
to declare (~ war)	declarar guerra	[dekla'rar 'gɛha]
aggression	agressão (f)	[agre'sãw]
to attack (invade)	atacar (vt)	[ata'kar]

to invade (vt)	invadir (vt)	[ĩva'dʒir]
invader	invasor (m)	[ĩva'zor]
conqueror	conquistador (m)	[kõkista'dor]

defense	defesa (f)	[de'feza]
to defend (a country, etc.)	defender (vt)	[defẽ'der]
to defend (against ...)	defender-se (vr)	[defẽ'dersi]

enemy	inimigo (m)	[ini'migu]
foe, adversary	adversário (m)	[adʒiver'sarju]
enemy (as adj)	inimigo	[ini'migu]

| strategy | estratégia (f) | [istra'tɛʒa] |
| tactics | tática (f) | ['tat∫ika] |

order	ordem (f)	['ordẽ]
command (order)	comando (m)	[ko'mãdu]
to order (vt)	ordenar (vt)	[orde'nar]
mission	missão (f)	[mi'sãw]
secret (adj)	secreto	[se'krɛtu]

| battle | batalha (f) | [ba'taʎa] |
| combat | combate (m) | [kõ'bat∫i] |

attack	ataque (m)	[a'taki]
charge (assault)	assalto (m)	[a'sawtu]
to storm (vt)	assaltar (vt)	[asaw'tar]

siege (to be under ~)	assédio, sítio (m)	[a'sɛdʒu], ['sitʃu]
offensive (n)	ofensiva (f)	[ɔfẽ'siva]
to go on the offensive	tomar à ofensiva	[to'mar a ofẽ'siva]
retreat	retirada (f)	[hetʃi'rada]
to retreat (vi)	retirar-se (vr)	[hetʃi'rarse]
encirclement	cerco (m)	['serku]
to encircle (vt)	cercar (vt)	[ser'kar]
bombing (by aircraft)	bombardeio (m)	[bõbar'deju]
to drop a bomb	lançar uma bomba	[lã'sar 'uma 'bõba]
to bomb (vt)	bombardear (vt)	[bõbar'dʒjar]
explosion	explosão (f)	[isplo'zãw]
shot	tiro (m)	['tʃiru]
to fire (~ a shot)	dar um tiro	[dar ũ 'tʃiru]
firing (burst of ~)	tiroteio (m)	[tʃiro'teju]
to aim (to point a weapon)	apontar para ...	[apõ'ta 'para]
to point (a gun)	apontar (vt)	[apõ'ta]
to hit (the target)	acertar (vt)	[aser'tar]
to sink (~ a ship)	afundar (vt)	[afũ'dar]
hole (in a ship)	brecha (f)	['brɛʃa]
to founder, to sink (vi)	afundar-se (vr)	[afũ'darse]
front (war ~)	frente (m)	['frẽtʃi]
evacuation	evacuação (f)	[evakwa'sãw]
to evacuate (vt)	evacuar (vt)	[eva'kwar]
trench	trincheira (f)	[trĩ'ʃejra]
barbwire	arame (m) enfarpado	[a'rami ẽfar'padu]
barrier (anti tank ~)	barreira (f) anti-tanque	[ba'hejra ãtʃi-'tãki]
watchtower	torre (f) de vigia	['tohi de vi'ʒia]
military hospital	hospital (m) militar	[ospi'taw mili'tar]
to wound (vt)	ferir (vt)	[fe'rir]
wound	ferida (f)	[fe'rida]
wounded (n)	ferido (m)	[fe'ridu]
to be wounded	ficar ferido	[fi'kar fe'ridu]
serious (wound)	grave	['gravi]

156. Weapons

weapons	arma (f)	['arma]
firearms	arma (f) de fogo	['arma de 'fogu]
cold weapons (knives, etc.)	arma (f) branca	['arma 'brãka]
chemical weapons	arma (f) química	['arma 'kimika]

nuclear (adj)	**nuclear**	[nu'kljar]
nuclear weapons	**arma** (f) **nuclear**	['arma nu'kljar]
bomb	**bomba** (f)	['bõba]
atomic bomb	**bomba** (f) **atômica**	['bõba a'tomika]
pistol (gun)	**pistola** (f)	[pis'tɔla]
rifle	**rifle** (m)	['hifli]
submachine gun	**semi-automática** (f)	[semi-awto'matʃika]
machine gun	**metralhadora** (f)	[metraʎa'dora]
muzzle	**boca** (f)	['boka]
barrel	**cano** (m)	['kanu]
caliber	**calibre** (m)	[ka'libri]
trigger	**gatilho** (m)	[ga'tʃiʎu]
sight (aiming device)	**mira** (f)	['mira]
magazine	**carregador** (m)	[kahega'dor]
butt (shoulder stock)	**coronha** (f)	[ko'rɔɲa]
hand grenade	**granada** (f) **de mão**	[gra'nada de mãw]
explosive	**explosivo** (m)	[isplo'zivu]
bullet	**bala** (f)	['bala]
cartridge	**cartucho** (m)	[kar'tuʃu]
charge	**carga** (f)	['karga]
ammunition	**munições** (f pl)	[muni'sõjs]
bomber (aircraft)	**bombardeiro** (m)	[bõbar'dejru]
fighter	**avião** (m) **de caça**	[a'vjãw de 'kasa]
helicopter	**helicóptero** (m)	[eli'kɔpteru]
anti-aircraft gun	**canhão** (m) **antiaéreo**	[ka'ɲãw ãtʃa'ɛrju]
tank	**tanque** (m)	['tãki]
tank gun	**canhão** (m)	[ka'ɲãw]
artillery	**artilharia** (f)	[artʃiʎa'ria]
gun (cannon, howitzer)	**canhão** (m)	[ka'ɲãw]
to lay (a gun)	**fazer a pontaria**	[fa'zer a põta'ria]
shell (projectile)	**projétil** (m)	[pro'ʒɛtʃiw]
mortar bomb	**granada** (f) **de morteiro**	[gra'nada de mor'tejru]
mortar	**morteiro** (m)	[mor'tejru]
splinter (shell fragment)	**estilhaço** (m)	[istʃi'ʎasu]
submarine	**submarino** (m)	[subma'rinu]
torpedo	**torpedo** (m)	[tor'pedu]
missile	**míssil** (m)	['misiw]
to load (gun)	**carregar** (vt)	[kahe'gar]
to shoot (vi)	**disparar, atirar** (vi)	[dʒispa'rar], [atʃi'rar]
to point at (the cannon)	**apontar para ...**	[apõ'tar 'para]

bayonet	baioneta (f)	[bajo'neta]
rapier	espada (f)	[is'pada]
saber (e.g., cavalry ~)	sabre (m)	['sabri]
spear (weapon)	lança (f)	['lãsa]
bow	arco (m)	['arku]
arrow	flecha (f)	['flɛʃa]
musket	mosquete (m)	[mos'ketʃi]
crossbow	besta (f)	['besta]

157. Ancient people

primitive (prehistoric)	primitivo	[primi'tʃivu]
prehistoric (adj)	pré-histórico	[prɛ-is'tɔriku]
ancient (~ civilization)	antigo	[ã'tʃigu]

Stone Age	Idade (f) da Pedra	[i'dadʒi da 'pɛdra]
Bronze Age	Idade (f) do Bronze	[i'dadʒi du 'brõzi]
Ice Age	Era (f) do Gelo	['ɛra du 'ʒelu]

tribe	tribo (f)	['tribu]
cannibal	canibal (m)	[kani'baw]
hunter	caçador (m)	[kasa'dor]
to hunt (vi, vt)	caçar (vi)	[ka'sar]
mammoth	mamute (m)	[ma'mutʃi]

cave	caverna (f)	[ka'vɛrna]
fire	fogo (m)	['fogu]
campfire	fogueira (f)	[fo'gejra]
cave painting	pintura (f) rupestre	[pĩ'tura hu'pɛstri]

tool (e.g., stone ax)	ferramenta (f)	[feha'mẽta]
spear	lança (f)	['lãsa]
stone ax	machado (m) de pedra	[ma'ʃadu de 'pɛdra]
to be at war	guerrear (vt)	[ge'hjar]
to domesticate (vt)	domesticar (vt)	[domestʃi'kar]

idol	ídolo (m)	['idolu]
to worship (vt)	adorar, venerar (vt)	[ado'ra˞], [vene'rar]
superstition	superstição (f)	[superstʃi'sãw]
rite	ritual (m)	[hi'twaw]

evolution	evolução (f)	[evolu'sãw]
development	desenvolvimento (m)	[dʒizẽvowvi'mẽtu]
disappearance (extinction)	extinção (f)	[istʃĩ'sãw]
to adapt oneself	adaptar-se (vr)	[adap'tarse]

archeology	arqueologia (f)	[arkjolo'ʒia]
archeologist	arqueólogo (m)	[ar'kjɔlogu]
archeological (adj)	arqueológico	[arkjo'lɔʒiku]
excavation site	escavação (f)	[iskava'sãw]

excavations	escavações (f pl)	[iskava'sõjs]
find (object)	achado (m)	[a'ʃadu]
fragment	fragmento (m)	[frag'mẽtu]

158. Middle Ages

people (ethnic group)	povo (m)	['povu]
peoples	povos (m pl)	['povus]
tribe	tribo (f)	['tribu]
tribes	tribos (f pl)	['tribus]
barbarians	bárbaros (pl)	['barbarus]
Gauls	gauleses (pl)	[gaw'lezes]
Goths	godos (pl)	['godus]
Slavs	eslavos (pl)	[iʃ'lavus]
Vikings	viquingues (pl)	['vikĩgis]
Romans	romanos (pl)	[ho'manus]
Roman (adj)	romano	[ho'manu]
Byzantines	bizantinos (pl)	[bizã'tʃinus]
Byzantium	Bizâncio	[bi'zãsju]
Byzantine (adj)	bizantino	[bizã'tʃinu]
emperor	imperador (m)	[ĩpera'dor]
leader, chief (tribal ~)	líder (m)	['lider]
powerful (~ king)	poderoso	[pode'rozu]
king	rei (m)	[hej]
ruler (sovereign)	governante (m)	[gover'nãtʃi]
knight	cavaleiro (m)	[kava'lejru]
feudal lord	senhor feudal (m)	[se'nor few'daw]
feudal (adj)	feudal	[few'daw]
vassal	vassalo (m)	[va'salu]
duke	duque (m)	['duki]
earl	conde (m)	['kõdʒi]
baron	barão (m)	[ba'rãw]
bishop	bispo (m)	['bispu]
armor	armadura (f)	[arma'dura]
shield	escudo (m)	[is'kudu]
sword	espada (f)	[is'pada]
visor	viseira (f)	[vi'zejra]
chainmail	cota (f) de malha	['kɔta de 'maʎa]
Crusade	cruzada (f)	[kru'zada]
crusader	cruzado (m)	[kru'zadu]
territory	território (m)	[tehi'tɔrju]
to attack (invade)	atacar (vt)	[ata'kar]

| to conquer (vt) | conquistar (vt) | [kõkis'tar] |
| to occupy (invade) | ocupar, invadir (vt) | [oku'parsi], [ĩva'dʒir] |

siege (to be under ~)	assédio, sítio (m)	[a'sɛdʒu] ['sitʃu]
besieged (adj)	sitiado	[si'tʃjadu]
to besiege (vt)	assediar, sitiar (vt)	[ase'dʒjaʳ], [si'tʃjar]

inquisition	inquisição (f)	[ĩkizi'sãw]
inquisitor	inquisidor (m)	[ĩkizi'dor]
torture	tortura (f)	[tor'tura]
cruel (adj)	cruel	[kru'ɛw]
heretic	herege (m)	[e'reʒi]
heresy	heresia (f)	[ere'zia]

seafaring	navegação (f) marítima	[navega'sãu ma'ritʃima]
pirate	pirata (m)	[pi'rata]
piracy	pirataria (f)	[pirata'ria]
boarding (attack)	abordagem (f)	[abor'daʒẽ]
loot, booty	presa (f), butim (m)	['preza], [bu'tĩ]
treasures	tesouros (m pl)	[te'zorus]

discovery	descobrimento (m)	[dʒiskobri'mẽtu]
to discover (new land, etc.)	descobrir (vt)	[dʒisko'bʳir]
expedition	expedição (f)	[ispedʒi'sãw]

musketeer	mosqueteiro (m)	[moske'tejru]
cardinal	cardeal (m)	[kar'dʒjaw]
heraldry	heráldica (f)	[e'rawdʒika]
heraldic (adj)	heráldico	[e'rawdʒiku]

159. Leader. Chief. Authorities

king	rei (m)	[hej]
queen	rainha (f)	[ha'iɲa]
royal (adj)	real	[he'aw]
kingdom	reino (m)	['hejnu]

| prince | príncipe (m) | ['prĩsipi] |
| princess | princesa (f) | [prĩ'seza] |

president	presidente (m)	[prezi'dẽtʃi]
vice-president	vice-presidente (m)	['visi-prezi'dẽtʃi]
senator	senador (m)	[sena'dor]

monarch	monarca (m)	[mo'narka]
ruler (sovereign)	governante (m)	[gover'nãtʃi]
dictator	ditador (m)	[dʒita'dor]
tyrant	tirano (m)	[tʃi'ranu]
magnate	magnata (m)	[mag'nata]
director	diretor (m)	[dʒire'tor]

chief	chefe (m)	['ʃɛfi]
manager (director)	gerente (m)	[ʒe'rẽtʃi]
boss	patrão (m)	[pa'trãw]
owner	dono (m)	['donu]

head (~ of delegation)	chefe (m)	['ʃɛfi]
authorities	autoridades (f pl)	[awtori'dadʒis]
superiors	superiores (m pl)	[supe'rjores]

governor	governador (m)	[governa'dor]
consul	cônsul (m)	['kõsuw]
diplomat	diplomata (m)	[dʒiplo'mata]
mayor	Presidente (m) da Câmara	[prezi'dẽtʃi da 'kamara]
sheriff	xerife (m)	[ʃe'rifi]

emperor	imperador (m)	[ĩpera'dor]
tsar, czar	czar (m)	['kzar]
pharaoh	faraó (m)	[fara'ɔ]
khan	cã, khan (m)	[kã]

160. Breaking the law. Criminals. Part 1

bandit	bandido (m)	[bã'dʒidu]
crime	crime (m)	['krimi]
criminal (person)	criminoso (m)	[krimi'nozu]

thief	ladrão (m)	[la'drãw]
to steal (vi, vt)	roubar (vt)	[ho'bar]
stealing (larceny)	furto (m)	['furtu]
theft	furto (m)	['furtu]

to kidnap (vt)	raptar, sequestrar (vt)	[hap'tar], [sekwes'trar]
kidnapping	sequestro (m)	[se'kwɛstru]
kidnapper	sequestrador (m)	[sekwestra'dor]

| ransom | resgate (m) | [hez'gatʃi] |
| to demand ransom | pedir resgate | [pe'dʒir hez'gatʃi] |

to rob (vt)	roubar (vt)	[ho'bar]
robbery	assalto, roubo (m)	[a'sawtu], ['hobu]
robber	assaltante (m)	[asaw'tãtʃi]

to extort (vt)	extorquir (vt)	[istor'kir]
extortionist	extorsionário (m)	[istorsjo'narju]
extortion	extorsão (f)	[istor'sãw]

to murder, to kill	matar, assassinar (vt)	[ma'tar], [asasi'nar]
murder	homicídio (m)	[omi'sidʒju]
murderer	homicida, assassino (m)	[omi'sida], [asa'sinu]
gunshot	tiro (m)	['tʃiru]

to fire (~ a shot)	dar um tiro	[dar ũ 'ʧiru]
to shoot to death	matar a tiro	[ma'tar a 'ʧiru]
to shoot (vi)	disparar, atirar (vi)	[dʒispa'rar], [atʃi'rar]
shooting	tiroteio (m)	[tʃiro'teju]

incident (fight, etc.)	incidente (m)	[ĩsi'dẽʧ]
fight, brawl	briga (f)	['briga]
Help!	Socorro!	[so'kohu]
victim	vítima (f)	['vitʃima]

to damage (vt)	danificar (vt)	[danifi'kar]
damage	dano (m)	['danu]
dead body, corpse	cadáver (m)	[ka'daver]
grave (~ crime)	grave	['gravi]

to attack (vt)	atacar (vt)	[ata'kar]
to beat (to hit)	bater (vt)	[ba'ter]
to beat up	espancar (vt)	[ispã'kar]
to take (rob of sth)	tirar (vt)	[tʃi'rar]
to stab to death	esfaquear (vt)	[isfaki'ɛr]
to maim (vt)	mutilar (vt)	[mutʃi'lar]
to wound (vt)	ferir (vt)	[fe'rir]

blackmail	chantagem (f)	[ʃã'taʒẽ]
to blackmail (vt)	chantagear (vt)	[ʃãta'ʒjar]
blackmailer	chantagista (m)	[ʃãta'ʒista]

protection racket	extorsão (f)	[istor'sãw]
racketeer	extorsionário (m)	[istorsjo'narju]
gangster	gângster (m)	['gãŋster]
mafia, Mob	máfia (f)	['mafja]

pickpocket	punguista (m)	[pũ'gista]
burglar	assaltante, ladrão (m)	[asaw'tãtʃi], [la'drãw]
smuggling	contrabando (m)	[kõtra'bãdu]
smuggler	contrabandista (m)	[kõtrabã'dʒista]

forgery	falsificação (f)	[fawsifika'sãw]
to forge (counterfeit)	falsificar (vt)	[fawsifi'kar]
fake (forged)	falsificado	[fawsifi'kadu]

161. Breaking the law. Criminals. Part 2

rape	estupro (m)	[is'tupru]
to rape (vt)	estuprar (vt)	[istu'prar]
rapist	estuprador (m)	[istupra'dor]
maniac	maníaco (m)	[ma'niaku]

| prostitute (fem.) | prostituta (f) | [prostʃi'uta] |
| prostitution | prostituição (f) | [prostʃitwi'sãw] |

pimp	cafetão (m)	[kafe'tãw]
drug addict	drogado (m)	[dro'gadu]
drug dealer	traficante (m)	[trafi'kãtʃi]

to blow up (bomb)	explodir (vt)	[isplo'dʒir]
explosion	explosão (f)	[isplo'zãw]
to set fire	incendiar (vt)	[ĩsẽ'dʒjar]
arsonist	incendiário (m)	[ĩsẽ'dʒjarju]

terrorism	terrorismo (m)	[teho'rizmu]
terrorist	terrorista (m)	[teho'rista]
hostage	refém (m)	[he'fẽ]

to swindle (deceive)	enganar (vt)	[ẽga'nar]
swindle, deception	engano (m)	[ẽ'gãnu]
swindler	vigarista (m)	[viga'rista]

to bribe (vt)	subornar (vt)	[subor'nar]
bribery	suborno (m)	[su'bornu]
bribe	suborno (m)	[su'bornu]

poison	veneno (m)	[ve'nɛnu]
to poison (vt)	envenenar (vt)	[ẽvene'nar]
to poison oneself	envenenar-se (vr)	[ẽvene'narsi]

suicide (act)	suicídio (m)	[swi'sidʒju]
suicide (person)	suicida (m)	[swi'sida]

to threaten (vt)	ameaçar (vt)	[amea'sar]
threat	ameaça (f)	[ame'asa]
to make an attempt	atentar contra a vida de ...	[atẽ'tar 'kõtra a 'vida de]
attempt (attack)	atentado (m)	[atẽ'tadu]

to steal (a car)	roubar (vt)	[ho'bar]
to hijack (a plane)	sequestrar (vt)	[sekwes'trar]

revenge	vingança (f)	[vĩ'gãsa]
to avenge (get revenge)	vingar (vt)	[vĩ'gar]

to torture (vt)	torturar (vt)	[tortu'rar]
torture	tortura (f)	[tor'tura]
to torment (vt)	atormentar (vt)	[atormẽ'tar]

pirate	pirata (m)	[pi'rata]
hooligan	desordeiro (m)	[dʒizor'dejru]
armed (adj)	armado	[ar'madu]
violence	violência (f)	[vjo'lẽsja]
illegal (unlawful)	ilegal	[ile'gaw]

spying (espionage)	espionagem (f)	[ispio'naʒẽ]
to spy (vi)	espionar (vi)	[ispjo'nar]

162. Police. Law. Part 1

justice	justiça (f)	[ʒus'tʃisa]
court (see you in ~)	tribunal (m)	[tribu'naw]
judge	juiz (m)	[ʒwiz]
jurors	jurados (m pl)	[ʒu'radɹs]
jury trial	tribunal (m) do júri	[tribu'naw du 'ʒuri]
to judge, to try (vt)	julgar (vt)	[ʒuw'gar]
lawyer, attorney	advogado (m)	[adʒivo'gadu]
defendant	réu (m)	['hɛw]
dock	banco (m) dos réus	['bãku dus hɛws]
charge	acusação (f)	[akuza sãw]
accused	acusado (m)	[aku'zadu]
sentence	sentença (f)	[sẽ'tẽsa]
to sentence (vt)	sentenciar (vt)	[sẽtẽ'siar]
guilty (culprit)	culpado (m)	[kuw'padu]
to punish (vt)	punir (vt)	[pu'nir]
punishment	punição (f)	[puni'sãw]
fine (penalty)	multa (f)	['muwta]
life imprisonment	prisão (f) perpétua	[pri'zãw per'pɛtwa]
death penalty	pena (f) de morte	['pena de 'mortʃi]
electric chair	cadeira (f) elétrica	[ka'dejra e'lɛtrika]
gallows	forca (f)	['forka]
to execute (vt)	executar (vt)	[ezekʊ'tar]
execution	execução (f)	[ezekʊ'sãw]
prison, jail	prisão (f)	[pri'zãw]
cell	cela (f) de prisão	['sɛla de pri'zãw]
escort (convoy)	escolta (f)	[is'kɔwta]
prison guard	guarda (m) prisional	['gwarda prizjo'naw]
prisoner	preso (m)	['prezu]
handcuffs	algemas (f pl)	[aw'ʒɛmas]
to handcuff (vt)	algemar (vt)	[awʒe mar]
prison break	fuga, evasão (f)	['fuga], [eva'zãw]
to break out (vi)	fugir (vi)	[fu'ʒir]
to disappear (vi)	desaparecer (vi)	[dʒizapare'ser]
to release (from prison)	soltar, libertar (vt)	[sow'tar], [liber'tar]
amnesty	anistia (f)	[anis'tʃia]
police	polícia (f)	[po'lis̩a]
police officer	polícia (m)	[po'lis̩a]

police station	delegacia (f) de polícia	[delega'sia de po'lisja]
billy club	cassetete (m)	[kase'tɛtʃi]
bullhorn	megafone (m)	[mega'foni]

patrol car	carro (m) de patrulha	['kaho de pa'truʎa]
siren	sirene (f)	[si'rɛni]
to turn on the siren	ligar a sirene	[li'gar a si'rɛni]
siren call	toque (m) da sirene	['tɔki da si'rɛni]

crime scene	cena (f) do crime	['sɛna du 'krimi]
witness	testemunha (f)	[teste'muɲa]
freedom	liberdade (f)	[liber'dadʒi]
accomplice	cúmplice (m)	['kũplisi]
to flee (vi)	escapar (vi)	[iska'par]
trace (to leave a ~)	traço (m)	['trasu]

163. Police. Law. Part 2

search (investigation)	procura (f)	[pro'kura]
to look for ...	procurar (vt)	[proku'rar]
suspicion	suspeita (f)	[sus'pejta]
suspicious (e.g., ~ vehicle)	suspeito	[sus'pejtu]
to stop (cause to halt)	parar (vt)	[pa'rar]
to detain (keep in custody)	deter (vt)	[de'ter]

case (lawsuit)	caso (m)	['kazu]
investigation	investigação (f)	[ĩvestʃiga'sãw]
detective	detetive (m)	[dete'tʃivi]
investigator	investigador (m)	[ĩvestʃiga'dor]
hypothesis	versão (f)	[ver'sãw]

motive	motivo (m)	[mo'tʃivu]
interrogation	interrogatório (m)	[ĩtehoga'tɔrju]
to interrogate (vt)	interrogar (vt)	[ĩteho'gar]
to question (~ neighbors, etc.)	questionar (vt)	[kestʃo'nar]
check (identity ~)	verificação (f)	[verifika'sãw]

round-up (raid)	batida (f) policial	[ba'tʃida poli'sjaw]
search (~ warrant)	busca (f)	['buska]
chase (pursuit)	perseguição (f)	[persegi'sãw]
to pursue, to chase	perseguir (vt)	[perse'gir]
to track (a criminal)	seguir, rastrear (vt)	[se'gir], [has'trjar]

arrest	prisão (f)	[pri'zãw]
to arrest (sb)	prender (vt)	[prẽ'der]
to catch (thief, etc.)	pegar, capturar (vt)	[pe'gar], [kaptu'rar]
capture	captura (f)	[kap'tura]
document	documento (m)	[doku'mẽtu]
proof (evidence)	prova (f)	['prɔva]

to prove (vt)	**provar** (vt)	[pro'var]
footprint	**pegada** (f)	[pe'gada]
fingerprints	**impressões** (f pl) **digitais**	[impre'sõjs dʒiʒi'tajs]
piece of evidence	**prova** (f)	['prɔva]
alibi	**álibi** (m)	['alibi]
innocent (not guilty)	**inocente**	[ino'sẽtʃi]
injustice	**injustiça** (f)	[ĩʒus'tʃisa]
unjust, unfair (adj)	**injusto**	[ĩ'ʒustu]
criminal (adj)	**criminal**	[krimi'naw]
to confiscate (vt)	**confiscar** (vt)	[kõfis'kar]
drug (illegal substance)	**droga** (f)	['drɔga]
weapon, gun	**arma** (f)	['arma]
to disarm (vt)	**desarmar** (vt)	[dʒizar'mar]
to order (command)	**ordenar** (vt)	[orde'nar]
to disappear (vi)	**desaparecer** (vi)	[dʒizapaɾe'ser]
law	**lei** (f)	[lej]
legal, lawful (adj)	**legal**	[le'gaw]
illegal, illicit (adj)	**ilegal**	[ile'gaw]
responsibility (blame)	**responsabilidade** (f)	[hespõsabili'dadʒi]
responsible (adj)	**responsável**	[hespõ'savew]

NATURE

The Earth. Part 1

164. Outer space

space	espaço, cosmo (m)	[is'pasu], ['kɔzmu]
space (as adj)	espacial, cósmico	[ispa'sjaw], ['kɔzmiku]
outer space	espaço (m) cósmico	[is'pasu 'kɔzmiku]
world	mundo (m)	['mũdu]
universe	universo (m)	[uni'vɛrsu]
galaxy	galáxia (f)	[ga'laksja]
star	estrela (f)	[is'trela]
constellation	constelação (f)	[kõstela'sãw]
planet	planeta (m)	[pla'neta]
satellite	satélite (m)	[sa'tɛlitʃi]
meteorite	meteorito (m)	[meteo'ritu]
comet	cometa (m)	[ko'meta]
asteroid	asteroide (m)	[aste'rɔjdʒi]
orbit	órbita (f)	['ɔrbita]
to revolve (~ around the Earth)	girar (vi)	[ʒi'rar]
atmosphere	atmosfera (f)	[atmos'fɛra]
the Sun	Sol (m)	[sɔw]
solar system	Sistema (m) Solar	[sis'tɛma so'lar]
solar eclipse	eclipse (m) solar	[e'klipsi so'lar]
the Earth	Terra (f)	['tɛha]
the Moon	Lua (f)	['lua]
Mars	Marte (m)	['martʃi]
Venus	Vênus (f)	['venus]
Jupiter	Júpiter (m)	['ʒupiter]
Saturn	Saturno (m)	[sa'turnu]
Mercury	Mercúrio (m)	[mer'kurju]
Uranus	Urano (m)	[u'ranu]
Neptune	Netuno (m)	[ne'tunu]
Pluto	Plutão (m)	[plu'tãw]
Milky Way	Via Láctea (f)	['via 'laktja]

| Great Bear (Ursa Major) | **Ursa Maior** (f) | [ursa ma'jɔr] |
| North Star | **Estrela Polar** (f) | [is'trela po'lar] |

Martian	**marciano** (m)	[mar'sjanu]
extraterrestrial (n)	**extraterrestre** (m)	[estrate'hɛstri]
alien	**alienígena** (m)	[alje'niʒena]
flying saucer	**disco** (m) **voador**	['dʒisku vwa'dor]

spaceship	**nave** (f) **espacial**	['navi ispa'sjaw]
space station	**estação** (f) **orbital**	[eʃta'sãw orbi'taw]
blast-off	**lançamento** (m)	[lãsa'mẽtu]

engine	**motor** (m)	[mo'tor]
nozzle	**bocal** (m)	[bo'kaw]
fuel	**combustível** (m)	[kõbus'tʃivew]

cockpit, flight deck	**cabine** (f)	[ka'bini]
antenna	**antena** (f)	[ã'tɛna]
porthole	**vigia** (f)	[vi'ʒia]
solar panel	**bateria** (f) **solar**	[bate'ria so'lar]
spacesuit	**traje** (m) **espacial**	['traʒi ispa'sjaw]

| weightlessness | **imponderabilidade** (f) | [ĩpõderabili'dadʒi] |
| oxygen | **oxigênio** (m) | [oksi'ʒenju] |

| docking (in space) | **acoplagem** (f) | [ako'plaʒẽ] |
| to dock (vi, vt) | **fazer uma acoplagem** | [fa'zer 'uma ako'plaʒẽ] |

observatory	**observatório** (m)	[observa'tɔrju]
telescope	**telescópio** (m)	[tele'skɔpju]
to observe (vt)	**observar** (vt)	[obser'var]
to explore (vt)	**explorar** (vt)	[isplo'rar]

165. The Earth

the Earth	**Terra** (f)	['tɛha]
the globe (the Earth)	**globo** (m) **terrestre**	['globu te'hɛstri]
planet	**planeta** (m)	[pla'neta]

atmosphere	**atmosfera** (f)	[atmos fɛra]
geography	**geografia** (f)	[ʒeogra'fia]
nature	**natureza** (f)	[natu'reza]

globe (table ~)	**globo** (m)	['globu]
map	**mapa** (m)	['mapa]
atlas	**atlas** (m)	['atlas]

Europe	**Europa** (f)	[ew'rɔpa]
Asia	**Ásia** (f)	['azja]
Africa	**África** (f)	['afrika]

Australia	**Austrália** (f)	[aws'tralja]
America	**América** (f)	[a'mɛrika]
North America	**América** (f) **do Norte**	[a'mɛrika du 'nɔrtʃi]
South America	**América** (f) **do Sul**	[a'mɛrika du suw]

| Antarctica | **Antártida** (f) | [ã'tartʃida] |
| the Arctic | **Ártico** (m) | ['artʃiku] |

166. Cardinal directions

north	**norte** (m)	['nɔrtʃi]
to the north	**para norte**	['para 'nɔrtʃi]
in the north	**no norte**	[nu 'nɔrtʃi]
northern (adj)	**do norte**	[du 'nɔrtʃi]

south	**sul** (m)	[suw]
to the south	**para sul**	['para suw]
in the south	**no sul**	[nu suw]
southern (adj)	**do sul**	[du suw]

west	**oeste, ocidente** (m)	['wɛstʃi], [osi'dẽtʃi]
to the west	**para oeste**	['para 'wɛstʃi]
in the west	**no oeste**	[nu 'wɛstʃi]
western (adj)	**ocidental**	[osidẽ'taw]

east	**leste, oriente** (m)	['lɛstʃi], [o'rjẽtʃi]
to the east	**para leste**	['para 'lɛstʃi]
in the east	**no leste**	[nu 'lɛstʃi]
eastern (adj)	**oriental**	[orjẽ'taw]

167. Sea. Ocean

sea	**mar** (m)	[mah]
ocean	**oceano** (m)	[o'sjanu]
gulf (bay)	**golfo** (m)	['gowfu]
straits	**estreito** (m)	[is'trejtu]

land (solid ground)	**terra** (f) **firme**	['tɛha 'firmi]
continent (mainland)	**continente** (m)	[kõtʃi'nẽtʃi]
island	**ilha** (f)	['iʎa]
peninsula	**península** (f)	[pe'nĩsula]
archipelago	**arquipélago** (m)	[arki'pɛlagu]

bay, cove	**baía** (f)	[ba'ia]
harbor	**porto** (m)	['portu]
lagoon	**lagoa** (f)	[la'goa]
cape	**cabo** (m)	['kabu]
atoll	**atol** (m)	[a'tɔw]

reef	recife (m)	[he'sifi]
coral	coral (m)	[ko'raw]
coral reef	recife (m) de coral	[he'sifi de ko'raw]

deep (adj)	profundo	[pro'fũdu]
depth (deep water)	profundidade (f)	[profũdʒi'dadʒi]
abyss	abismo (m)	[a'bizmɹ]
trench (e.g., Mariana ~)	fossa (f) oceânica	['fɔsa o'sjanika]

| current (Ocean ~) | corrente (f) | [ko'hẽtʃ] |
| to surround (bathe) | banhar (vt) | [ba'ɲar] |

| shore | litoral (m) | lito'raw] |
| coast | costa (f) | ['kɔsta] |

flow (flood tide)	maré (f) alta	[ma'rɛ 'awta]
ebb (ebb tide)	refluxo (m)	[he'fluksu]
shoal	restinga (f)	[hes'tʃĩɕa]
bottom (~ of the sea)	fundo (m)	['fũdu]
wave	onda (f)	['õda]
crest (~ of a wave)	crista (f) da onda	['krista da 'õda]
spume (sea foam)	espuma (f)	[is'puma]

storm (sea storm)	tempestade (f)	[tẽpes'tadʒi]
hurricane	furacão (m)	[fura'kãw]
tsunami	tsunami (m)	[tsu'nami]
calm (dead ~)	calmaria (f)	[kawma'ria]
quiet, calm (adj)	calmo	['kawmu]

| pole | polo (m) | ['pɔlu] |
| polar (adj) | polar | [po'lar] |

latitude	latitude (f)	[latʃi'tucʒi]
longitude	longitude (f)	[lõʒi'tudʒi]
parallel	paralela (f)	[para'lɛla]
equator	equador (m)	[ekwa'cor]

sky	céu (m)	[sɛw]
horizon	horizonte (m)	[ori'zõtʃ]
air	ar (m)	[ar]

lighthouse	farol (m)	[fa'rɔw]
to dive (vi)	mergulhar (vi)	[mergu'ʎar]
to sink (ab. boat)	afundar-se (vr)	[afũ'darse]
treasures	tesouros (m pl)	[te'zorus]

168. Mountains

| mountain | montanha (f) | [mõ'taɲa] |
| mountain range | cordilheira (f) | [kordʒi'ʎejra] |

mountain ridge	**serra** (f)	['sɛha]
summit, top	**cume** (m)	['kumi]
peak	**pico** (m)	['piku]
foot (~ of the mountain)	**pé** (m)	[pɛ]
slope (mountainside)	**declive** (m)	[de'klivi]

volcano	**vulcão** (m)	[vuw'kãw]
active volcano	**vulcão** (m) **ativo**	[vuw'kãw a'tʃivu]
dormant volcano	**vulcão** (m) **extinto**	[vuw'kãw is'tʃĩtu]

eruption	**erupção** (f)	[erup'sãw]
crater	**cratera** (f)	[kra'tɛra]
magma	**magma** (m)	['magma]
lava	**lava** (f)	['lava]
molten (~ lava)	**fundido**	[fũ'dʒidu]

canyon	**cânion, desfiladeiro** (m)	['kanjon], [dʒisfila'dejru]
gorge	**garganta** (f)	[gar'gãta]
crevice	**fenda** (f)	['fẽda]
abyss (chasm)	**precipício** (m)	[presi'pisju]

pass, col	**passo, colo** (m)	['pasu], ['kɔlu]
plateau	**planalto** (m)	[pla'nawtu]
cliff	**falésia** (f)	[fa'lɛzja]
hill	**colina** (f)	[ko'lina]

glacier	**geleira** (f)	[ʒe'lejra]
waterfall	**cachoeira** (f)	[kaʃ'wejra]
geyser	**gêiser** (m)	['ʒɛjzer]
lake	**lago** (m)	['lagu]

plain	**planície** (f)	[pla'nisi]
landscape	**paisagem** (f)	[paj'zaʒẽ]
echo	**eco** (m)	['ɛku]

alpinist	**alpinista** (m)	[awpi'nista]
rock climber	**escalador** (m)	[iskala'dor]
to conquer (in climbing)	**conquistar** (vt)	[kõkis'tar]
climb (an easy ~)	**subida, escalada** (f)	[su'bida], [iska'lada]

169. Rivers

river	**rio** (m)	['hiu]
spring (natural source)	**fonte, nascente** (f)	['fõtʃi], [na'sẽtʃi]
riverbed (river channel)	**leito** (m) **de rio**	['lejtu de 'hiu]
basin (river valley)	**bacia** (f)	[ba'sia]
to flow into ...	**desaguar no ...**	[dʒiza'gwar nu]

| tributary | **afluente** (m) | [a'flwẽtʃi] |
| bank (of river) | **margem** (f) | ['marʒẽ] |

current (stream)	corrente (f)	[ko'hētʃi]
downstream (adv)	rio abaixo	['hiu a'baɪʃu]
upstream (adv)	rio acima	['hiu a'sima]

inundation	inundação (f)	[ĩtrodu'sâw]
flooding	cheia (f)	['ʃeja]
to overflow (vi)	transbordar (vi)	[trãzbor'dar]
to flood (vt)	inundar (vt)	[inũ'dar]

| shallow (shoal) | banco (m) de areia | ['bãku de a'reja] |
| rapids | corredeira (f) | [kohe'dejra] |

dam	barragem (f)	[ba'haʒẽ]
canal	canal (m)	[ka'naw]
reservoir (artificial lake)	reservatório (m) de água	[hezerva'torju de 'agwa]
sluice, lock	eclusa (f)	[e'kluza]

water body (pond, etc.)	corpo (m) de água	['korpu de 'agwa]
swamp (marshland)	pântano (m)	['pãtanu]
bog, marsh	lamaçal (m)	[lama'saw]
whirlpool	rodamoinho (m)	[hodamo'iɲu]

stream (brook)	riacho (m)	['hjaʃu]
drinking (ab. water)	potável	[po'tavew]
fresh (~ water)	doce	['dosi]

| ice | gelo (m) | ['ʒelu] |
| to freeze over (ab. river, etc.) | congelar-se (vr) | [kõʒe'larsi] |

170. Forest

| forest, wood | floresta (f), bosque (m) | [flo'rɛsta], ['bɔski] |
| forest (as adj) | florestal | [flores'taw] |

thick forest	mata (f) fechada	['mata fe'ʃada]
grove	arvoredo (m)	[arvo'redu]
forest clearing	clareira (f)	[kla'rejra]

| thicket | matagal (m) | [mata'gaw] |
| scrubland | mato (m), caatinga (f) | ['matu], [ka'tʃĩga] |

| footpath (troddenpath) | trilha, vereda (f) | ['triʎa], [ve'reda] |
| gully | ravina (f) | [ha'vina] |

tree	árvore (f)	['arvori]
leaf	folha (f)	['foʎa]
leaves (foliage)	folhagem (f)	[fo'ʎaʒẽ]
fall of leaves	queda (f) das folhas	['kɛda das 'foʎas]
to fall (ab. leaves)	cair (vi)	[ka'ir]

top (of the tree)	topo (m)	['topu]
branch	ramo (m)	['hamu]
bough	galho (m)	['gaʎu]
bud (on shrub, tree)	botão (m)	[bo'tãw]
needle (of pine tree)	agulha (f)	[a'guʎa]
pine cone	pinha (f)	['piɲa]

tree hollow	buraco (m) de árvore	[bu'raku de 'arvori]
nest	ninho (m)	['niɲu]
burrow (animal hole)	toca (f)	['tɔka]

trunk	tronco (m)	['trõku]
root	raiz (f)	[ha'iz]
bark	casca (f) de árvore	['kaska de 'arvori]
moss	musgo (m)	['muzgu]

to uproot (remove trees or tree stumps)	arrancar pela raiz	[ahã'kar 'pɛla ha'iz]
to chop down	cortar (vt)	[kor'tar]
to deforest (vt)	desflorestar (vt)	[dʒisflores'tar]
tree stump	toco, cepo (m)	['toku], ['sepu]

campfire	fogueira (f)	[fo'gejra]
forest fire	incêndio (m) florestal	[ĩ'sẽdʒiu flores'taw]
to extinguish (vt)	apagar (vt)	[apa'gar]

forest ranger	guarda-parque (m)	['gwarda 'parki]
protection	proteção (f)	[prote'sãw]
to protect (~ nature)	proteger (vt)	[prote'ʒer]
poacher	caçador (m) furtivo	[kasa'dor fur'tʃivu]
steel trap	armadilha (f)	arma'dʒiʎa]

| to gather, to pick (vt) | colher (vt) | [ko'ʎer] |
| to lose one's way | perder-se (vr) | [per'dersi] |

171. Natural resources

natural resources	recursos (m pl) naturais	[he'kursus natu'rajs]
minerals	minerais (m pl)	[mine'rajs]
deposits	depósitos (m pl)	[de'pɔzitus]
field (e.g., oilfield)	jazida (f)	[ʒa'zida]

to mine (extract)	extrair (vt)	[istra'jir]
mining (extraction)	extração (f)	[istra'sãw]
ore	minério (m)	[mi'nɛrju]
mine (e.g., for coal)	mina (f)	['mina]
shaft (mine ~)	poço (m) de mina	['posu de 'mina]
miner	mineiro (m)	[mi'nejru]
gas (natural ~)	gás (m)	[gajs]
gas pipeline	gasoduto (m)	[gazo'dutu]

oil (petroleum)	petróleo (m)	[pe'trɔlju]
oil pipeline	oleoduto (m)	[oljo'dutu]
oil well	poço (m) de petróleo	['posu de pe'trɔlju]
derrick (tower)	torre (f) petrolífera	['tohi petro'lifera]
tanker	petroleiro (m)	[petro'lejru]

sand	areia (f)	[a'reja]
limestone	calcário (m)	[kaw'karju]
gravel	cascalho (m)	[kas'kaʎu]
peat	turfa (f)	['turfa]
clay	argila (f)	[ar'ʒila]
coal	carvão (m)	[kar'vãw]

iron (ore)	ferro (m)	['fɛhu]
gold	ouro (m)	['oru]
silver	prata (f)	['prata]
nickel	níquel (m)	['nikew]
copper	cobre (m)	['kɔbri]

zinc	zinco (m)	['zĩku]
manganese	manganês (m)	[mãga'nes]
mercury	mercúrio (m)	[mer'kurju]
lead	chumbo (m)	['ʃũbu]

mineral	mineral (m)	[mine'raw]
crystal	cristal (m)	[kris'taw]
marble	mármore (m)	['marmori]
uranium	urânio (m)	[u'ranju]

The Earth. Part 2

172. Weather

weather	**tempo** (m)	['tẽpu]
weather forecast	**previsão** (f) **do tempo**	[previ'zãw du 'tẽpu]
temperature	**temperatura** (f)	[tẽpera'tura]
thermometer	**termômetro** (m)	[ter'mometru]
barometer	**barômetro** (m)	[ba'romɛtru]
humid (adj)	**úmido**	['umidu]
humidity	**umidade** (f)	[umi'dadʒi]
heat (extreme ~)	**calor** (m)	[ka'lor]
hot (torrid)	**tórrido**	['tɔhidu]
it's hot	**está muito calor**	[is'ta 'mwĩtu ka'lor]
it's warm	**está calor**	[is'ta ka'lor]
warm (moderately hot)	**quente**	['kẽtʃi]
it's cold	**está frio**	[is'ta 'friu]
cold (adj)	**frio**	['friu]
sun	**sol** (m)	[sɔw]
to shine (vi)	**brilhar** (vi)	[bri'ʎar]
sunny (day)	**de sol, ensolarado**	[de sɔw], [ẽsola'radu]
to come up (vi)	**nascer** (vi)	[na'ser]
to set (vi)	**pôr-se** (vr)	['porsi]
cloud	**nuvem** (f)	['nuvẽj]
cloudy (adj)	**nublado**	[nu'bladu]
rain cloud	**nuvem** (f) **preta**	['nuvẽj 'preta]
somber (gloomy)	**escuro**	[is'kuru]
rain	**chuva** (f)	['ʃuva]
it's raining	**está a chover**	[is'ta a ʃo'ver]
rainy (~ day, weather)	**chuvoso**	[ʃu'vozu]
to drizzle (vi)	**chuviscar** (vi)	[ʃuvis'kar]
pouring rain	**chuva** (f) **torrencial**	['ʃuva tohẽ'sjaw]
downpour	**aguaceiro** (m)	[agwa'sejru]
heavy (e.g., ~ rain)	**forte**	['fortʃi]
puddle	**poça** (f)	['posa]
to get wet (in rain)	**molhar-se** (vr)	[mo'ʎarsi]
fog (mist)	**nevoeiro** (m)	[nevo'ejru]
foggy	**de nevoeiro**	[de nevu'ejru]

| snow | neve (f) | ['nɛvi] |
| it's snowing | está nevando | [is'ta ne'vãdu] |

173. Severe weather. Natural disasters

thunderstorm	trovoada (f)	[tro'vwada]
lightning (~ strike)	relâmpago (m)	[he'lãpɐgu]
to flash (vi)	relampejar (vi)	[helãpe'ʒar]

thunder	trovão (m)	[tro'vãw]
to thunder (vi)	trovejar (vi)	[trove'ʒar]
it's thundering	está trovejando	[is'ta trove'ʒãdu]

| hail | granizo (m) | [gra'nizu] |
| it's hailing | esta caindo granizo | [is'ta kɐ'idu gra'nizu] |

| to flood (vt) | inundar (vt) | [inũ'dar] |
| flood, inundation | inundação (f) | [ĩtrodu'sãw] |

earthquake	terremoto (m)	[tehe'motu]
tremor, shoke	abalo, tremor (m)	[a'balu], [tre'mor]
epicenter	epicentro (m)	[epi'sẽtru]

| eruption | erupção (f) | [erup'sãw] |
| lava | lava (f) | ['lava] |

twister	tornado (m)	[tor'nadu]
tornado	tornado (m)	[tor'nadu]
typhoon	tufão (m)	[tu'fãw]

hurricane	furacão (m)	[fura'kãw]
storm	tempestade (f)	[tẽpes'tadʒi]
tsunami	tsunami (m)	[tsu'nami]

cyclone	ciclone (m)	[si'klɔni]
bad weather	mau tempo (m)	[maw 'tẽpu]
fire (accident)	incêndio (m)	[ĩ'sẽdʒiu]
disaster	catástrofe (f)	[ka'tastrofi]
meteorite	meteorito (m)	[meteo'ritu]

avalanche	avalanche (f)	[ava'lãʃi]
snowslide	deslizamento (m) de neve	[dʒizliza'mẽtu de 'nɛvi]
blizzard	nevasca (f)	[ne'vaska]
snowstorm	tempestade (f) de neve	[tẽpes'tadʒi de 'nɛvi]

Fauna

174. Mammals. Predators

predator	**predador** (m)	[preda'dor]
tiger	**tigre** (m)	['tʃigri]
lion	**leão** (m)	[le'ãw]
wolf	**lobo** (m)	['lobu]
fox	**raposa** (f)	[ha'pozu]
jaguar	**jaguar** (m)	[ʒa'gwar]
leopard	**leopardo** (m)	[ljo'pardu]
cheetah	**chita** (f)	['ʃita]
black panther	**pantera** (f)	[pã'tɛra]
puma	**puma** (m)	['puma]
snow leopard	**leopardo-das-neves** (m)	[ljo'pardu das 'nɛvis]
lynx	**lince** (m)	['lĩsi]
coyote	**coiote** (m)	[ko'jotʃi]
jackal	**chacal** (m)	[ʃa'kaw]
hyena	**hiena** (f)	['jena]

175. Wild animals

animal	**animal** (m)	[ani'maw]
beast (animal)	**besta** (f)	['besta]
squirrel	**esquilo** (m)	[is'kilu]
hedgehog	**ouriço** (m)	[o'risu]
hare	**lebre** (f)	['lɛbri]
rabbit	**coelho** (m)	[ko'eʎu]
badger	**texugo** (m)	[te'ʃugu]
raccoon	**guaxinim** (m)	[gwaʃi'nĩ]
hamster	**hamster** (m)	['amster]
marmot	**marmota** (f)	[mah'mɔta]
mole	**toupeira** (f)	[to'pejra]
mouse	**rato** (m)	['hatu]
rat	**ratazana** (f)	[hata'zana]
bat	**morcego** (m)	[mor'segu]
ermine	**arminho** (m)	[ar'miɲu]
sable	**zibelina** (f)	[zibe'lina]

marten	marta (f)	['mahta]
weasel	doninha (f)	[do'niɲa]
mink	visom (m)	[vi'zõ]
beaver	castor (m)	[kas'to‐]
otter	lontra (f)	['lõtra]
horse	cavalo (m)	[ka'valu]
moose	alce (m)	['awsi]
deer	veado (m)	['vjadu˖]
camel	camelo (m)	[ka'meˑu]
bison	bisão (m)	[bi'zãw]
wisent	auroque (m)	[aw'rɔki]
buffalo	búfalo (m)	['bufalu]
zebra	zebra (f)	['zebra˖
antelope	antílope (m)	[ã'tʃilopi]
roe deer	corça (f)	['korsa]
fallow deer	gamo (m)	['gamu]
chamois	camurça (f)	[ka'mursa]
wild boar	javali (m)	[ʒava'li]
whale	baleia (f)	[ba'leja]
seal	foca (f)	['fɔka]
walrus	morsa (f)	['mɔhsa]
fur seal	urso-marinho (m)	['ursu ma'riɲu]
dolphin	golfinho (m)	[gow'fiɲu]
bear	urso (m)	['ursu]
polar bear	urso (m) polar	['ursu po'lar]
panda	panda (m)	['pãda]
monkey	macaco (m)	[ma'kaku]
chimpanzee	chimpanzé (m)	[ʃĩpã'zɛ]
orangutan	orangotango (m)	[orãgu'tãgu]
gorilla	gorila (m)	[go'rila]
macaque	macaco (m)	[ma'kaku]
gibbon	gibão (m)	[ʒi'bãw]
elephant	elefante (m)	[ele'fãtʃi]
rhinoceros	rinoceronte (m)	[hinose'rõtʃi]
giraffe	girafa (f)	[ʒi'rafa]
hippopotamus	hipopótamo (m)	[ipo'pɔtamu]
kangaroo	carguru (m)	[kãgu'ru]
koala (bear)	coala (m)	['kwala]
mongoose	mangusto (m)	[mã'gustu]
chinchilla	chinchila (f)	[ʃĩ'ʃila]
skunk	cangambá (f)	[kã'gãba]
porcupine	porco-espinho (m)	['pɔrku is'piɲu]

176. Domestic animals

cat	gata (f)	['gata]
tomcat	gato (m) macho	['gatu 'maʃu]
dog	cão (m)	['kãw]

horse	cavalo (m)	[ka'valu]
stallion (male horse)	garanhão (m)	[gara'ɲãw]
mare	égua (f)	['ɛgwa]

cow	vaca (f)	['vaka]
bull	touro (m)	['toru]
ox	boi (m)	[boj]

sheep (ewe)	ovelha (f)	[o'veʎa]
ram	carneiro (m)	[kar'nejru]
goat	cabra (f)	['kabra]
billy goat, he-goat	bode (m)	['bɔdʒi]

| donkey | burro (m) | ['buhu] |
| mule | mula (f) | ['mula] |

pig, hog	porco (m)	['porku]
piglet	leitão (m)	[lej'tãw]
rabbit	coelho (m)	[ko'eʎu]

| hen (chicken) | galinha (f) | [ga'liɲa] |
| rooster | galo (m) | ['galu] |

duck	pata (f)	['pata]
drake	pato (m)	['patu]
goose	ganso (m)	['gãsu]

| tom turkey, gobbler | peru (m) | [pe'ru] |
| turkey (hen) | perua (f) | [pe'rua] |

domestic animals	animais (m pl) domésticos	[ani'majs do'mɛstʃikus]
tame (e.g., ~ hamster)	domesticado	[domestʃi'kadu]
to tame (vt)	domesticar (vt)	[domestʃi'kar]
to breed (vt)	criar (vt)	[krjar]

farm	fazenda (f)	[fa'zẽda]
poultry	aves (f pl) domésticas	['avis do'mɛstʃikas]
cattle	gado (m)	['gadu]
herd (cattle)	rebanho (m), manada (f)	[he'baɲu], [ma'nada]

stable	estábulo (m)	[is'tabulu]
pigpen	chiqueiro (m)	[ʃi'kejru]
cowshed	estábulo (m)	[is'tabulu]
rabbit hutch	coelheira (f)	[kue'ʎejra]
hen house	galinheiro (m)	[gali'ɲejru]

177. Dogs. Dog breeds

dog	cão (m)	['kãw]
sheepdog	cão pastor (m)	['kãw pas'tor]
German shepherd	pastor-alemão (m)	[pas'tor ale'mãw]
poodle	poodle (m)	['pudw]
dachshund	linguicinha (f)	[lĩgwi'siɲa]
bulldog	buldogue (m)	[buw'dogi]
boxer	boxer (m)	['boksər]
mastiff	mastim (m)	[mas'tʃĩ]
Rottweiler	rottweiler (m)	[hɔt'vejler]
Doberman	dóberman (m)	['dɔberman]
basset	basset (m)	[ba'sɛt]
bobtail	pastor inglês (m)	[pas'tor ĩ'gles]
Dalmatian	dálmata (m)	['dalmata]
cocker spaniel	cocker spaniel (m)	['kɔker spa'njel]
Newfoundland	terra-nova (m)	['tɛha-'nova]
Saint Bernard	são-bernardo (m)	[sãw-ber'nardu]
husky	husky (m) siberiano	['aski sibe'rjanu]
Chow Chow	Chow-chow (m)	[ʃou'ʃou]
spitz	spitz alemão (m)	['spits ale'mãw]
pug	pug (m)	[pug]

178. Sounds made by animals

barking (n)	latido (m)	[la'tʃidu]
to bark (vi)	latir (vi)	[la'tʃir]
to meow (vi)	miar (vi)	[mjar]
to purr (vi)	ronronar (vi)	[hõho'nar]
to moo (vi)	mugir (vi)	[mu'ʒ r]
to bellow (bull)	bramir (vi)	[bra'mir]
to growl (vi)	rosnar (vi)	[hoz'nar]
howl (n)	uivo (m)	['wivu]
to howl (vi)	uivar (vi)	[wi'var]
to whine (vi)	ganir (vi)	[ga'ni˺]
to bleat (sheep)	balir (vi)	[ba'li˺]
to oink, to grunt (pig)	grunhir (vi)	[gru'ɲir]
to squeal (vi)	guinchar (vi)	[gĩ'ʃaɾ]
to croak (vi)	coaxar (vi)	[koa'ʃar]
to buzz (insect)	zumbir (vi)	[zũ'bi˺]
to chirp (crickets, grasshopper)	ziziar (vi)	[zi'zjar]

179. Birds

bird	pássaro (m), ave (f)	['pasaru], ['avi]
pigeon	pombo (m)	['põbu]
sparrow	pardal (m)	[par'daw]
tit (great tit)	chapim-real (m)	[ʃa'pĩ-he'aw]
magpie	pega-rabuda (f)	['pega-ha'buda]
raven	corvo (m)	['korvu]
crow	gralha-cinzenta (f)	['graʎa sĩ'zẽta]
jackdaw	gralha-de-nuca-cinzenta (f)	['graʎa de 'nuka sĩ'zẽta]
rook	gralha-calva (f)	['graʎa 'kawvu]
duck	pato (m)	['patu]
goose	ganso (m)	['gãsu]
pheasant	faisão (m)	[faj'zãw]
eagle	águia (f)	['agja]
hawk	açor (m)	[a'sor]
falcon	falcão (m)	[faw'kãw]
vulture	abutre (m)	[a'butri]
condor (Andean ~)	condor (m)	[kõ'dor]
swan	cisne (m)	['sizni]
crane	grou (m)	[grow]
stork	cegonha (f)	[se'goɲa]
parrot	papagaio (m)	[papa'gaju]
hummingbird	beija-flor (m)	[bejʒa'flor]
peacock	pavão (m)	[pa'vãw]
ostrich	avestruz (m)	[aves'truz]
heron	garça (f)	['garsa]
flamingo	flamingo (m)	[fla'mĩgu]
pelican	pelicano (m)	[peli'kanu]
nightingale	rouxinol (m)	[hoʃi'nɔw]
swallow	andorinha (f)	[ãdo'riɲa]
thrush	tordo-zornal (m)	['tɔrdu-zor'nal]
song thrush	tordo-músico (m)	['tɔrdu-'muziku]
blackbird	melro-preto (m)	['mɛwhu 'pretu]
swift	andorinhão (m)	[ãdori'ɲãw]
lark	laverca, cotovia (f)	[la'verka], [kutu'via]
quail	codorna (f)	[ko'dɔrna]
woodpecker	pica-pau (m)	['pika 'paw]
cuckoo	cuco (m)	['kuku]
owl	coruja (f)	[ko'ruʒa]

eagle owl	bufo-real (m)	['bufu-he'aw]
wood grouse	tetraz-grande (m)	[tɛ'tras-'grãdʒi]
black grouse	tetraz-lira (m)	[tɛ'tras-'lira]
partridge	perdiz-cinzenta (f)	[per'dis sĩ'zẽta]

starling	estorninho (m)	[istor'niɲu]
canary	canário (m)	[ka'narju]
hazel grouse	galinha-do-mato (f)	[ga'liɲa du 'matu]
chaffinch	tentilhão (m)	[tẽtʃi'ʎ̃ãw]
bullfinch	dom-fafe (m)	[dõ'fafi]

seagull	gaivota (f)	[gaj'vɔta]
albatross	albatroz (m)	[alba'trɔs]
penguin	pinguim (m)	[pĩ'gwĩ]

180. Birds. Singing and sounds

to sing (vi)	cantar (vi)	[kã'tar]
to call (animal, bird)	gritar, chamar (vi)	[gri'tar], [ʃa'mar]
to crow (rooster)	cantar (vi)	[kã'tar]
cock-a-doodle-doo	cocorocó (m)	[kokuru'kɔ]

to cluck (hen)	cacarejar (vi)	[kakare'ʒar]
to caw (crow call)	crocitar, grasnar (vi)	[krosi'tar], [graz'nar]
to quack (duck call)	grasnar (vi)	[graz'nar]
to cheep (vi)	piar (vi)	[pjar]
to chirp, to twitter	chilrear, gorjear (vi)	[ʃiw'hjar], [gor'ʒjar]

181. Fish. Marine animals

bream	brema (f)	['brema]
carp	carpa (f)	['karpa]
perch	perca (f)	['pehka]
catfish	siluro (m)	[si'luru]
pike	lúcio (m)	['lusju]

| salmon | salmão (m) | [saw'mãw] |
| sturgeon | esturjão (m) | [istur'ʒãw] |

herring	arenque (m)	[a'rẽk]
Atlantic salmon	salmão (m) do Atlântico	[saw'mãw du at'lãtʃiku]
mackerel	cavala, sarda (f)	[ka'vala], ['sarda]
flatfish	solha (f), linguado (m)	['soʎa], [lĩ'gwadu]

zander, pike perch	lúcio perca (m)	['lusju 'perka]
cod	bacalhau (m)	[baka'ʎaw]
tuna	atum (m)	[a'tũ]
trout	truta (f)	['truta]

eel	enguia (f)	[ẽ'gia]
electric ray	raia (f) elétrica	['haja e'lɛtrika]
moray eel	moreia (f)	[mo'reja]
piranha	piranha (f)	[pi'raɲa]

shark	tubarão (m)	[tuba'rãw]
dolphin	golfinho (m)	[gow'fiɲu]
whale	baleia (f)	[ba'leja]

crab	caranguejo (m)	[karã'geʒu]
jellyfish	água-viva (f)	['agwa 'viva]
octopus	polvo (m)	['powvu]

starfish	estrela-do-mar (f)	[is'trela du 'mar]
sea urchin	ouriço-do-mar (m)	[o'risu du 'mar]
seahorse	cavalo-marinho (m)	[ka'valu ma'riɲu]

oyster	ostra (f)	['ostra]
shrimp	camarão (m)	[kama'rãw]
lobster	lagosta (f)	[la'gosta]
spiny lobster	lagosta (f)	[la'gosta]

182. Amphibians. Reptiles

| snake | cobra (f) | ['kɔbra] |
| venomous (snake) | venenoso | [vene'nozu] |

| viper | víbora (f) | ['vibora] |
| cobra | naja (f) | ['naʒa] |

| python | píton (m) | ['pitɔn] |
| boa | jiboia (f) | [ʒi'bɔja] |

grass snake	cobra-de-água (f)	[kɔbra de 'agwa]
rattle snake	cascavel (f)	[kaska'vɛw]
anaconda	anaconda, sucuri (f)	[ana'kõda], [sukuri]

lizard	lagarto (m)	[la'gartu]
iguana	iguana (f)	[i'gwana]
monitor lizard	varano (m)	[va'ranu]
salamander	salamandra (f)	[sala'mãdra]

| chameleon | camaleão (m) | [kamale'ãu] |
| scorpion | escorpião (m) | [iskorpi'ãw] |

| turtle | tartaruga (f) | [tarta'ruga] |
| frog | rã (f) | [hã] |

| toad | sapo (m) | ['sapu] |
| crocodile | crocodilo (m) | [kroko'dʒilu] |

183. Insects

insect, bug	inseto (m)	[iˈsɛtu]
butterfly	borboleta (f)	[borboˈleta]
ant	formiga (f)	[forˈmiga]
fly	mosca (f)	[ˈmoska]
mosquito	mosquito (m)	[mosˈkitu]
beetle	escaravelho (m)	[iskaraˈveʎu]
wasp	vespa (f)	[ˈvespa]
bee	abelha (f)	[aˈbeʎa]
bumblebee	mamangaba (f)	[mamãˈgaba]
gadfly (botfly)	moscardo (m)	[mosˈkardu]
spider	aranha (f)	[aˈraɲa]
spiderweb	teia (f) de aranha	[ˈteja de aˈraɲa]
dragonfly	libélula (f)	[liˈbɛlula]
grasshopper	gafanhoto (m)	[gafaˈɲotu]
moth (night butterfly)	traça (f)	[ˈtrasa]
cockroach	barata (f)	[baˈrata]
tick	carrapato (m)	[kahaˈpatu]
flea	pulga (f)	[ˈpuwga]
midge	borrachudo (m)	[bohaˈʃudu]
locust	gafanhoto-migratório (m)	[gafaˈɲotu-migraˈtɔrju]
snail	caracol (m)	[karaˈkɔw]
cricket	grilo (m)	[ˈgrilu]
lightning bug	pirilampo, vaga-lume (m)	[piriˈlãpu], [vaga-ˈlumi]
ladybug	joaninha (f)	[ʒwaˈniɲa]
cockchafer	besouro (m)	[beˈzoru]
leech	sanguessuga (f)	[sãgiˈsuga]
caterpillar	lagarta (f)	[laˈgarta]
earthworm	minhoca (f)	[miˈɲɔka]
larva	larva (f)	[ˈlarva]

184. Animals. Body parts

beak	bico (m)	[ˈbiku]
wings	asas (f pl)	[ˈazas]
foot (of bird)	pata (f)	[ˈpata]
feathers (plumage)	plumagem (f)	[pluˈmaʒẽ]
feather	pena, pluma (f)	[ˈpena], [ˈpluma]
crest	crista (f)	[ˈkrista]
gills	guelras (f pl)	[ˈgɛwhas]
spawn	ovas (f pl)	[ˈɔvas]

larva	larva (f)	['larva]
fin	barbatana (f)	[barba'tana]
scales (of fish, reptile)	escama (f)	[is'kama]

fang (canine)	presa (f)	['preza]
paw (e.g., cat's ~)	pata (f)	['pata]
muzzle (snout)	focinho (m)	[fo'siɲu]
maw (mouth)	boca (f)	['boka]
tail	cauda (f), rabo (m)	['kawda], ['habu]
whiskers	bigodes (m pl)	[bi'gɔdʒis]

| hoof | casco (m) | ['kasku] |
| horn | corno (m) | ['kornu] |

carapace	carapaça (f)	[kara'pasa]
shell (of mollusk)	concha (f)	['kõʃa]
eggshell	casca (f) de ovo	['kaska de 'ovu]

| animal's hair (pelage) | pelo (m) | ['pelu] |
| pelt (hide) | pele (f), couro (m) | ['pɛli], ['koru] |

185. Animals. Habitats

| habitat | hábitat (m) | ['abitatʃi] |
| migration | migração (f) | [migra'sãw] |

mountain	montanha (f)	[mõ'taɲa]
reef	recife (m)	[he'sifi]
cliff	falésia (f)	[fa'lɛzja]

forest	floresta (f)	[flo'rɛsta]
jungle	selva (f)	['sɛwva]
savanna	savana (f)	[sa'vana]
tundra	tundra (f)	['tũdra]

steppe	estepe (f)	[is'tɛpi]
desert	deserto (m)	[de'zɛrtu]
oasis	oásis (m)	[o'asis]

sea	mar (m)	[mah]
lake	lago (m)	['lagu]
ocean	oceano (m)	[o'sjanu]

swamp (marshland)	pântano (m)	['pãtanu]
freshwater (adj)	de água doce	[de 'agwa 'dosi]
pond	lagoa (f)	[la'goa]
river	rio (m)	['hiu]

| den (bear's ~) | toca (f) do urso | ['tɔka du 'ursu] |
| nest | ninho (m) | ['niɲu] |

tree hollow	**buraco** (m) **de árvore**	[bu'raku de 'arvori]
burrow (animal hole)	**toca** (f)	['tɔka]
anthill	**formigueiro** (m)	[formi'gejru]

Flora

186. Trees

tree	**árvore** (f)	['arvori]
deciduous (adj)	**decídua**	[de'sidwa]
coniferous (adj)	**conífera**	[ko'nifera]
evergreen (adj)	**perene**	[pe'rɛni]
apple tree	**macieira** (f)	[ma'sjejra]
pear tree	**pereira** (f)	[pe'rejra]
sweet cherry tree	**cerejeira** (f)	[sere'ʒejra]
sour cherry tree	**ginjeira** (f)	[ʒĩ'ʒejra]
plum tree	**ameixeira** (f)	[amej'ʃejra]
birch	**bétula** (f)	['bɛtula]
oak	**carvalho** (m)	[kar'vaʎu]
linden tree	**tília** (f)	['tʃilja]
aspen	**choupo-tremedor** (m)	['ʃopu-treme'dor]
maple	**bordo** (m)	['bɔrdu]
spruce	**espruce** (m)	[is'pruse]
pine	**pinheiro** (m)	[pi'ɲejru]
larch	**alerce, lariço** (m)	[a'lɛrse], [la'risu]
fir tree	**abeto** (m)	[a'bɛtu]
cedar	**cedro** (m)	['sɛdru]
poplar	**choupo, álamo** (m)	['ʃopu], ['alamu]
rowan	**tramazeira** (f)	[trama'zejra]
willow	**salgueiro** (m)	[saw'gejru]
alder	**amieiro** (m)	[a'mjejru]
beech	**faia** (f)	['faja]
elm	**ulmeiro, olmo** (m)	[ul'mejru], ['ɔwmu]
ash (tree)	**freixo** (m)	['frejʃu]
chestnut	**castanheiro** (m)	[kasta'ɲejru]
magnolia	**magnólia** (f)	[mag'nɔlja]
palm tree	**palmeira** (f)	[paw'mejra]
cypress	**cipreste** (m)	[si'prɛstʃi]
mangrove	**mangue** (m)	['mãgi]
baobab	**embondeiro, baobá** (m)	[ẽbõ'dejru], [bao'ba]
eucalyptus	**eucalipto** (m)	[ewka'liptu]
sequoia	**sequoia** (f)	[se'kwɔja]

187. Shrubs

bush	arbusto (m)	[ar'buʃtu]
shrub	arbusto (m), moita (f)	[ar'buʃtu], ['mɔjta]
grapevine	videira (f)	[vi'dejɾa]
vineyard	vinhedo (m)	[vi'ɲedu]
raspberry bush	framboeseira (f)	[frãboe'zejra]
blackcurrant bush	groselheira-negra (f)	[groze'ʎejra 'negra]
redcurrant bush	groselheira-vermelha (f)	[grozɛ'ʎejra ver'meʎa]
gooseberry bush	groselheira (f) espinhosa	[groze'ʎejra ispi'ɲoza]
acacia	acácia (f)	[a'kasˌa]
barberry	bérberis (f)	['bɛrberis]
jasmine	jasmim (m)	[ʒaz'mĩ]
juniper	junípero (m)	[ʒu'niperu]
rosebush	roseira (f)	[ho'zeˌra]
dog rose	roseira (f) brava	[ho'zeˌra 'brava]

188. Mushrooms

mushroom	cogumelo (m)	[kogu'mɛlu]
edible mushroom	cogumelo (m) comestível	[kogu'mɛlu komes'tʃivew]
poisonous mushroom	cogumelo (m) venenoso	[kogu'mɛlu vene'nozu]
cap (of mushroom)	chapéu (m)	[ʃa'pɛw]
stipe (of mushroom)	pe caule (m)	[pɛ], ['kauli]
cep (Boletus edulis)	boleto, porcino (m)	[bu'letu], [porsinu]
orange-cap boletus	boleto (m) alaranjado	[bu'letu alarã'ʒadu]
birch bolete	boleto (m) de bétula	[bu'letu de 'bɛtula]
chanterelle	cantarelo (m)	[kãta'rɛlu]
russula	rússula (f)	['rusula]
morel	morchella (f)	[mor'ʃɛla]
fly agaric	agário-das-moscas (m)	[a'garju das 'moskas]
death cap	cicuta (f) verde	[si'kuta 'verdʒi]

189. Fruits. Berries

fruit	fruta (f)	['fruta]
fruits	frutas (f pl)	['frutas]
apple	maçã (f)	[ma'sã]
pear	pera (f)	['pera]
plum	ameixa (f)	[a'mejʃa]
strawberry (garden ~)	morango (m)	[mo'rãgu]

sour cherry	ginja (f)	['ʒĩʒa]
sweet cherry	cereja (f)	[se'reʒa]
grape	uva (f)	['uva]
raspberry	framboesa (f)	[frãbo'eza]
blackcurrant	groselha (f) negra	[gro'zɛʎa 'negra]
redcurrant	groselha (f) vermelha	[[gro'zɛʎa ver'meʎa]
gooseberry	groselha (f) espinhosa	[gro'zɛʎa ispi'ɲoza]
cranberry	oxicoco (m)	[oksi'koku]
orange	laranja (f)	[la'rãʒa]
mandarin	tangerina (f)	[tãʒe'rina]
pineapple	abacaxi (m)	[abaka'ʃi]
banana	banana (f)	[ba'nana]
date	tâmara (f)	['tamara]
lemon	limão (m)	[li'mãw]
apricot	damasco (m)	[da'masku]
peach	pêssego (m)	['pesegu]
kiwi	quiuí (m)	[ki'vi]
grapefruit	toranja (f)	[to'rãʒa]
berry	baga (f)	['baga]
berries	bagas (f pl)	['bagas]
cowberry	arando (m) vermelho	[a'rãdu ver'meʎu]
wild strawberry	morango-silvestre (m)	[mo'rãgu siw'vɛstri]
bilberry	mirtilo (m)	[mih'tʃilu]

190. Flowers. Plants

flower	flor (f)	[flɔr]
bouquet (of flowers)	buquê (m) de flores	[bu'ke de 'floris]
rose (flower)	rosa (f)	['hɔza]
tulip	tulipa (f)	[tu'lipa]
carnation	cravo (m)	['kravu]
gladiolus	gladíolo (m)	[gla'dʒiolu]
cornflower	escovinha (f)	[isko'viɲa]
harebell	campainha (f)	[kampa'iɲa]
dandelion	dente-de-leão (m)	['dẽtʃi] de le'ãw]
camomile	camomila (f)	[kamo'mila]
aloe	aloé (m)	[alo'ɛ]
cactus	cacto (m)	['kaktu]
rubber plant, ficus	fícus (m)	['fikus]
lily	lírio (m)	['lirju]
geranium	gerânio (m)	[ʒe'ranju]
hyacinth	jacinto (m)	[ʒa'sĩtu]

mimosa	mimosa (f)	[mi'mɔza]
narcissus	narciso (m)	[nar'sizu]
nasturtium	capuchinha (f)	[kapu'ʃiɲa]

orchid	orquídea (f)	[or'kidʒia]
peony	peônia (f)	[pi'onia]
violet	violeta (f)	[vjo'leta]

pansy	amor-perfeito (m)	[a'mor per'fejtu]
forget-me-not	não-me-esqueças (m)	['nãw mi is'kesas]
daisy	margarida (f)	[marga'rida]

poppy	papoula (f)	[pa'pola]
hemp	cânhamo (m)	['kaɲamu]
mint	hortelã, menta (f)	[orte'lã], ['mẽta]
lily of the valley	lírio-do-vale (m)	['lirju du 'vali]
snowdrop	campânula-branca (f)	[kã'panula-'brãka]

nettle	urtiga (f)	[ur'tʃiga]
sorrel	azedinha (f)	[aze'dʒinha]
water lily	nenúfar (m)	[ne'nufar]
fern	samambaia (f)	[samã'baja]
lichen	líquen (m)	['likẽ]

conservatory (greenhouse)	estufa (f)	[is'tufa]
lawn	gramado (m)	[gra'madu]
flowerbed	canteiro (m) de flores	[kã'tejru de 'floris]

plant	planta (f)	['plãta]
grass	grama (f)	['grama]
blade of grass	folha (f) de grama	['foʎa de 'grama]

leaf	folha (f)	['foʎa]
petal	pétala (f)	['pɛtala]
stem	talo (m)	['talu]
tuber	tubérculo (m)	[tu'berkulu]

| young plant (shoot) | broto, rebento (m) | ['brotu], [he'bẽtu] |
| thorn | espinho (m) | [is'piɲu] |

to blossom (vi)	florescer (vi)	[flore'ser]
to fade, to wither	murchar (vi)	[mur'ʃar]
smell (odor)	cheiro (m)	['ʃejru]
to cut (flowers)	cortar (vt)	[kor'tar]
to pick (a flower)	colher (vt)	[ko'ʎer]

191. Cereals, grains

| grain | grão (m) | ['grãw] |
| cereal crops | cereais (m pl) | [se'rjajs] |

ear (of barley, etc.)	espiga (f)	[is'piga]
wheat	trigo (m)	['trigu]
rye	centeio (m)	[sẽ'teju]
oats	aveia (f)	[a'veja]
millet	painço (m)	[pa'ĩsu]
barley	cevada (f)	[se'vada]

corn	milho (m)	['miʎu]
rice	arroz (m)	[a'hoz]
buckwheat	trigo-sarraceno (m)	['trigu-saha'sẽnu]

pea plant	ervilha (f)	[er'viʎa]
kidney bean	feijão (m) roxo	[fej'ʒãw 'hoʃu]
soy	soja (f)	['soʒa]
lentil	lentilha (f)	[lẽ'tʃiʎa]
beans (pulse crops)	feijão (m)	[fej'ʒãw]

REGIONAL GEOGRAPHY

Countries. Nationalities

192. Politics. Government. Part 1

politics	política (f)	[po'litʃika]
political (adj)	político	[po'litʃiku]
politician	político (m)	[po'litʃiku]
state (country)	estado (m)	[i'stadu]
citizen	cidadão (m)	[sida'dãw]
citizenship	cidadania (f)	[sidaca'nia]
national emblem	brasão (m) de armas	[bra'zãw de 'armas]
national anthem	hino (m) nacional	['inu nasjo'naw]
government	governo (m)	[go'vernu]
head of state	Chefe (m) de Estado	['ʃɛfi də i'stadu]
parliament	parlamento (m)	[parla mẽtu]
party	partido (m)	[par'tʃidu]
capitalism	capitalismo (m)	[kapita'lizmu]
capitalist (adj)	capitalista	[kapita'lista]
socialism	socialismo (m)	[sosja'lizmu]
socialist (adj)	socialista	[sosja'lista]
communism	comunismo (m)	[komu'nizmu]
communist (adj)	comunista	[komu'nista]
communist (n)	comunista (m)	[komu'nista]
democracy	democracia (f)	[demckra'sia]
democrat	democrata (m)	[demc'krata]
democratic (adj)	democrático	[demc'kratʃiku]
Democratic party	Partido (m) Democrático	[par'tʃidu demo'kratʃiku]
liberal (n)	liberal (m)	[libe'rɛw]
liberal (adj)	liberal	[libe'rɛw]
conservative (n)	conservador (m)	[kõserva'dor]
conservative (adj)	conservador	[kõserva'dor]
republic (n)	república (f)	[he'puolika]
republican (n)	republicano (m)	[hepubli'kanu]

Republican party	**Partido** (m) **Republicano**	[par'tʃidu hepubli'kanu]
elections	**eleições** (f pl)	[elej'sõjs]
to elect (vt)	**eleger** (vt)	[ele'ʒer]
elector, voter	**eleitor** (m)	[elej'tor]
election campaign	**campanha** (f) **eleitoral**	[kã'paɲa elejto'raw]

voting (n)	**votação** (f)	[vota'sãw]
to vote (vi)	**votar** (vi)	[vo'tar]
suffrage, right to vote	**sufrágio** (m)	[su'fraʒu]

candidate	**candidato** (m)	[kãdʒi'datu]
to be a candidate	**candidatar-se** (vi)	[kãdʒida'tarsi]
campaign	**campanha** (f)	[kã'paɲa]

opposition (as adj)	**da oposição**	[da opozi'sãw]
opposition (n)	**oposição** (f)	[opozi'sãw]

visit	**visita** (f)	[vi'zita]
official visit	**visita** (f) **oficial**	[vi'zita ofi'sjaw]
international (adj)	**internacional**	[ĩternasjo'naw]

negotiations	**negociações** (f pl)	[negosja'sõjs]
to negotiate (vi)	**negociar** (vi)	[nego'sjar]

193. Politics. Government. Part 2

society	**sociedade** (f)	[sosje'dadʒi]
constitution	**constituição** (f)	[kõstʃitwi'sãw]
power (political control)	**poder** (m)	[po'der]
corruption	**corrupção** (f)	[kohup'sãw]

law (justice)	**lei** (f)	[lej]
legal (legitimate)	**legal**	[le'gaw]

justice (fairness)	**justeza** (f)	[ʒus'teza]
just (fair)	**justo**	['ʒustu]

committee	**comitê** (m)	[komi'te]
bill (draft law)	**projeto-lei** (m)	[pro'ʒɛtu-'lej]
budget	**orçamento** (m)	[orsa'mẽtu]
policy	**política** (f)	[po'litʃika]
reform	**reforma** (f)	[he'fɔrma]
radical (adj)	**radical**	[hadʒi'kaw]

power (strength, force)	**força** (f)	['forsa]
powerful (adj)	**poderoso**	[pode'rozu]
supporter	**partidário** (m)	[partʃi'darju]
influence	**influência** (f)	[ĩ'flwẽsja]
regime (e.g., military ~)	**regime** (m)	[he'ʒimi]
conflict	**conflito** (m)	[kõ'flitu]

| conspiracy (plot) | conspiração (f) | [kõspira'sãw] |
| provocation | provocação (f) | [provoka'sãw] |

to overthrow (regime, etc.)	derrubar (vt)	[dehu bar]
overthrow (of government)	derrube (m), queda (f)	[de'rube], ['kɛda]
revolution	revolução (f)	[hevolu'sãw]

| coup d'état | golpe (m) de Estado | ['gowpi de i'stadu] |
| military coup | golpe (m) militar | ['gowpi mili'tar] |

crisis	crise (f)	['krizi]
economic recession	recessão (f) econômica	[hesep'sãw eko'nomika]
demonstrator (protester)	manifestante (m)	[manifəs'tãtʃi]
demonstration	manifestação (f)	[manifəsta'sãw]
martial law	lei (f) marcial	[lej mar'sjaw]
military base	base (f) militar	['bazi mili'tar]

| stability | estabilidade (f) | [istabil 'dadʒi] |
| stable (adj) | estável | [is'tavɛw] |

| exploitation | exploração (f) | [isplora'sãw] |
| to exploit (workers) | explorar (vt) | [isplo'rar] |

racism	racismo (m)	[ha'sizmu]
racist	racista (m)	[ha'sista]
fascism	fascismo (m)	[fa'sizmu]
fascist	fascista (m)	[fa'sista]

194. Countries. Miscellaneous

foreigner	estrangeiro (m)	[istrã'ʒejru]
foreign (adj)	estrangeiro	[istrã'ʒejru]
abroad (in a foreign country)	no estrangeiro	[no istrã'ʒejru]

emigrant	emigrante (m)	[emi'grãtʃi]
emigration	emigração (f)	[emigra'sãw]
to emigrate (vi)	emigrar (vi)	[emi'grar]

the West	Ocidente (m)	[osi'dẽtʃ]
the East	Oriente (m)	[o'rjẽtʃi]
the Far East	Extremo Oriente (m)	[is'trɛmu o'rjẽtʃi]

civilization	civilização (f)	[siviliza'sãw]
humanity (mankind)	humanidade (f)	[umani'dadʒi]
the world (earth)	mundo (m)	['mũdu]
peace	paz (f)	[pajz]
worldwide (adj)	mundial	[mũ'dʒjaw]
homeland	pátria (f)	['patrja]
people (population)	povo (m)	['povu]

population	população (f)	[popula'sãw]
people (a lot of ~)	gente (f)	['ʒẽtʃi]
nation (people)	nação (f)	[na'sãw]
generation	geração (f)	[ʒera'sãw]
territory (area)	território (m)	[tehi'tɔrju]
region	região (f)	[he'ʒjãw]
state (part of a country)	estado (m)	[i'stadu]
tradition	tradição (f)	[tradʒi'sãw]
custom (tradition)	costume (m)	[kos'tumi]
ecology	ecologia (f)	[ekolo'ʒia]
Indian (Native American)	índio (m)	['ĩdʒju]
Gypsy (masc.)	cigano (m)	[si'ganu]
Gypsy (fem.)	cigana (f)	[si'gana]
Gypsy (adj)	cigano	[si'ganu]
empire	império (m)	['ĩpɛrju]
colony	colônia (f)	[ko'lonja]
slavery	escravidão (f)	[iskravi'dãw]
invasion	invasão (f)	[ĩva'zãw]
famine	fome (f)	['fɔmi]

195. Major religious groups. Confessions

religion	religião (f)	[heli'ʒãw]
religious (adj)	religioso	[heli'ʒozu]
faith, belief	crença (f)	['krẽsa]
to believe (in God)	crer (vt)	[krer]
believer	crente (m)	['krẽtʃi]
atheism	ateísmo (m)	[ate'izmu]
atheist	ateu (m)	[a'tew]
Christianity	cristianismo (m)	[kristʃja'nizmu]
Christian (n)	cristão (m)	[kris'tãw]
Christian (adj)	cristão	[kris'tãw]
Catholicism	catolicismo (m)	[katoli'sizmu]
Catholic (n)	católico (m)	[ka'tɔliku]
Catholic (adj)	católico	[ka'tɔliku]
Protestantism	protestantismo (m)	[protestã'tʃizmu]
Protestant Church	Igreja (f) Protestante	[i'greʒa protes'tãtʃi]
Protestant (n)	protestante (m)	[protes'tãtʃi]
Orthodoxy	ortodoxia (f)	[ortodok'sia]
Orthodox Church	Igreja (f) Ortodoxa	[i'greʒa orto'dɔksa]

Orthodox (n)	ortodoxo (m)	[orto'dɔksu]
Presbyterianism	presbiterianismo (m)	[prezbitərja'nizmu]
Presbyterian Church	Igreja (f) Presbiteriana	[i'greʒa prezbite'rjana]
Presbyterian (n)	presbiteriano (m)	[prezbitə'rjanu]

| Lutheranism | luteranismo (m) | [lutera'nizmu] |
| Lutheran (n) | luterano (m) | [lute'ranu] |

| Baptist Church | Igreja (f) Batista | [i'greʒa ba'tʃista] |
| Baptist (n) | batista (m) | [ba'tʃista] |

| Anglican Church | Igreja (f) Anglicana | [i'greʒa ãgli'kana] |
| Anglican (n) | anglicano (m) | [ãgli'kanu] |

| Mormonism | mormonismo (m) | [mormo'nizmu] |
| Mormon (n) | mórmon (m) | ['mɔrmõ] |

| Judaism | Judaísmo (m) | [ʒuda'izmu] |
| Jew (n) | judeu (m) | [ʒu'dew] |

| Buddhism | budismo (m) | [bu'dʒizmu] |
| Buddhist (n) | budista (m) | [bu'dʒista] |

| Hinduism | hinduísmo (m) | [ĩ'dwizmu] |
| Hindu (n) | hincu (m) | [ĩ'du] |

Islam	Islã (m)	[iz'lã]
Muslim (n)	muçulmano (m)	[musuw'manu]
Muslim (adj)	muçulmano	[musuw'manu]

| Shiah Islam | xiismo (m) | [ʃi'iʒmu] |
| Shiite (n) | xiita (m) | [ʃi'ita] |

| Sunni Islam | sunismo (m) | [su'nizmu] |
| Sunnite (n) | sunita (m) | [su'nita] |

196. Religions. Priests

| priest | padre (m) | ['padri] |
| the Pope | Papa (m) | ['papa] |

monk, friar	monge (m)	['mõʒi]
nun	freira (f)	['frejra]
pastor	pastor (m)	[pas'tor]

abbot	abade (m)	[a'badʒi]
vicar (parish priest)	vigário (m)	[vi'garju]
bishop	bispo (m)	['bispu]
cardinal	cardeal (m)	[kar'dʒjaw]
preacher	pregador (m)	[prega'dor]

preaching	**sermão** (m)	[ser'mãw]
parishioners	**paroquianos** (pl)	[paro'kjanus]
believer	**crente** (m)	['krẽtʃi]
atheist	**ateu** (m)	[a'tew]

197. Faith. Christianity. Islam

Adam	**Adão**	[a'dãw]
Eve	**Eva**	['ɛva]
God	**Deus** (m)	['dews]
the Lord	**Senhor** (m)	[se'ɲor]
the Almighty	**Todo Poderoso** (m)	['todu pode'rozu]
sin	**pecado** (m)	[pe'kadu]
to sin (vi)	**pecar** (vi)	[pe'kar]
sinner (masc.)	**pecador** (m)	[peka'dor]
sinner (fem.)	**pecadora** (f)	[peka'dora]
hell	**inferno** (m)	[ĩ'fɛrnu]
paradise	**paraíso** (m)	[para'izu]
Jesus	**Jesus**	[ʒe'zus]
Jesus Christ	**Jesus Cristo**	[ʒe'zus 'kristu]
the Holy Spirit	**Espírito** (m) **Santo**	[is'piritu 'sãtu]
the Savior	**Salvador** (m)	[sawva'dor]
the Virgin Mary	**Virgem Maria** (f)	['virʒẽ ma'ria]
the Devil	**Diabo** (m)	['dʒjabu]
devil's (adj)	**diabólico**	[dʒja'bɔliku]
Satan	**Satanás** (m)	[sata'nas]
satanic (adj)	**satânico**	[sa'taniku]
angel	**anjo** (m)	['ãʒu]
guardian angel	**anjo** (m) **da guarda**	['ãʒu da 'gwarda]
angelic (adj)	**angelical**	[ãʒeli'kaw]
apostle	**apóstolo** (m)	[a'pɔstolu]
archangel	**arcanjo** (m)	[ar'kãʒu]
the Antichrist	**anticristo** (m)	[ãtʃi'kristu]
Church	**Igreja** (f)	[i'greʒa]
Bible	**Bíblia** (f)	['biblja]
biblical (adj)	**bíblico**	['bibliku]
Old Testament	**Velho Testamento** (m)	['vɛʎu testa'mẽtu]
New Testament	**Novo Testamento** (m)	['novu testa'mẽtu]
Gospel	**Evangelho** (m)	[evã'ʒɛʎu]

| Holy Scripture | Sagradas Escrituras (f pl) | [sa'gradas iskri'turas] |
| Heaven | Céu (m) | [sɛw] |

Commandment	mandamento (m)	[mãda'mẽtu]
prophet	profeta (m)	[pro'fɛta]
prophecy	profecia (f)	[profɛ'sia]

Allah	Alá (m)	[a'la]
Mohammed	Maomé (m)	[mao'nɛ]
the Koran	Alcorão (m)	[awkɔ'rãw]

mosque	mesquita (f)	[mes'kita]
mullah	mulá (m)	[mu'la]
prayer	oração (f)	[ora'sãw]
to pray (vi, vt)	rezar, orar (vi)	[he'zar], [o'rar]

pilgrimage	peregrinação (f)	[pereçrina'sãw]
pilgrim	peregrino (m)	[pere'grinu]
Mecca	Meca (f)	['mɛkɐ]

church	igreja (f)	[i'greʒa]
temple	templo (m)	['tẽplu]
cathedral	catedral (f)	[kate'craw]
Gothic (adj)	gótico	['gɔtʃiku]
synagogue	sinagoga (f)	[sina'gɔga]
mosque	mesquita (f)	[mes'kita]

chapel	capela (f)	[ka'pɛla]
abbey	abadia (f)	[aba'dʒia]
convent	convento (m)	[kõ'vẽtu]
monastery	mosteiro, monastério (m)	[mos'tejru], [monas'tɛrju]

bell (church ~s)	sino (m)	['sinu]
bell tower	campanário (m)	[kãpa'narju]
to ring (ab. bells)	repicar (vi)	[hepi'kar]

cross	cruz (f)	[kruz]
cupola (roof)	cúpula (f)	['kupula]
icon	ícone (m)	['ikoni]

soul	alma (f)	['awma]
fate (destiny)	destino (m)	[des'tʃinu]
evil (n)	mal (m)	[maw]
good (n)	bem (m)	[bẽj]

vampire	vampiro (m)	[vã'piru]
witch (evil ~)	bruxa (f)	['bruʃa]
demon	demônio (m)	[de'monju]
spirit	espírito (m)	[is'piritʊ]

| redemption (giving us ~) | recenção (f) | [hedẽ'sãw] |
| to redeem (vt) | recimir (vt) | [hedʒi'mir] |

church service, mass	**missa** (f)	['misa]
to say mass	**celebrar a missa**	[sele'brar a 'misa]
confession	**confissão** (f)	[kõfi'sãw]
to confess (vi)	**confessar-se** (vr)	[kõfe'sarsi]

saint (n)	**santo** (m)	['sãtu]
sacred (holy)	**sagrado**	[sa'gradu]
holy water	**água** (f) **benta**	['agwa 'bẽta]

ritual (n)	**ritual** (m)	[hi'twaw]
ritual (adj)	**ritual**	[hi'twaw]
sacrifice	**sacrifício** (m)	[sakri'fisju]

superstition	**superstição** (f)	[superstʃi'sãw]
superstitious (adj)	**supersticioso**	[superstʃi'sjozu]
afterlife	**vida** (f) **após a morte**	['vida a'pɔjs a 'mortʃi]
eternal life	**vida** (f) **eterna**	['vida e'terna]

MISCELLANEOUS

198. Various useful words

background (green ~)	**fundo** (m)	['fũdu]
balance (of situation)	**equilíbrio** (m)	[eki'librju]
barrier (obstacle)	**barreira** (f)	[ba'hejra]
base (basis)	**base** (f)	['bazi]
beginning	**começo, início** (m)	[ko'mesu], [i'nisju]
category	**categoria** (f)	[katego'ria]
cause (reason)	**causa** (f)	['kawza]
choice	**variedade** (f)	[varje'dadʒi]
coincidence	**coincidência** (f)	[koïsi'dẽsja]
comfortable (~ chair)	**cómodo**	['komcdu]
comparison	**comparação** (f)	[kõpara'sãw]
compensation	**compensação** (f)	[kõpẽsa'sãw]
degree (extent, amount)	**grau** (m)	[graw]
development	**desenvolvimento** (m)	[dʒizẽvowvi'mẽtu]
difference	**diferença** (f)	[dʒife'rẽsa]
effect (e.g., of drugs)	**efeito** (m)	[e'fejtu]
effort (exertion)	**esforço** (m)	[is'forsu]
element	**elemento** (m)	[ele'mẽtu]
end (finish)	**fim** (m)	[fĩ]
example (illustration)	**exemplo** (m)	[e'zẽplu]
fact	**fato** (m)	['fatu]
frequent (adj)	**frequente**	[fre'kwẽtʃi]
growth (development)	**crescimento** (m)	[kresi'mẽtu]
help	**ajuda** (f)	[a'ʒuda]
ideal	**ideal** (m)	[ide'jaw]
kind (sort, type)	**tipo** (m)	['tʃipu]
labyrinth	**labirinto** (m)	[labi'rĩtu]
mistake, error	**erro** (m)	['ehu]
moment	**momento** (m)	[mo'mẽtu]
object (thing)	**objeto** (m)	[ɔb'ʒɛtu]
obstacle	**obstáculo** (m)	[ob'stakulu]
original (original copy)	**original** (m)	[oriʒi'naw]
part (~ of sth)	**parte** (f)	['partʃi]
particle, small part	**partícula** (f)	[par'tʃikula]
pause (break)	**pausa** (f)	['pawza]

position	posição (f)	[pozi'sãw]
principle	princípio (m)	[prĩ'sipju]
problem	problema (m)	[prob'lɛma]

process	processo (m)	[pru'sɛsu]
progress	progresso (m)	[pro'grɛsu]
property (quality)	propriedade (f)	[proprje'dadʒi]
reaction	reação (f)	[hea'sãw]
risk	risco (m)	['hisku]

secret	segredo (m)	[se'gredu]
series	série (f)	['sɛri]
shape (outer form)	forma (f)	['fɔrma]
situation	situação (f)	[sitwa'sãw]
solution	solução (f)	[solu'sãw]

standard (adj)	padrão	[pa'drãw]
standard (level of quality)	padrão (m)	[pa'drãw]
stop (pause)	paragem (f)	[pa'raʒẽ]
style	estilo (m)	[is'tʃilu]

system	sistema (m)	[sis'tɛma]
table (chart)	tabela (f)	[ta'bɛla]
tempo, rate	ritmo (m)	['hitʃmu]
term (word, expression)	termo (m)	['termu]

thing (object, item)	coisa (f)	['kojza]
truth (e.g., moment of ~)	verdade (f)	[ver'dadʒi]
turn (please wait your ~)	vez (f)	[vez]
type (sort, kind)	tipo (m)	['tʃipu]
urgent (adj)	urgente	[ur'ʒẽtʃi]

urgently (adv)	urgentemente	[urʒẽte'mẽtʃi]
utility (usefulness)	utilidade (f)	[utʃili'dadʒi]
variant (alternative)	variante (f)	[va'rjãtʃi]
way (means, method)	modo (m)	['mɔdu]
zone	zona (f)	['zɔna]

www.ingramcontent.com/pod-product-compliance
Lightning Source LLC
LaVergne TN
LVHW051303080426
835509LV00020B/3123